ROUTLEDGE LIBRA
19TH CENTURY

Volume 18

THE INTELLECTUAL CRISIS IN ENGLISH CATHOLICISM

THE INTELLECTUAL CRISIS IN ENGLISH CATHOLICISM

Liberal Catholics, Modernists, and the
Vatican in the Late Nineteenth and
Early Twentieth Centuries

WILLIAM J. SCHOENL

Routledge
Taylor & Francis Group

LONDON AND NEW YORK

First published in 1982 by Garland Publishing, Inc.

This edition first published in 2018
by Routledge
2 Park Square, Milton Park, Abingdon, Oxon OX14 4RN

and by Routledge
711 Third Avenue, New York, NY 10017

Routledge is an imprint of the Taylor & Francis Group, an informa business

British Library Cataloguing in Publication Data
A catalogue record for this book is available from the British Library

ISBN: 978-1-138-06800-1 (Set)
ISBN: 978-1-315-10089-0 (Set) (ebk)
ISBN: 978-1-138-07896-3 (Volume 18) (hbk)
ISBN: 978-1-138-07898-7 (Volume 18) (pbk)
ISBN: 978-1-315-11443-9 (Volume 18) (ebk)

Publisher's Note
The publisher has gone to great lengths to ensure the quality of this reprint but points out that some imperfections in the original copies may be apparent.

Disclaimer
The publisher has made every effort to trace copyright holders and would welcome correspondence from those they have been unable to trace.

Preface to the reissue edition

In his classical essay, "Politics and the English Language," George Orwell criticized the misuse of abstract words that were not tied down to objects. He observed that when certain topics were raised, the concrete melted into the abstract. The papal encyclical *Pascendi* condemning "modernism" is an example of misuse of an abstract word. It had fabricated "modernism" in the Church: no Catholic intellectual held the system condemned as "modernism" in *Pascendi*. Critics of *Pascendi* who promote ideologies, however, are also an example: ideologies abstract from and oversimplify reality.

The present book does not focus on the abstraction Catholic "modernism." It focuses on individuals and their real actions, attitudes, and behaviors. In particular, it describes five liberal Catholics in England: Wilfrid Ward, Friedrich von Hugel, George Tyrrell, Francis Aidan Gasquet, and Edmund Bishop. It demonstrates major differences in temperament and view among them.

I use the term "liberal Catholic" to refer to those who attempted to reconcile their Church with knowledge and contemporary culture in the late nineteenth and early twentieth centuries. They sought to find a new *modus vivendi* for Catholicism within contemporary culture. The historian must use some term to refer to those who made these attempts. "Liberal Catholic" presents at least no more problem than alternative terms, such as "progressive Catholic." "*Aggiornamento*" (renewal)—a term popular during the time of the Second Vatican Council—would be anachronistic applied to the period 1890–1914. I use the term "modernist" to refer to those liberal Catholics who became more radical and after the turn of the century called into question the idea of dogma and/or the authority of the ecclesiastical authorities.

I wish to add a comment on Alfred Loisy, a modernist. His *L'Evangile et l'Eglise* (1902) was relatively moderate compared to some of his later statements after Cardinal Richard, the Archbishop of Paris, condemned his book. For example, he later wrote: "Historically speaking, I did not admit that Christ founded the Church or the Sacraments; I professed that dogmas formed themselves gradually and that they were not unchangeable; and it was the same for ecclesiastical authority which I conceived of as a ministry of human education. . . ." "M. von Hugel who defends me so bravely believes very differently from me in the divinity of Jesus Christ. Setting aside metaphysical phraseology, I do not believe in the divinity of Jesus any more than [Adolf von] Harnack or Jean Reville, and I look on the personal Incarnation of God as a philosophic myth" (Loisy, *Memoires*, II, pp. 168, 397).

I wish also to add comments about two English liberal Catholics—Francis Aidan Gasquet and Wilfrid Ward. Even after Pope Pius X appointed him to supervise the revision of the Vulgate, Gasquet retained a liberal Catholic inclination. In a letter to his friend Edmund Bishop, June 28, 1907, he wrote that it was an honor for us English that he had been offered this appointment, but that it would mean great labor and three to four months each year away from England. He told Bishop that we had always complained that we English were left out of all things and this weighed with him (Gasquet Papers, Downside Abbey).

After *Pascendi* Wilfrid Ward gave up his attempts to serve as a liaison officer between orthodox Catholic positions and modern thought in England. He accepted *Pascendi*, and he subsequently turned to literary subjects. Although his biographer Maisie Ward said that eventually he came to think that he had overrated the strength of theological thought to counter modernist thought at the time and looked upon the modernist crisis as calling for unusual action by the ecclesiastical authorities, I believe that *Pascendi* and subsequent acts continued to bother him. From 1908 to 1916 only two of the more than thirty articles appearing over his name in the *Dublin Review* directly concerned reconciling Christian beliefs with modern thought, and both were commentaries on recently published books.

In recent years some social scientists have challenged "naturalistic" assumptions in the social sciences—assumptions that tried to explain everything in physical terms. In his book *Between Naturalism and Religion* (2008), for example, Juergen Habermas, an important European thinker, refrained from passing judgment on truths of faith but insisted on a strict demarcation between knowledge and faith. His thought insisted on the difference between faith and knowledge, but it eschewed the rationalist "presumption" that it could itself decide the rationality or irrationality of aspects of religious doctrines (pp. 140, 143). He thought that to speak with one another, the religious side should accept the authority of reason as to the fallible results of the sciences and, conversely, "secular reason may not set itself up as the judge concerning truths of faith" (Habermas, *An Awareness of What Is Missing* 2010, p. 16). Naturalistic assumptions as well as knowledge and faith were root issues in the modernist crisis.

William Schoenl

THE INTELLECTUAL CRISIS IN ENGLISH CATHOLICISM ★ Liberal Catholics, Modernists, and the Vatican in the Late Nineteenth and Early Twentieth Centuries

William J. Schoenl

Garland Publishing, Inc.
New York & London ★ 1982

Library of Congress Cataloging in Publication Data

Schoenl, William J., 1941–
  The intellectual crisis in English Catholicism.

  (Modern British history)
  Bibliography: p.
  Includes index.
  1. Liberalism (Religion)—Catholic Church—History—
19th century.   2. Liberalism (Religion)—Catholic Church
—History—20th century.   3. Modernism—Catholic Church
—History—19th century.   4. Modernism—Catholic Church
—History—20th century.   5. Liberalism (Religion)—
England—History—19th century.   6. Liberalism (Religion)
—England—History—20th century.   7. Catholic Church—
England—History—19th century.   8. Catholic Church—
England—History—20th century.   I. Title.   II. Series.
BX1396.2.S36   1982   282'.42   81-48368
ISBN 0-8240-5164-5

All volumes in this series are printed on acid-free,
250-year-life paper.
Printed in the United States of America

Dedicated to Colleagues Who Have Suffered

from Intolerance--whether from the

Left, Right, or Center

It should be presupposed that every good Christian
ought to be more ready to give a good sense to the
doubtful proposition of another than to condemn it;
and if he cannot give a good sense to it, let him
inquire how the other understands it, and if he is
in error, let him correct him with charity.

The Spiritual Exercises of
Saint Ignatius of Loyola*

---

*Trans. W. H. Longridge (London and Oxford:
A. R. Mowbray, 1919; 4th edition, 1950), pp. 24-25.

CONTENTS

PREFACE

      This study treats the attempts of English liberal
Catholics to reconcile their Church with secular culture in
the late nineteenth and early twentieth centuries. Since
many of the underlying issues in the crisis enveloping them
also confronted members of other religious bodies I have
placed their endeavor in a broad cultural setting. This
work was written not only for specialists in religious
history but for all readers who might be interested in a
seminal period of Catholicism. It is a study in religious,
intellectual, and cultural history, or, more precisely, in
their intersections. It attempts to provide an account of
the development of liberal Catholicism in England in the
late nineteenth and early twentieth centuries.

      It is the first study of the main English liberal
Catholics of that period as a group. Viewed together they
form a spectrum of liberal Catholic thought that ranged
from moderately liberal to extremely so. As time went on
they frequently disagreed with each other on major issues
yet they did sound a common keynote. Above all, their
endeavor to find a new _modus_ _vivendi_ for Catholicism within
contemporary culture and their emphasis on that aim were
what they had in common. This study calls attention to
both the essential similarity and the divergent views among
them. I have tried to show the many fine shades of
diversity in their attitudes. I have examined the various
impacts of actions of the Vatican on them and have considered their involvement in the Catholic modernist controversy.

Although historical writing on the period has in recent years focused on the modernists, intellectual ferment and significant attempts at renewal in the Roman Church were by no means limited to the modernists. Besides modernism the broader phenomenon of liberal Catholicism needs to be examined if a balanced and accurate understanding of Roman Catholicism during the period is eventually to be achieved. In England at least, modernists stood in a definite relation to liberal Catholicism, one partially of similarity but more significantly of difference. I have viewed them as a distinct subgroup that eventually emerged among the larger English liberal Catholic group. I believe this book shows that there was a spectrum of liberal Catholicism of which the Catholic modernists were but a part, ultimately diverging from the others.

The intellectual crisis in English Catholicism was much broader than the specifically modernist crisis. It arose from the apparent conflict between Roman Catholicism and contemporary thought, but it was not only a conflict of ideas. It was also a conflict of the public actions of men and their often passionate debates. Since their actions often took the form of periodical articles and letters to newspapers and many of the controversies were fought in the press, I have made extensive use of the relevant periodical literature. The crisis was deepened by the various controversies that arose between liberal Catholic writers and ecclesiastical officials and among the liberal Catholics themselves. These controversies began in the 1890's, became more vehement with the emergence of a modernist group among the liberal Catholics after 1900, and continued until the crisis reached its climax with the papal condemnation of modernism in 1907. The virulent anti-modernist reaction that ensued affected the Roman Church's development in the twentieth century. Beyond resulting in the virtually

complete suppression of modernism, it damaged moderate
liberal Catholic efforts at reconciling the Church with
contemporary culture. I have sought to present a balanced
view of the crisis of more than seventy years ago. Some of
its underlying issues still confront Christian communions
today, although present problems cannot be recapitulated in
late nineteenth and early twentieth-century categories.
While indebted to numerous sources, this is the first study
that has attempted to treat as a whole the intellectual
crisis and post-1890 English liberal Catholicism. As
Thomas Michael Loome has suggested in his recent book,
Liberal Catholicism, Reform Catholicism, Modernism: A Contribution to a New Orientation in Modernist Research (Mainz,
Germany, 1979): "It is only when one stresses one crisis
manifest in many highly diverse controversies that one can
do justice to the complexity of the crisis and make room
for the widely differing controversies through which the
crisis unfolded" (p. 195). So far as English Catholicism
in the late nineteenth and early twentieth centuries is
concerned, I believe my study demonstrates that there was
one intellectual crisis, as I have called it, manifest in
many widely differing controversies involving the Vatican
and liberal Catholics in England.

For aid and encouragement I am grateful to several
present and past colleagues in the Department of Humanities
at Michigan State University; I wish to thank in particular
Professors Samuel J. Thomas and Ronald R. Nelson for reading parts of this work. I am thankful to Professor Loome
for reading a section, and for encouragement at a trying
time. I am grateful to Professors Robert K. Webb and
Robert D. Cross who read a much earlier version of this
study at Columbia University. The thoughtful criticisms of
these scholars enabled me to avoid numerous errors of content and style. I alone am responsible for shortcomings
that may be found in this book.

I wish to thank the National Endowment for the
Humanities and the Penrose Fund of the American Philosophical Society for grants that enabled me to do research in
manuscript sources. Of course, my findings, conclusions,
etc., do not necessarily represent the views of those
institutions. I am grateful to Rosemary Sheed Middleton
for access to the Wilfrid Ward Family Papers (now in the
St. Andrews University Library); the librarians of the
Department of Manuscripts, the British Museum, for letting
me see the George Tyrrell, Friedrich von Hügel, and Maude
Petre manuscripts there; Dom Mark Pontifex and Dom Daniel
Rees for showing me the Edmund Bishop Papers and the
Francis Cardinal Gasquet Papers at Downside Abbey; R. N.
Smart, Keeper of Manuscripts, St. Andrews University
Library, for sending me copies of Bishop's letters to
Hügel, letters in the Ward-Hügel correspondence, and, in
addition, Tyrrell's correspondence with Ward; Elizabeth R.
Poyser, Archivist of the Archbishop of Westminster, for
showing me papers of Herbert Cardinal Vaughan; Major T. L.
Ingram, Archivist for the Earl of Halifax, for letting me
see the copies (made by Wilfrid Ward in 1910 and sent to
Lord Halifax) of some letters of Tyrrell to Ward; the
librarians of the Cambridge University Library; and Walter
W. Burinski and the interlibrary loan staff of the Michigan
State University Library. Finally, I am grateful to
Jo Grandstaff who typed my manuscript with expertise and
good humor.

William J. Schoenl

October, 1980

INTRODUCTION

Since the Scientific Revolution and the Enlighten-
ment, traditional Christian beliefs have been challenged by
the rise of a naturalistic world view excluding the supernatural from anything in reality. To take well-known
nineteenth-century examples, naturalistic assumptions were
made by Strauss and Renan in their "scientific" Biblical
criticism, and evolution was transmuted into a philosophy
of life under the guise of science by Huxley, Spencer,
Haeckel, and others. The rapid development of science in
the nineteenth century would, in any case, have tested
Christian beliefs. Intermingled with naturalism, it confronted the churches with a dilemma.[1]

Historically, Christianity has been at once both
transcendentally oriented and culturally adaptable. If the
churches now attempted to uphold their traditional dogmas,
they ran the risk of alienating themselves from contemporary
culture with its scientific idiom. If they adjusted dogma
to the conclusions of the science of the age, they risked
emptying Christianity of its transcendent content. Liberal
Catholicism stood for an extrication from this predicament.
Contemporary Christian doctrines and scientific criticism
might be reconciled without sacrificing the dogmas and their
transcendent references. The scientific methods and those
conclusions of modern science that had definitely been proven
or were probable were to be accepted. Unessential accretions that appeared in day-to-day preaching and in theologians' statements of the dogmas' meanings and implications
were to be susceptible of modification or elimination. The
essence of each dogma was to be upheld. It was hoped that

1

acceptance of this policy would preserve the full transcendent content of Christianity, but permit a reconciliation with scientific criticism. The story of the efforts to reconcile Catholicism with science is a large part of the history of nineteenth-century liberal Catholicism and its various attempts to reconcile the Roman Church with contemporary culture.[2]

Radicals among liberal Catholics were less willing to respect contemporary Catholic doctrines and ecclesiastical officials than moderate liberal Catholics. But not until after 1900 did Catholic modernism, the most challenging form of radical liberal Catholicism, emerge. Pressed by scientific criticism, the modernists called into question the meaning of dogma and the traditional understanding of the authority of the Church. Thus, moderate liberal Catholicism and modernism represented two different responses to scientific criticism. The dominant response within the Roman Church, however, proved to be reliance on ecclesiastical authority, particularly the pope.

One of the functions of authority in a church is to preserve the fundamental beliefs of that church. This in itself is a conservative function. But questions may arise as to how belief can best be preserved in the face of new intellectual challenges. The decisions made by ecclesiastical authorities in these instances depend, to a significant degree, on their assessment of the challenges. Here the roles of the ecclesiastical official and the intellectual meet, and conflict sometimes results.

The exercise of authority within the Church in response to the challenge of science created problems for the liberal Catholics. While accepting the principle of the authority of the Church, liberal Catholics emphasized the need to come to grips with scientific criticism. They recognized that scholars and thinkers had played a

2

significant role in the history of the Church by meeting
intellectual challenges with intellectual answers and by
presenting the Church's beliefs in contemporary terms.
They hoped to defend belief by showing how firmly it stood
in the face of criticism and how it was sometimes enlightened
by criticism. The ecclesiastical authorities, on the other
hand, tended to rely on authority and obedience to defend
belief. In a period of crisis like the nineteenth century,
it was probable that conflicts between Catholic intellectuals
and ecclesiastical officials would occur. Under pressure,
both found it more difficult to distinguish between intellectual suppression and legitimate demands for obedience.
Furthermore, intellectual inquiry requires a high degree of
freedom and the acceptance of the inevitability of some
mistakes, whereas periods of crisis generally breed
intolerance.

The tension in the Church reached its peak during
the 1860's. Not only had the challenge of science become
steadily more apparent, but Pius IX had just been stripped
of the papal states by Italy in the process of unification.
In these circumstances, he was further inclined to defensive
reaction against the challenges of the modern world. Since
ascending to the papal throne in 1846, he had been confronted with several dilemmas. He had sympathized with
some of the ideas of political liberalism, but had been
forced by revolutionaries to flee Rome in 1848; moreover,
political liberalism, particularly in Italy, was often
accompanied by atheism and anti-clericalism. Given these
circumstances, could he have reconciled himself with
liberalism? He was sympathetic toward Italian nationalist
aspirations, but he was the universal head of the Church and
support of Italian unification would have involved war
against Catholic Austria. Finally, there was the problem of
the papal states. Pius was not primarily interested in

3

temporal power, but he believed that the papal states were a necessary material guarantee against interference by a secular power in the pope's exercise of his spiritual office. In his view, therefore, he could not relinquish control over them. He was thus torn between some of his original sympathies and the biddings of his conscience. In addition, he could grasp political realities; he realized that his policies would be unpopular in Europe and were opposed to currents of political liberalism and nationalism.

A number of Roman Catholics were making vigorous attempts to come to terms with the challenges of political liberalism and nineteenth-century science. Count Charles de Montalembert (1810-1870) led those who urged acceptance of political liberalism and the separation of church and state. J. J. I. von Döllinger (1799-1890) advocated that the Church accept the new historical criticism, adjust to developments in science, and allow Catholic scholars to pursue scientific inquiry free from intervention by ecclesiastical officials. In England, Sir John (later Lord) Acton (1834-1902), a pupil of Döllinger, employed a periodical-- first the Rambler, then the Home and Foreign Review--to broadcast the call for free intellectual inquiry. Both Döllinger and Acton thought it incumbent on Roman Catholics to submit to the dogmas of the Church, but were inclined to urge absolute freedom for Catholic intellectuals except in instances of real dogmatic error.[3]

At first, these liberal Catholics had regarded the threat to the papal states as an act of unprovoked and unjust aggression against Pius IX; moreover, they feared that an Italian state in possession of the papal territories might interfere in the pope's independent exercise of his spiritual office. To the liberal Catholics the issue was a temporal affair and involved neither questions of one's fundamental loyalty to the Church nor theological questions

4

as such. When Döllinger, Acton, and other liberal Catholics became convinced that the downfall of the papal states was inevitable, their ardor for that cause cooled. To the neo-ultramontanes,[4] the cause of the papal states was the cause of the whole Church, for the Pope had decided to attempt to retain his territories. Consequently, they were inclined to consider criticism or even lukewarmness toward that cause as indicative of a lack of loyalty to the Pope and the Church.

As a fervent neo-ultramontane, Henry Edward Manning-- a convert from Anglicanism in 1851 and Provost of the Chapter of Westminster since 1857--vehemently supported the cause of the papal states. He remembered how the Erastian- ism of England had exerted what he regarded as a sinister influence on Anglican ecclesiastical authority in the Gorham judgment (1850); he feared that the loss of the papal states would expose the papacy to similar influences from a new Italian state. In using some extreme theological argu- ments, he gave the impression that the temporal power of the pope might in due course become a dogma of faith; more- over, he cited prophecies to support his argument that the city of Rome would abandon the faith and become an "anti- Christ." So extreme was he on the latter count that there was even some talk in Rome of placing his works in defense of the temporal power on the Index.[5]

In contrast to Manning, Acton and his associates of the English liberal Catholic periodical, The Rambler, viewed the question of the papal states not as a matter of obedience to the pope but as a contemporary political and historical question. They considered it subject to individual inquiry and opinion as were other political and historical questions. The basic division between the insistence of Action and his Rambler colleagues on free scientific inquiry and the insistence of the neo-ultramontanes on ecclesiastical

authority was thus expressed in their differences over the
question of the papal states. Moreover, Acton and his
associates objected to Manning's dragging theological considerations into the question. It was not long before the
Rambler received a rebuke from Rome for its views on the
papal states. The instigator of this rebuke was Manning's
friend in Rome, Monsignor Talbot, an Englishman who was a
chamberlain to Pius IX.[6]

In regard to the question of the papal states, John
Henry Newman occupied, as was typical of him, an inter-
mediate position between the neo-ultramontanes and the
liberal Catholics, although he was more sympathetic toward
the views of the latter. He objected completely to the neo-
ultramontanes' making the temporal power a test of Catholic
loyalty. In 1860 he disliked the temporal power more than
Acton did, but he refrained from questioning it publicly.[7]
Newman's attitude reflected his tendency to uphold the
rights of scientific inquiry into nontheological problems.
His silence, on the other hand, reflected his reluctance to
place himself in a position of outright opposition to the
representatives of ecclesiastical authority, for which he
had high regard. Nevertheless, his silence remained an
implicit indictment of the temporal power. This did not
escape Manning's notice. In 1866 he wrote to Talbot about
Newman:

> Whether he knows it or not, he has become the centre
> of those who hold low views about the Holy See, are
> anti-Roman, cold and silent, to say no more, about
> the Temporal Power. . . . I see no danger of a
> Cisalpine Club rising again, but I see much danger
> of an English Catholicism, of which Newman is the
> highest type. It is the old Anglican, patristic,
> literary, Oxford tone transplanted into the Church.
> It takes the line of deprecating exaggerations,
> foreign devotions, Ultramontanism, anti-national
> sympathies. In one word, it is worldly Catholicism,
> and it will have the worldly on its side, and will
> deceive many.[8]

It was, however, a difference in perspective and not a difference in belief or loyalty that separated Newman from Manning and liberal Catholics from neo-ultramontanes. Most of the liberal Catholic and neo-ultramontane leaders could agree with Acton's later statement that the Church's "Communion is dearer to me than life."[9] The liberals focused their attention on the future benefits that the Church could derive from accepting the advances in scientific knowledge and method and the establishment of political liberties. Liberal Catholic intellectuals believed that the new scientific methods would lead to the discovery of fresh knowledge that must ultimately coincide with dogma at the very least, while causing to be discarded accretions which encumbered the Church's preaching of its faith. They argued that rejection of the new science would be futile for the Church because its methods and discoveries would be widely accepted among the educated classes; more importantly, like Newman, they feared that rejection itself would tend in the long run to discredit religious belief. Those liberals mainly interested in the political developments affecting the Church believed that liberal political ideas were not in themselves contrary to the Catholic faith. These ideas also would be generally accepted; if the Church should reject them, it would be alienated further from modern society. The neo-ultramontanes, on the other hand, tended to focus their attention on the present attacks of science on theology and of liberal revolutions on the Church. To some neo-ultramontanes, agnostic scientists seemed to be simply blasphemers, and advocates of political liberalism merely thieves. With all the new scientific challenges to traditional religious beliefs and with the threat of revolutions with strong anti-clerical or atheistic elements, the ecclesiastical authorities on the whole were inclined, like Manning in England, to accept the neo-ultramontane view of the Church in the modern world.

Since Pius IX's experience with the new Italy was his primary experience with the modern world, it sealed his acceptance of the neo-ultramontane view. To him, modern civilization meant the Roman Republic, the murder of his minister Rossi, and his flight to Gaeta. It meant Cavour, anti-clerical legislation, the suppressing of monasteries and convents, and the seizure of the papal states. And it signified Mazzini and the proclamation of a new religion of humanity in the same breath as the proclamation of political liberalism.[10]

The collision between the defensive reaction of Pius IX and the sanguine hopes of the liberal Catholics occurred in 1863-64. In August 1863, Montalembert urged his ideas of political liberalism on a French and Belgian Catholic congress at Malines. Shortly thereafter at a German Catholic congress in Munich, Döllinger advocated free scientific inquiry and the general acceptance of the new historical methods in theology. This was too much for the beleaguered Pope. In February 1864, Montalembert's ideas were censured by the Pope in a private but official letter. In March, a papal brief censuring Döllinger's efforts to bring about freedom of scientific inquiry from intervention by ecclesiastical authorities was published. The brief insisted that Catholic intellectuals respect not only the dogmas and acts of infallible authority but also the ordinary magisterium (teaching authority) of the Church and the doctrinal decisions of the Roman congregations. Since virtually complete freedom of intellectual inquiry was the basic principle of Acton's Home and Foreign Review, the brief implicitly censured his journal. To avoid placing himself in a position of outright opposition to the Pope, Acton discontinued publication.

Döllinger and Acton had raised the question of the legitimate roles of the intellectual and of authority within the Roman Church, and the Pope had given what they regarded as an unsatisfactory answer. In sympathy with the aims if not with all the views of the liberal Catholics, John Henry Newman wrote to Acton that he found no difficulty in acquiescing in the letter and the principle of the points made in the brief, but that he dreaded their application.[11] The series of papal censures culminated at the end of 1864 when Pius IX promulgated the Syllabus of Errors. It condemned the proposition that the pope "can and should reconcile and harmonize himself with progress, with liberalism, and with recent civilization." For the time being at least, the Vatican had rejected the liberal Catholic policy of reconciliation.

In England, Newman had sympathized with the liberal Catholic aim of preserving belief by coming to grips intellectually with the challenges to it. Sometimes Newman's sensitivity, however, had made him appear indecisive. It was difficult for him to favor unreservedly any one course of action or any one group when he saw merits in other claims as well. Moreover, he sometimes disagreed with the specific views and tactics of the leading liberal Catholics of his day. Thus he had been unable to give himself wholeheartedly to their cause, even if he agreed with their general aims or basic positions on many issues. Enthusiastic liberal Catholics sometimes wrongly attributed to timidity his refusals to back them to the extent they desired,[12] while neo-ultramontanes mistakenly suspected him of being less than wholehearted in his espousal of Catholic beliefs.

Indeed, Newman had proposed to assist the Roman Church in England by coming to grips intellectually with the challenges to belief, but it was preoccupied with serious

9

pastoral problems. Moreover, it was isolated from the main currents of English civic and social life. Although English Catholics in 1829 had been given the right to hold nearly all public offices--which made them in theory virtually equal to other Englishmen--they remained a group apart. The anti-papal agitation of the early 1850's had showed that England's traditional hostility to Roman Catholicism was not dead. Besides these historical residues, the Roman Church in England faced several problems due to recent growth. Large-scale Irish immigration to English cities during the 1840's had swelled its ranks. If the immigrants were not to drift away from the Church in their new urban environments, more priests had to be provided and more churches built. In addition to the problem of finding these resources, the old clash of Irish and English interests and prejudices had to be dealt with. During the 1840's also, converts from Anglicanism had followed Newman to Rome in the wake of the Oxford Movement. The old English Catholics and the new converts often continued to feel toward each other the same antagonism that had long existed between "Papists" and Englishmen in general.

Even if preoccupied with pastoral problems, the ecclesiastical authorities of the Roman Church in England could not but notice that traditional religious beliefs were being challenged in the name of science. Within the Anglican Church, the "Broad Church" group, attaching relatively little importance to dogma, was ready to accommodate itself at dogma's expense to opinions of science. The publication of Essays and Reviews (1860) had crystallized in England the challenge of science to traditional religious beliefs. In this work, a group of Anglican churchmen seemed to compromise in favor of scientific criticism doctrines regarding the inspiration and authenticity of Scripture.[13] Would some educated English Roman Catholics do likewise? It did not take the papal actions of the 1860's to sound the alarm over science's challenge--conflicts at home had already done so. But there were different responses to the challenge.

A comparison between Newman and Manning will be illustrative. Manning was especially quick to draw lessons from the conflicts within the Anglican Church. Recognizing that the Christian churches were faced with a crisis, he identified a major cause as rationalism or the belief that man's reason, not revelation or the authority of the Church, was the ultimate judge in questions of dogma. He was convinced that rationalism was the tendency of religious belief in Anglicanism; he pointed to the Anglican Bishop Colenso-- who shortly after Essays and Reviews had also raised doubts concerning the inspiration and authenticity of the Biblical books--as a sample of it, even if the majority of Anglican clergymen were presently against Colenso. He believed that the Roman Church, with its dogma and authoritative claims, was the only church that stood with certainty against the advancing tide of rationalism.[14]

Like some other churchmen who looked with apprehension at the advances of science, Manning was not an obscurantist. He did not think that Scripture had laid down a particular system of chronology and did not hold that it contained a revelation of the physical sciences; he admitted that some of its narratives taken as history seemed incredible. He thought some of the difficulty might lie in the understanding of Scripture. More typically, he maintained that the science of his day generalized too hastily on the evidence it had discovered and tended too much to regard its conclusions as established once and for all. There was indeed a tendency in the Victorian era to accept unquestioningly the judgments of science. It was true, moreover, that--even as some churchmen were attacking

11

science--some Victorian scientists, led by Huxley, were belligerently attacking religion. Manning reacted with characteristic vigor to what he considered, with some justice, to be a mistaken faith in science. In his view, "science unscientifically handled" was challenging the principles of belief with principles of naturalistic atheism. Consequently, he referred to himself as a ringleader of Catholics who abhorred the science fashionable in his day, which he scornfully called "'the brutal philosophy,' to wit, there is no God, and the ape is our Adam."[15] He was inclined to fear that attempts to reconcile advances in scientific knowledge with opinions current among Catholic theologians would lead to heresy and the flouting of ecclesiastical authority. He concluded that it was best to rest assured in one's faith and to leave the intellectual questions raised by science unresolved. To the English Catholic Academia, he remarked: "It would inspire us with more confidence in their science and humility, if our geologists said: 'If the facts of geology are contrary to the Catholic faith, let geology look to its facts. . . .' Even in our own short lifetime we have seen the facts of geology to be made, unmade, remade, and made over again, I know not how many times."[16]

Both Manning and Newman affirmed the claims of revelation, dogma, and the authority of the Church. Newman was also apprehensive about the scientific developments of his age. Fearing that startling conclusions resulting from scientific inquiries could awaken religious doubts in weak minds, he thought that they were best discussed in serious, not light, publications. He objected to the use of scientific arguments as either a conclusive proof or disproof of the inspiration and authority of Scripture and other doctrinal matters. But he also objected to the exaltation of theological opinions into dogmas of faith and to attempts

to thwart or cast aspersions on strictly scientific research
into physical phenomena and into the Bible and its times.
Regarding the publication of Darwin's Origin of Species, he
remarked: "I either go whole hog with Darwin, or, dispens-
ing with time and history altogether, hold, not only the
theory of distinct species, but that also of the creation
of fossil-bearing rocks."[17] He feared the growth of suspicions and doubts about religion among educated persons if
the Church thwarted scientific inquiry or if it failed to
come to grips with intellectual problems raised by science.
The case of Galileo was intensely relevant to him. In
1876, he wrote to his fellow Roman Catholic, the biologist
St. George Mivart: "Those who would not allow Galileo to
reason 300 years ago, will not allow anyone else now. The
past is no lesson for them for the present and the future:
and their notion of stability in faith is ever to be repeating errors and then repeating retractations of them."[18]
Certain that scientific truth could not ultimately contradict the truth of revelation, he counselled forbearance by
both scientists and divines. He warned educated people
about mistaking popular theological opinions for dogmas of
faith. If temporary conflicts arose between science and
religion, he was convinced that supposed scientific facts
would turn out to be either untrue or not really contradictory to revelation, even if they denied something con-
fused with revelation. He considered it "the highest wisdom
to accept truth of whatever kind, wherever it is clearly
ascertained to be such, though there be difficulty in
adjusting it with other known truth."[19]

Newman ascribed the irreligious tendency associated
with the advances of science to the naturalistic assumptions
of scientists, not to the scientific method. Rejecting the
nineteenth century's faith in science and progress, he
believed that life's meaning and mankind's happiness could

be found only in Christianity.[20] He thought the Church
would eventually have to grapple with science, the intellectual challenge of the nineteenth century, as it had with
Aristotelian philosophy, the challenge in the High Middle
Ages. In contrast to Manning, he was inclined to fear not
heresies but indifference toward religious beliefs because
of lack of understanding of them; he advised capable churchmen to promote better understanding by taking up scientific
studies and not allowing the use of them to be monopolized
by unbelievers. He did not expect, however, any speedy
reconciliation of the Church with scientific developments
in the near future. He foresaw a current of unbelief drifting in the following direction: unbelievers would maintain
that religious beliefs were a waste of time since one could
not scientifically prove them to be true; they would conclude that mankind, having already wasted centuries on
religious beliefs, should ignore them in the future.
Newman tended to think that unbelief would become powerful
and popular for a time since the sheer allurement of science
and the effects of specialization in only one branch of
study would prejudice minds a priori against religious
beliefs.[21]

He regarded the education of Christian minds that
could resist the rising tide of unbelief as his special
work.[22] In view of conditions in many Catholic institutions of learning during the nineteenth century, this work
took on all the more importance. In France, for instance,
the so-called Cartesian scholasticism was widespread in the
seminaries. Moreover, numerous Catholic centers of learning had been destroyed by the French Revolution and were
yet to be replaced. Not much work was being done in the
new scientific Biblical and historical criticism. While a
seminarian, Renan's study of Cartesian scholasticism
stimulated his doubts about his faith and acquainted him

14

with the philosophies of opponents such as Kant which it attempted to refute. Weakened by philosophical doubt, his faith was destroyed when he became acquainted with philological criticism of the Bible. After abandoning his studies for the priesthood, he became an exponent of the faith in science and a leading rationalist who rejected dogma because he could not rationally verify it.[23]

Although Newman stood directly opposed to the naturalistic assumptions of works such as Renan's _Vie de Jésus_, he was alive to the plausibility of scepticism in matters of belief. In _An Essay in Aid of a Grammar of Assent_ (1870), he replied to scepticism by attempting to show that believers could have valid grounds for their religious convictions without being able to present arguments that would necessarily convince unbelievers. In analyzing the psychology of the believer and unbeliever, Newman held that they did not see the same evidence; unbelief resulted from assuming false first principles that precluded full knowledge of the evidence for belief.[24] His non-scholastic approach to the problem of certitude was characterized by its individuality.

The different policies advocated by Newman and Manning for the higher education of Roman Catholics in England reflected their different views on the conflict between science and religion. Even after Oxford and Cambridge agreed to admit Roman Catholics, Manning, who had become Archbishop of Westminster in 1865, maintained a prohibition against Catholics attending them. He believed that their anti-Catholic atmosphere would be injurious to faith and piety; moreover, he regarded them as centers of growing unbelief. Better that young Catholics not attend university at all.[25]

While recognizing the risk that intellectual challenges by their very nature present to belief, Newman hoped

to see Catholics pursue higher scientific and humanistic
studies. He was convinced that a "University as such,
involves as one of its necessary conditions, a risk to the
faith of these or those members of it. . . . It would be
melancholy, if they [the authorities of a university] were
commanded to impose restraints upon its members, which were
destructive of the very life of a University."[26] He thought
it would be a sufficient safeguard if he founded at Oxford
a residence where Roman Catholic students could receive
intellectual and spiritual guidance in their religion at
the same time that they received training in other subjects.
But most of the English Roman Catholic hierarchy, whose
views on the subject were similar to Manning's, opposed his
plans. Ultimately submissive to authority, Newman eventually
abandoned his project.

Manning realized that university education was not
unimportant, but his conception of it as a means of advancing the interests of Roman Catholics in the modern world was
quite different from Newman's. Newman hoped that it would
result in enlargement of mind, put Roman Catholics abreast
of modern knowledge, and tend to remove suspicions that
modern knowledge was necessarily destructive of religious
belief. Manning believed that it should provide young
Catholics with training for the professions. This training
could be secured in a protective Catholic environment.
Manning's attempt to found a Catholic university at
Kensington reflected his conception of university education
for Catholics.[27]

Although Newman's efforts to work toward the reconciliation of the Church and modern knowledge had been
frustrated,[28] he had left an intellectual legacy that could
be claimed by the English liberal Catholics of the 1890's.
In his views on the way to deal with the challenge of
science to religious belief, they could find a confirmation

16

of the policy of reconciliation that they advocated. In his upholding the rights of free scientific inquiry while retaining the claims of dogma and legitimate ecclesiastical authority, the liberals could see an image of their perspective on the Church and the Catholic intellectual. And in his firm belief that the conflict between science and religion could not be ultimate, they could find reassurance that their goal of reconciliation, no matter how difficult, was possible to attain. Newman himself was aware that his work might be meaningful to the generation after him. He wrote in his journal in January 1868, not long after his plans for the education of Catholics at Oxford had again been frustrated: "Perhaps my name is to be turned to account as a sanction and outset by which others, who agree with me in opinion, should write and publish instead of me, and thus begin the transmission of views in religious and intellectual matters congenial with my own, to the generation after me."[29]

The Vatican Council convened by Pius IX in 1869 brought down the curtain on the liberal Catholicism of the mid-nineteenth century. After the Munich brief and the Syllabus of Errors, liberal Catholicism had been able to do little more than try to limit the reach of the neoultramontane triumph. The convening of the Vatican Council aroused fears among liberal Catholics--especially the fear of excessive papal authority. Unsuccessfully they turned to the bishops at the Council to oppose the increasing power of the pope.[30] It was not, however, the doctrine of papal infallibility in itself, as defined by the Council, that affected their cause. With a few exceptions, most notably Döllinger, they assented to the dogma when it had been defined. The significance of the Vatican Council for their cause lay in the fact that the Council demonstrated that the Church was looking to the papacy for leadership.

17

Pius IX had already decided that the liberal Catholic view of the Church in the modern world was wrong. Moreover, the majority of the episcopate as well as lay opinion supported the neo-ultramontane view.[31] It was conceivable that another pope in other circumstances might come to a different decision on the liberal Catholic policy of seeking a new modus vivendi for the Church within contemporary culture, but for at least the near future Pius IX's decision seemed irreversible. Neo-ultramontism and the First Vatican Council accelerated the development of a more centralized, disciplined church--the Roman Church as it was to be for another century.

After the Vatican Council the liberal Catholic view of the Church in the modern world went into eclipse. Some frustrated liberal Catholics ended their efforts to reconcile their Church to the new scientific and political ideas; they now occupied themselves with more secular concerns. Acton turned to preoccupation with history, and his Rambler associate Richard Simpson to Shakespearean literature. In France and Germany, many members of the younger generation of Catholics tended to be caught up in the general movement toward Roman Catholic cohesiveness that was accelerated by the Vatican Council, republican anticlericalism in France, and the Kulturkampf in Germany. Among the older generation of liberal-minded Catholics, Montalembert, the leader in France, had died, Döllinger in Germany had been excommunicated for refusing to submit to the Council's decrees, and the aging Newman in England tended to withdraw into retirement. Between 1870 and 1890, therefore, few calls were heard for the reconciliation of the Roman Church with contemporary culture and for the intellectual freedom necessary to achieve this end.

Given the increasing absorption of naturalistic assumptions and philosophies of life into European culture during the nineteenth century, a defensive reliance on authority was perhaps the likely response of the Roman Church to the challenge of contemporary thought and criticism during the period. Given the history of the Roman Church, it was also likely that Catholic intellectuals would again attempt, sooner or later, to reconcile Catholicism with scientific criticism. But knowledge was becoming more specialized; research was being done by professional scholars trained in scientific methods. The nonprofessional found it more difficult to compete with, or even to keep informed of, the results of professional scholarship. If Catholicism was to find a _modus_ _vivendi_ within contemporary culture, there seemed to be a need for Catholic scholars trained in the new historical methods and for theologians and philosophers who were familiar with the results of recent scholarship in areas of vital interest to Christianity.

In response to this need, a new group of liberal Catholics emerged in England during the 1890's. To illustrate English liberal Catholicism from 1890 to 1907, I have selected its leading figures: the theologian George Tyrrell (1861-1909), the philosopher and Biblical critic Baron Friedrich von Hügel (1852-1925),[32] the biographer and essayist Wilfrid Ward (1856-1916), the Benedictine historian Francis Aidan Gasquet (1846-1929), and the historian of liturgy Edmund Bishop (1846-1917). Each could claim to be employing the new historical methods or to be familiar with results of recent scholarship, and each produced works of some influence. All five men became involved in major ecclesiastical controversies affecting the reconciliation of Roman Catholicism with contemporary culture. They represent, moreover, the different positions that eventually developed within English liberal Catholicism under the pressure of the controversies. Tyrrell and Hügel became leading modernists, although Hügel's modernism was largely confined to the area of Biblical criticism. Ward best represented moderate English liberal Catholicism. For the sake of candor, I must state that I admire Ward for trying to find a middle course between modernism and ultra-conservativism. Yet I do not think that he found a suitable course--have we even today?--and he was at times too apologetical for actions and policies of ecclesiastical authorities. Gasquet generally stood somewhat to the right of Ward on issues. Like the others, Bishop saw a need for liberal Catholic works but he shared little of the other men's optimism about the probable outcome of their efforts to reconcile Roman Catholicism with contemporary thought and criticism. If one placed these five figures on the spectrum of religious thought and ecclesiastical views that developed within English liberal Catholicism, Tyrrell would stand near the far left, Hügel on the left center, Ward in the middle, Gasquet to the right, and Bishop would sometimes appear with Gasquet to the right of Ward and at other times to the left.[33] Ultimately Hügel and Ward possessed a remarkable centrality, as I hope this book will show.

Divisions only gradually emerged; in the early 1890's, liberal Catholics generally agreed on ends and means. By encouraging attitudes of objectivity and tolerance within the Roman Church and among its critics as well, they hoped to enable Catholic intellectuals to meet the challenges of scholarship and criticism. They also hoped that the Roman ecclesiastical authorities would allow Catholic intellectuals freedom of inquiry within the necessary limits of the Church's dogma and discipline.

The body of this book will attempt to provide an account of the development of liberal Catholicism in England

20

in the late nineteenth and early twentieth centuries. It is the first study of the main English liberal Catholics of the period after 1890 as a group. It will try to show that there was one intellectual crisis manifest in many widely differing controversies involving the Vatican and liberal Catholics in England. It will also try to demonstrate that there was a spectrum of liberal Catholicism of which the Catholic modernists were but a part, ultimately diverging from the others.

CHAPTER I

THE REAPPEARANCE OF ENGLISH

LIBERAL CATHOLICISM

The actions of the papacy under Pius IX had been
decisive in frustrating the hopes of Montalembert, Döllinger,
Acton, Newman, and other liberal-minded Catholics in the
1860's when the tension between Roman Catholicism and the
modern world reached its peak. So too the actions of the
papacy under Leo XIII were decisive in encouraging the hopes
of the new generation of liberal Catholics that appeared on
the ecclesiastical scene in the early 1890's. Although Leo
was not himself a student of science, he was a scholar and
a diplomat who realized that some familiarity with the
scientific idiom of the age was necessary to restore
Catholicism's intellectual prestige. Consequently, he
encouraged historical studies, and had dramatized his bene-
diction to these studies by opening the Vatican archives to
Catholic and non-Catholic scholars. He seemed inclined to
allow much freedom of inquiry to Roman Catholics seriously
dealing with questions of religion. In the early 1890's,
he inaugurated his _ralliement_ policy. These actions, so
different from those of his predecessor, clearly indicated
that Leo hoped for at least some reconciliation with modern
society and thought.

In spite of the risk of opposition from ecclesiastical authorities in the two decades following the Vatican
Council, Catholic scholars were at work with the new
scientific methods. In the field of history, some Roman

Catholic scholars were using the Rankean methods to study the history of religion. The French abbé Louis Duchesne (1843-1922) became the leading Catholic advocate and exemplar of the new historical methods. In the area of Biblical criticism, Father Gustav Bickell (1838-1906) of Innsbruck and abbé Alfred Loisy (1857-1940) of the Institut Catholique in Paris were doing some distinguished work. In the Catholic institutes that had grown up in France after 1875, other scholars using the new methods were also at work.

Another factor that led to the reappearance of liberal Catholicism in the 1890's was the passing away of those who had been involved in the liberal Catholic-neo-ultramontane conflicts of the 1860's. Of the neo-ultramontanes, Pius IX had died in 1878, William George Ward in 1882, Louis Veuillot in 1883, and Henry Edward Manning in 1892; of the liberal Catholics, Montalembert died in 1870, Newman in 1890, Döllinger in 1890, and Acton after the Vatican Council eschewed ecclesiastical contro-versy.[1] A new generation of Catholics unscarred by the battles of the 1860's had grown up and was ready to take its place in ecclesiastical affairs by 1890.

By the late nineteenth century historical criticism, particularly criticism of the Bible, was becoming ever more the focal point of the conflict of science and religion. Within Protestantism, dogmatic religion was giving way in the face of this challenge. The presupposition that ortho-doxy had been irretrievably discredited represented a growing feeling in England. It was precisely this assump-tion that liberal Catholicism refused to grant. It was precisely the growth of this feeling that Newman had long ago feared. Liberal Catholicism as well as liberal Protestantism was attempting to find a new modus vivendi for Christianity within contemporary culture. But unlike

23

liberal Protestantism, the new generation of liberal
Catholics was not inclined to accept wholesale the conclusions of Biblical and historical criticism, to reject the
traditional Christian dogmas, and to begin preaching a new
gospel.

The leading new liberal Catholics of the early
1890's, Friedrich von Hügel, Wilfrid Ward, Francis Aidan
Gasquet, and Edmund Bishop hoped to take up the work of
reconciliation that had been abandoned amid the conflicts
that had arisen in mid-century. Except for Gasquet, who
was later to become a cardinal, these new liberal Catholics
were laymen.[2] None was directly involved in ecclesiastical
administration in the 1890's, but they thought they had an
intellectual role to fulfill within the Church. They tried
to carry out the dual intellectual function of transmitting
Catholicism while subjecting it to criticism. Their outlook on the contemporary problems of Christianity tended to
be historical: they saw the problems confronting
Christianity as products of historical developments rather
than as simply conflicts of irreconcilable basic principles.

Gasquet turned to historical scholarship after ill
health had forced him to resign his strenuous duties as
Prior of Downside Abbey. His first major historical work,
Henry VIII and the English Monasteries (2 volumes, 1888-89),
was an immediate success. It quickly went through several
editions, and altered the unfavorable popular English view
of Catholic monasticism during the Reformation period.
Indeed, before Gasquet's work even Cardinal Manning had
thought little could be said in favor of the monasteries.[3]
In the preface to his work, Gasquet stated his aims and
methods:

24

The present work has no pretence to be more than the title page claims for it, "an attempt to illustrate the history" of a great event in our national annals. My sympathies are naturally engaged, but I have striven to avoid anything like presenting or pleading a case, which, indeed, I felt would defeat my purpose. If I have insisted more on the facts which tell in favour of the monasteries than on those which tell against them, it is because the latter are well known and have been repeated, improved on and emphasized for three centuries and a half, whilst that there is anything to say on the other hand for the monks, has been little recognized even by those who would be naturally predisposed in their favour. My belief is, that the facts speak strongly enough for themselves, and I have endeavoured to add as little as possible of my own to the story they tell. All I desire is that my readers should judge from the letters, documents and opinions, which will be found in the following pages, whether bare justice has hitherto been done to the memory of the monastic order in England.[4]

In writing this history in accord with the criteria of the new scientific historical method, Gasquet acknowledged a debt to his friend "Edmund Bishop, who, from first to last, has aided me by counsel and suggestion as well as by his careful examination of every proof sheet. . . ."[5] Later, when Bishop was no longer available to insist on strict adherence to the historical method and when Gasquet was partially preoccupied by new administrative duties, Gasquet would lapse into an all too apologetical manner of writing history. Nevertheless, his early historical works were not of this nature, and established his reputation.

Edmund Bishop had converted to Roman Catholicism from High Anglicanism in 1867. In his papers at Downside Abbey, his own account of his state of mind at age seventeen shows that his study of the Arian controversy and the ancient Council of Nicaea influenced him on his way toward Rome: "A new question, that of the Church and Church authority, rose up before me. As time went on one difficulty struck me. It was this. How is it, if the Council of Nicaea, for instance, had power and authority to, and did in effect, decide and pronounce and define the true and saving doctrine of the Faith, that this no longer holds good today? . . . With very little alteration of phraseology my Anglican excuses for refusing to submit to the Catholic Church of today would serve the turn for refusing to admit the authority of the Nicene Council." He remarked that the Arians could have quoted against the Creed of Nicaea "several ugly passages from ante-Nicene Fathers at least as cogent against the doctrine of Nicaea as are these instances against Papal Supremacy."[6]

Bishop nevertheless regarded the papal actions of 1864 as a "crushing" of free lay intellectual activity. In his view, the papacy had denied the layman a role in the intellectual life of the Church for at least the foreseeable future. Even Leo XIII's pontificate did not change Bishop's view, which he retained for the rest of his life. This settled belief, as well as the fact that publication was not the primary concern with him in his historical research, decisively affected his liberal Catholic activities. He became a liberal Catholic who was content to help raise the level of English Roman Catholic scholarship and intellectual life through the influences of his learning and personality on promising scholars, particularly among the Benedictines of Downside Abbey, where he had been a postulant in the late 1880's. Pessimistic as to the immediate future of the liberal Catholic cause, he tended to be indifferent toward any attempts to reconcile Catholicism with contemporary culture that went beyond his self-imposed limitation of being a scholar and a scholar only. Bishop possessed a wide knowledge of the documents of medieval history, but his area of special scholarly interest was the rather esoteric field of the history of Western liturgy. Although most of his published writings were contributions to Catholic periodicals, he had acquired before 1890 a well-deserved scholarly reputation on the Continent, particularly among critical scholars in Germany.[7] In England he remained practically unknown. His only work that received public attention there was Edward VI and the Book of Common Prayer (1890), which he wrote with Gasquet. The scholarly, non-controversial intent of this work was stated in its preface: "Though treating of liturgy the object of the work is strictly historical. Unless a clear and intelligible idea can be gained of the liturgical changes in the reign of Edward VI, it is impossible to understand a period which is the turning point in the religious history of England."[8] The work was, however, of obvious interest to Anglicans because of the claims of the Anglo-Catholic party. It would become of even more interest when the Anglican orders controversy began a few years later.

Although Hügel had specialized knowledge of the methods and results of Biblical criticism and kept abreast of contemporary developments in that field, he was not a productive Biblical scholar. His deepest interest really lay elsewhere, for he was concerned above all with shedding light on the problems, present and historical, that he considered to be involved in living a spiritual life. Not until many years later did he begin publishing his profound major works on religion and establishing his intellectual reputation in England. Nevertheless, his interest in science on the one hand and the spiritual life on the other naturally affected his basic outlook on the conflict of science and religion in the 1890's.

To Hügel, the intrinsic value of scientific inquiry had to be accepted for its own sake, but if research were to be of full benefit to an individual it also had to become an integral part of his spiritual life. Indeed, he believed that it was through an earnestness and enthusiasm for the discovery of truth, similar in its way to devotion to living a spiritual life, that science itself was able to advance. Although he thought that scientific work by Catholics was vitally necessary to alleviate the intellectual difficulties that some individuals were experiencing, he believed that in this earthly life one could not hope to see the reconciliation of all the conflicts between the teachings of religion and those of science; therefore, one had to accept the inevitability of some tension between religious and scientific beliefs. He regarded the free acceptance of this tension as a purifying agent for the soul and as one of life's necessary crosses. His faith in the supernatural alongside his belief in the inevitability of this tension enabled him throughout his long life to accept without reservation both the teachings of the Church and those of science, even in the cases where their teachings appeared to be contradictory. Hügel perhaps expressed his views most succinctly in the following passage:

> The inclusion and proper utilising of the phenomenal, determinist-seeming facts and method of science, within the total activity and growth of human personality, so as to feed, check, purify and render fruitful the metaphysical and spiritual convictions and interpretations of the soul, which, in their turn, alone give full meaning and value to that phenomenal·series: all this has for men of faith and study become more and more inevitable, urgent, difficult, crucifying. Yet it brings with it the sure fruits of the accepted Cross, a humble, humiliating creative power, and a peace which no man can give or take away.[9]

To justify his position intellectually, he seems in the 1890's to have made use of the Kantian distinction between phenomena and noumena. He tended at this time to regard science and religion as dealing with two different worlds: science with the world of phenomena, and religion with the real noumenal world beyond appearances. He would later reject the epistemological basis of Kant's position and repudiate certain consequences that others were drawing from it. But he never abandoned his basic views that the work of liberal Catholics toward the reconciliation of science and religion was necessary, that simultaneously one must accept the inevitability of tension between religious and scientific beliefs, and, above all, that the spiritual life was superior to the purely intellectual life.[10]

Ward was primarily concerned with the problem of the relationship between ecclesiastical authority and the Catholic intellectual. Unlike Hügel, he was only indirectly interested in the scholarly problems of scientific specialists. Although the son of William George Ward, he preferred in intellectual matters to follow his father's old opponent, Newman. In fact, among the leading new liberal Catholics, Wilfrid Ward had the deepest admiration for Newman, and tried to follow his lead and ideas most faithfully. Ward's views concerning the problem of the role of intellectuals and of authorities within the Church were based on his reading of the past. In his view, the Church was historically and essentially assimilative of the cultures in which it had existed. It had always rejected rival theories of life, but once their aggressiveness had been broken it assimilated what it found true in them. There were, however, two enemies of this wise conservatism that had preserved the Church from heresy and the abandonment of God's revelation on one hand and from stagnation and decay on the other. There were those foes on the left who would pull the Church down by revolutionizing or rejecting its dogma and basic institutions, and there were those on the right who would make life in the Church unbearable at present by

29

refusing to allow any change or renewal whatsoever.[11]   It
was precisely in the transmission of revelation and the
simultaneous assimilation of contemporary thought that
ecclesiastical authority and the Catholic intellectual each
had a complementary role to play. Ward's conception of the
relationship between the intellectual and authority in the
Church, a conception that was always basic to him, was ably
summarized many years later in an article in the Dublin
Review:

> Both periods [the Patristic and the Mediaeval] prove
> how wide a liberty can exist within the Church side
> by side with submission to authority. But the
> history of these periods further elucidates the
> function of authority in regard to human thought.
> It does not belong to authority to build up schools
> of thought; you cannot demand that the Papacy should
> provide the world with ready-made systems of
> philosophy; that is the function of the Catholic
> body at large and of individual thinkers. But it
> does belong to the Papacy and the ecclesiastical
> authorities to determine whether new ideas or methods
> of thought are to be accepted into the institutional
> life of the Church. . . . For authority is set to
> foster and shield the life itself of the Catholic
> community--that life 'which is deeper than thought
> and deeper still than any analysis of thought.'
> . . . there can be no true intellectual progress
> which shatters the life it should nourish or dis-
> rupts that institutional existence which is to the
> invisible Christian Faith what the human body is to
> the soul. That briefly was the moral which Wilfrid
> Ward, led by Newman, drew from the reading of
> Church history, and it was the theme which he
> persistently laboured in all his apologetic writings.[12]

The liberal Catholics had no wish to see history
repeat itself because of ignorance of it. Their outlook on
their present situation was conditioned by their view of the
past. In the epilogue of Wilfrid Ward's biography (1893) of
his father, an epilogue that was almost a joint production
of Ward and Hügel,[13] the typical English liberal Catholic

view of their present situation in light of the past was
expressed. In their judgment, Döllinger, by disparaging
ecclesiastical authority, had represented the extreme
liberal Catholic reaction to the development of science,
while Veuillot, by exalting ecclesiastical authority beyond
due limits, had represented the extreme conservative reaction. Newman had stood for a moderate response in the
1860's. Now in the 1890's, Ward and Hügel hoped the new
liberal Catholics would avoid extremes and cast themselves
in the mediating role of Newman. They thought that Leo XIII
would allow them the freedom necessary to assume this
role.[14]

Issues confronting liberal Catholics, within both
the Anglican and Roman churches, were crystallized in
England in 1889 by the Anglican publication, Lux Mundi.
In this volume of essays a group of Anglo-Catholic clergymen attempted to take a step toward the reconciliation of
Christianity and modern thought. They were convinced that
Christianity needed "disencumbering, reinterpreting,
explaining" and that there must be "great changes in the
outlying departments of theology, where it is linked on to
other sciences. . . ." On the other hand, they had no
intention of abandoning Christian dogma. In his preface
to Lux Mundi, Charles Gore expressed the general outlook
of liberal Catholics:

> We grudge the name 'development,' on the one hand,
> to anything which fails to preserve the type of the
> Christian Creed and the Christian Church; for
> development is not innovation, it is not heresy:
> on the other hand, we cannot recognize as the true
> 'development of Christian doctrine' a movement
> which means merely an intensification of a current
> tendency from within, a narrowing and hardening of
> theology by simply giving it greater definiteness
> or multiplying its dogmas.

> The real development of theology is rather the
> process in which the Church, standing firm in her
> old truths, enters into the apprehension of the
> new social and intellectual movements of each
> age. . . .15

Lux Mundi became such a sensation that it ran through ten
editions in one year. It won admiration and also brought
down sharp criticism. Pusey's disciple, H. P. Liddon,
regarded it as a surrender to rationalist criticism. On
the other hand, the Church Times approved it with reserva-
tions.16 In any case, Lux Mundi aired the problem of the
relationship of Catholic thought to scientific criticism,
particularly Biblical criticism.

       A major problem recognized by the Lux Mundi
essayists in the contemporary conflict between religion and
science was the old problem of faith and reason. In the
view expressed in Lux Mundi, faith did not depend on reason
alone, but neither was it irrational. It was an act of the
whole man, including the reason. Man naturally expressed
his faith in terms of reason. Therefore, when methods of
thought changed, some change in the methods of expressing
faith was also necessary. These changes did not have to
affect the substantial truth of the Christian dogmas. But
if the dogmas remained substantially unchanged, it was
always possible to achieve a fuller understanding of them.
Moreover, critics of Christianity could not simply say that
dogmas necessarily fettered the reason. If the dogmas were
true, then they did not fetter the reason. The Church permitted full investigation of its Creeds. The claim that
the dogmas were final and authoritative did not mean that
they were to be accepted blindly, but meant that if they
were accepted as substantially true, then they were final
in a sense in which science's truths were not. However, no
tradition of theological interpretation, no matter how

venerable, could claim final authority; only dogma could make this claim. The primary question was the truth of the dogmas, and the challenge of science bore directly on that question. It had to be admitted that the sphere of religion could not be completely separated from the spheres of science and philosophy. In fact, nineteenth-century science had unwittingly done Christianity a service by overturning the deistic conception of God and forcing Christianity to return to the truer traditional conceptions of the Greek fathers. But the scientific critic must not make assumptions without realizing that he is doing so. Historical criticism bore directly on the question of Christ's life, death, and resurrection. If the resurrection of Christ was really an extraordinary event, then the evidence of it could not be treated simply as if it were a natural historical event.[17]

Since Biblical criticism became a crucial matter in Lux Mundi and within the Roman Catholic Church in the 1890's, a retrospective look at it will be useful before we proceed. The English liberal (Roman) Catholics of the mid-nineteenth century had not felt their own position threatened by the rising Biblical criticism but welcomed it as an effective point of argument against Protestantism. In their view it helped to show that Scripture was not the ultimate norm of faith, a claim Protestants had made for the Bible. Johann Adam Möhler (1796-1838) and the Catholic Tübingen School had earlier also taken an optimistic view of Biblical criticism. They maintained that the Catholic's faith is founded on a living tradition, not on the letter of Biblical texts, and that the Catholic critic, although certainly believing that Scripture substantiates the Church's traditional teaching concerning faith and morals, may freely

recognize human imperfections and errors in the Bible.[18]
In a similar vein Richard Simpson, writing in the English
liberal Catholic Home and Foreign Review in 1863, was
optimistic: "It has long since been admitted by Catholic
theologians that a book in Scripture need not be in fact
the work of the author to whom it has for many centuries
been ascribed, and by whom it apparently claims to be
written. . . . And it has long since been taken for granted
that an inspired saint, 'full of the Holy Ghost,' may be
fallible in his historical statements, . . . The inspiration of Scripture is a traditional belief of the Catholic
Church, which has, however, cautiously abstained from
defining the nature and limits of inspiration. . . ."[19]
Simpson maintained that Catholics, safe in the Church's
dogmatic infallibility, could permit without danger the
free scientific investigation of Scripture. Thus, he com-
bined his vindication of the Catholic position with an
appeal for freedom for Catholic scholars.[20]

Other English liberal Catholics of the mid-
nineteenth century were also optimistic regarding Biblical
criticism. Henry Nutcombe Oxenham, in evaluating Essays
and Reviews in which a number of Anglican Broad Church
scholars had applied literary and historical criticism to
the Bible, took the line that the Essayists were destroying
the foundations of Protestantism. In 1862 Acton wrote to
Döllinger that Benjamin Jowett, one of the contributors to
Essays and Reviews, had told him that Catholics could let
Biblical criticism pass without opposition more easily than
Protestants could.[21] In a letter in the Rambler in 1862
Acton said that there was no reason for Catholics "to
place the chronology of the Hebrew Version, the universality
of the Deluge, and the habits of carnivora, among the tests
of infallibility, and the articles by which the Church must
stand and fall. Protestants occupy towards the letter of

the Bible a position different from our own. Having no
authority to define and explain the portions which are of
doctrinal importance, they are unable to distinguish
between the authority of different passages." He went on
to say that, unlike Protestants, "the Catholic avoids a
collision between creation and revelation, because he
possesses a criterion which separates in the Bible its
natural and its supernatural character, and informs him of
those things which it teaches, and which belong neither to
history nor to physical science."[22] To defend the Church
but claim permission for criticism, Acton distinguished in
the Church's teaching between infallible dogma and fallible
human notions that form round it. He also made a distinction in Scripture between a supernatural core of revelation
and passages of natural opinion surrounding it.[23] English
liberal Catholics of the mid-nineteenth century were convinced that Biblical criticism, by threatening the Bible-
based existence of Protestantism, made their own position
advantageous. Although largely chary of the ecclesiastical
authorities and suspicious of the attitude of the Vatican
toward Scripture, they no more than dimly foresaw that the
Biblical question would later bring liberal Catholics into
conflict with the pope.[24]

A new perspective on the whole evolution of ancient
Israel arose in Old Testament studies during the late 1860's
and 1870's. The Biblical critic most often associated with
this new perspective is Julius Wellhausen (1844-1918), who
eventually presented a magisterial synthesis of the investi-
gations of numerous predecessors. While a venerable tradition affirmed that the Pentateuch consisted of the oldest
documents of Hebrew literature and, consequently, antedated
the prophets, Wellhausen's school placed the solemn promulgation of the Law after the Babylonian Exile and the composition of the main codes after the great prophetical

movement. According to this interpretation only the Book of the Covenant and, perhaps, the oldest editing of the Yahwistic and Elohistic narratives could have been earlier than the eighth century. The prophets ceased to be viewed as restorers of Mosaic monotheism; in the new perspective they, not Moses, were the first to build up and proclaim monotheism.

Earlier Biblical critics had utilized the tools developed by scholars of other ancient literatures to ascertain the circumstances of documents' origins and to determine their meaning within the context of the historical situation of the author or compiler. The Bible was thus evaluated as a historically conditioned expression of man's culture. Although some critics continued to regard the Bible as a source of divine revelation, they nevertheless as critics viewed the Scriptures as a body of human literature subject to the same canons of inquiry as secular documents. By the 1860's the consensus of a broad spectrum of critics was that four sources could be distinguished in the Pentateuch and that in chronological order they were: First Elohist or Priestly Source (P), Second Elohist (E), Jahwist (J), and Deuteronomist (D). The revolution in Old Testament studies occurred when this essentially literary study of the Pentateuch was coupled with an idea of the historical development of ancient Israel's law and cultus. The outlines of the "Wellhausenian" reconstruction began to take form in the 1860's through the work of several scholars, especially Karl Heinrich Graf who utilized suggestions by Abraham Kuenen. They put the Pentateuchal documents distinguished by literary methods into a new chronological order and claimed to discover a pattern of development of law and liturgy from patriarchal simplicity to post-exilic complexity. It was affirmed that the materials in J-E reflected a simple, unpriestly, decentralized mode of religious life earlier than the seventh century. The P material of the Pentateuch with its fully developed pattern of worship and elaborate sacrifices offered by priests and Levites was considered to be post-exilic; P was looked upon as the latest, rather than the earliest, of the Pentateuchal documents. The pre-exilic prophets, seen in this perspective, were ignorant of the "Mosaic" cult because it did not yet exist, not because an apostate nation had forgotten it. Thus the prophets, not Moses, were seen as the first major teachers of ethical monotheism. Their ethical preaching and the priestly traditions were looked upon as antithetical strands in Israel's religious evolution.

In Great Britain William Robertson Smith was the first leading scholar to set forth and defend the recon-struction of Old Testament history wrought by the work of Graf, Kuenen, and Wellhausen. His Old Testament and the Jewish Church appeared in 1881. Later, S. R. Driver, who succeeded Pusey as Regius Professor of Hebrew at Oxford in 1884, also presented an influential popularization of the "Wellhausenian" reconstruction in his Introduction to the Literature of the Old Testament (1891). However, at the time Robertson Smith's work appeared in 1881 Driver was not yet satisfied that all of Wellhausen's views were cor-rect; many seemed to him to be conjectures that ought not to be advanced and reasoned on as facts. Moreover, he thought that probabilities were being summed into certain-ties, that conclusions of a series of presuppositions were being announced in a too confident manner. Driver later was won over to the Wellhausenian reconstruction. As things turned out, it came to exercise a striking hold over Old Testament scholarship. Only in recent decades have studies utilizing historical and philological materials procured by archaeology challenged its main tenets.[25]

At the time of _Lux Mundi_ the question of the Higher Criticism in England turned round the Old Testament and still not the New Testament.[26] David Friedrich Strauss's _Leben Jesu_ (1835-36), which tried to resolve the Gospels into myth and was influenced by Hegel's philosophy, had won little support in England, although George Eliot published a translation (1846). Ernest Renan's _Vie de Jésus_ (1863) was far more successful there. In his interpretation of Jesus, Renan, like Strauss, assumed that the supernatural could be admitted in no part of human history. He interpreted persons and events in terms of what he regarded as morally and psychologically probable. Acceptance of the dictum, "Miracles do not happen," by many critics and their dismissal of Biblical narratives containing features considered to be miraculous were among the traits of the early critical movement that had engendered distrust of it.[27] The Cambridge scholars B. F. Westcott, F. J. A. Hort, and J. B. Lightfoot were the outstanding figures in the English theological world from 1865 to _Lux Mundi_. They derived from older liberals the view that the Bible must be investigated as other ancient works, but they added a conviction that the central teachings of Christianity would be established more fully.[28] Indeed, Westcott had influenced Charles Gore at Harrow by showing how an otherworldly religion and a critical mind could go together.[29] The work of Westcott and Lightfoot, such as in establishing that the most important writings of the New Testament were of a relatively early date, had done much to quiet fears regarding the challenge of German criticism to orthodoxy. Yet critics could reply that accretions of miracle and theological interpretation in the New Testament had been added more quickly than earlier critics had supposed.[30] The church historian Adolf von Harnack would advance that view in later controversy.

Besides the specific issues raised by critics of the Bible, there were larger questions. One such question is perhaps clearer in retrospect than it was at the time. To what extent were nineteenth-century Biblical and historical critics truly scientific? How far were they influenced by assumptions? Archbishop Arthur Michael Ramsey has written that critics of Charles Gore--historians more liberal than he--used an avowedly historical method that began with the record of Christ's life, investigated it with historical science, and then judged its value and significance. In carrying this out "they could be unconscious of any philosophical assumptions, but it was quite inevitable that they should have some--both in their treatment of evidence in connection with 'abnormal' events and in their criteria for value and appreciation. It is now possible to see that both Gore and his critics were at fault in claiming that they were offering 'just history', and in thinking that 'just history' can provide a basis upon which 'interpretation' can then be brought as a second stage."[31]

C. H. Dodd has commented that critics in the nineteenth century tended on the whole to say: "strip off the interpretation so far as possible; it only tells us what some early Christians thought or believed; the residue will be plain matter of fact." Dodd remarks that the effort to make a sharp division between fact and interpretation, setting them over against each other, is misguided--whether it seeks to establish the facts by eliminating the interpretation, or, attending exclusively to interpretation, it dismisses the question of fact as irrelevant.[32] He has observed that the quest of the Historical Jesus was the object of nineteenth-century criticism; close analysis and evaluation of the Gospels as historical documents was its method. "Its assumption, avowed or implicit, was that this

39

method would succeed in eliminating from the records a mass of intrusive material due to the faith and thought of the early Church (Gemeindetheologie). When this was done, the residue would lie before us as a solid nucleus of bare fact, upon which we might put our own interpretation, without regard to the interpretation given by the early Church in the documents themselves." Thus it attempted to reconstruct Christianity on a base of historical fact, scientifically assured. Dodd goes on to say that this method of criticism, in searching for bare facts, sought to eliminate anything in the Gospels that might be attributable to the Church's faith or experience; in doing so it neglected precisely those elements in the Gospels that, to their authors, made them worth writing--whereas it is necessary to do full justice to an author's intention in order to understand his work. Nevertheless, Dodd adds that "when all these contentions are admitted, they do not dispense us from the duty of asking, and if possible answering, the historical question."[33]

In Lux Mundi the crucial area of Biblical criticism received special attention from Charles Gore. His thought was conditioned at its roots by his conviction that Christianity was pre-eminently the historical religion: not only did it arise out of historical events but those events were involved in the substance of belief. Gore maintained that the historical facts testified to by the New Testament were to be verified by the method of historical criticism. He did not share, however, the assumption of some critics that the Jesus of History and the Christ of Faith were really different. In some works after Lux Mundi he perhaps overestimated the power of historical criticism to yield demonstrative evidence of the truth of the Gospels.

And he seems to have drawn a too rigid line between the Old Testament and the New Testament. He combatted, however, the philosophical assumptions of critics who denied the miraculous. He regarded this denial as a common element in the interpretations of Christ by Strauss, Renan, and, later, Adolf von Harnack. He considered it to be based on the view that nature is a system complete in itself.[34]

In his essay, "The Holy Spirit and Inspiration," in Lux Mundi, Gore attempted to clarify his basic orthodoxy and loyalty to the Church. Accepting the Christian creed as true, he saw no need for heresies, basic innovations, and fundamental rejections, but did see a need for some reform and restoration. He agreed that ecclesiastical authority had to be exerted sometimes to keep the fundamental principles of the Church intact, but, short of this, thought the Church was characteristically tolerant, both theologically and morally. While recognizing that the Christian creed was inseparably interwoven with certain historical facts, he maintained that the New Testament record could not be understood by a Christian simply as literary or historical documents; full understanding necessarily involved presuppositions, or a frame of mind, about God and other matters of belief. "It is, we may perhaps say, becoming more and more difficult to believe in the Bible without believing in the Church." "Thus in fact the Apostolic writings were written as occasion required, within the Church, and for the Church. They presuppose membership in it and familiarity with its tradition."[35]

On the other hand, Gore pointed out a need for historical understanding of the Bible as well. He cited the early Church father Chrysostom: "We must not then look at the facts in themselves only, but investigate with attention the period also, the cause, the motive, the difference of persons, and all the attendant circumstances:

41

so only can one get at the truth." The latter part of his
essay took up some of the specific questions that Biblical
criticism had raised regarding inspiration. He held that
while inspiration guaranteed the truth of Scripture, it
did not guarantee its historical truth in every instance.
Referring to the fact that all early history tended to
attribute to first founders subsequent institutional
developments, he mentioned as instances the attribution of
the Mosaic law to Moses, the Psalms to David, and the
Proverbs to Solomon. Although the truth of historical
facts was more vital in the New Testament, here the evidence was not remote as in the Old Testament. Inspiration
did not necessarily imply a miraculous revelation of new
facts to the Biblical writers. After all, even writers of
the New Testament used the knowledge and methods of their
age. While upholding the possibility of Old Testament
miracles, Gore left this area open to literary and historical criticism. He raised the question whether the Scripture
narratives referring to periods before Abraham were mythi-
cal, although containing an indistinguishable historical
germ. He believed that Biblical criticism was reaching
some results as sure as those reached by Galileo and other
physical scientists, and clearly implied that the Church
should accept them as it had all too reluctantly accepted
the conclusions of those earlier scientists. He suggested
a kenotic view of Christ and said that He observed the
limits of the scientific and historical knowledge of His
age. In concluding, Gore appealed for a fair and frank
discussion of the questions raised by Biblical criticism,
but a discussion consistent with loyalty to Christ and the
Church. He was convinced that such a course would remove
"great obstacles from the path to belief of many who certainly wish to believe, and do not exhibit any undue
scepticism."[36]

Liberal Roman Catholics in England agreed with Gore
and Lux Mundi in advocating a frank and open-minded consideration of the products of Biblical and historical
criticism. Wilfrid Ward thought that Lux Mundi "expressed
the claim of the younger generation of thoughtful Christians
to hold on to orthodox Christianity while admitting a
breadth of view at variance with certain theological traditions hitherto generally regarded as synonymous with orthodoxy."[37] While agreeing with the aims of Lux Mundi, Ward
nevertheless thought it had ceded some points too readily
to Biblical criticism. In an article entitled "New Wine
in Old Bottles" in the Nineteenth Century, Ward pointed to
a significant difference between the Anglican and Roman
churches.[38] When Anglican writers of such weight as the
Lux Mundi authors argued for the orthodoxy of certain
views, the limits of orthodoxy within the Anglican Church
had to be extended to these opinions, for there was no
higher ecclesiastical authority to decide nor any machinery
to check their propagation. In the Roman Church, a higher
ecclesiastical authority did exist and possessed the jurisdiction to decide on the orthodoxy of views. On the one
hand, therefore, it had to be careful not to accept new
views prematurely and had to take into consideration the
present state of all shades of belief, popular as well as
sophisticated, within the Church. Thus the significance
of the title of the article, "no man putteth new wine into
old bottles; otherwise the wine will burst the bottles, and
both the wine will be spilled and the bottles will be lost."
On the other hand, there was less danger in the Roman Church
that broad views would be accepted as orthodox simply
because they were being discussed. Views did not become
orthodox until they received the approval of Roman ecclesiastical authority. Thus, at least in theory, the Roman
Church could tolerate the discussion of liberal views with

43

less danger to orthodoxy than could Anglicanism. Ward and other liberal Catholics hoped that the Roman authorities would in practice tolerate moderate liberal views and exercise authority only when opinions became excessive or dangerous to the faith.

English Roman Catholics had already been given a small taste of the forthcoming scriptural controversies. In 1887, the liberal Catholic biologist St. George Mivart (1827-1900) had published in the Nineteenth Century an article entitled "The Catholic Church and Biblical Criticism."[39] Mivart accurately foresaw that Biblical criticism would become more and more the focal point of the conflict between science and religion, although he was somewhat too sanguine when he expressed his opinion that the conflict between the Roman Church and biological science was an affair of the past. His article was an attempt to state the limits of Catholic belief in regard to the Bible and, therefore, the conclusions of Biblical criticism that Catholics were free to accept. Since Mivart was not a specialist in theology, it was not surprising that Bishop Hedley of Newport, the leading English Roman Catholic bishop on matters of controversy with science, published an article criticizing Mivart's article.[40] The real crux of the matter, however, seems to have been Mivart's underlying tendency to refer all questions to the tribunal of reason for decision.[41] In his article, Mivart stated: "For, as I before pointed out, God has taught us by the actual facts of the history of Galileo that it is to men of science that He has committed the elucidation of scientific questions, scriptural or otherwise, and not to a consensus of theologians, or to ecclesiastical assemblies or tribunals."[42] Hedley replied that there were questions bound up with scientific matters, for instance, the Virgin Birth and the Resurrection, that the Church would not cede authority to science to decide. He held that scientific inquiry was not absolutely free to arrive at any conclusions whatever, and recalled the liberal Catholics of the 1860's and Pius IX's Munich Brief. The theologian "will steadfastly maintain that the Church of God has the power both to define indirectly points of science or history which are involved in revelation, and to judge when they are actually so involved."[43]

It was the agnostic James Fitzjames Stephen who seized upon the broader dimensions of the Biblical question raised by Mivart and upon his tendency to refer all questions to his reason for decision.[44] Stephen saw two principles underlying Mivart's article: (1) In all matters of physical science and historical criticism, science is the ultimate judge (not the authority of the Church), and (2) the Roman Church will benefit by admitting this in Biblical criticism as well as physical science. Stephen argued that acceptance of these principles could destroy the Apostles' Creed. If these principles and the same scientific method and criteria applied to the Old Testament by Kuenan, Wellhausen, Colenso, and Reuss were applied to the New Testament, the facts stated in the Creed would be rejected by science as untrue or at least doubtful. Thus, Christ's divinity, the Resurrection, and, in fact, all theological doctrine must likewise be rejected. The end result, as a commentator in the Saturday Review observed, could be that "the Roman Catholic Church . . . would be reduced to a kind of glorified Positivism, supplying the poetical and romantic element which Comte's system clumsily attempts but entirely fails to provide."[45]

Mivart was disconcerted by the criticism his article had aroused. He wrote to Edmund Bishop: "Indeed, having now said my say--what I felt I must say--I have no intention of ever writing one line more on the subjects

45

discussed. I wish to consider that a chapter closed."
For the next several years, Mivart hesitated to publish
anything that might again provoke ecclesiastical controversy.[46]

Since there were no Roman Catholic Biblical
scholars of major importance in England in 1890, English
liberal Catholics became only indirectly involved in the
issue of Biblical criticism. It, however, was to become
the most controversial issue in the Roman Church, and
Hügel kept the English liberal Catholics informed of its
progress. In particular, he made them aware of Alfred
Loisy's critical work. Loisy was convinced that the
progress of Biblical criticism had made popular teaching
about the Bible obsolete and, therefore, that acceptance
of the scientific study of Scripture by the Church was
imperative. Not until a number of years later did he put
forward a completely symbolical and evolutionary interpretation of dogma. As a seminarian, however, he had had an
experience similar to that of Renan; the rationalistic
theological manuals which he encountered during his training for the priesthood raised difficulties in his mind
about religious belief. Nevertheless, in 1879, he was
ordained. After learning Hebrew by himself and impressing
Duchesne during a brief period of studies at the newly
founded Institut Catholique in Paris, he received an invi-
tation to the Institut as a graduate student and instructor
of Hebrew. He hoped to master Renan's learning in order to
refute him. In 1883, Loisy's confidence was shaken. Never
doubting that Biblical and historical criticism were truly
scientific, he concluded from his critical studies that
Catholic ideas of dogma were irreconcilable with what he
regarded as the historical facts. He further concluded
that Catholic belief was holding back the intellectual
progress of humanity, but that man's future moral progress

and social solidarity were inconceivable without the Church. Desiring to serve humanity in and through the Church, he saw no reason to abandon the priesthood. He persisted in his belief that religion was "a tremendous force that had dominated and still did all of human history."[47]

Hoping to prepare the way gradually for a change in the Church's teaching, regarding Biblical criticism as a completely autonomous science, and seeing no need at the time to subject himself to ecclesiastical censure, Loisy did not state his theological views in his critical works. After his appointment in 1890 as professor of Holy Scripture at the Institut Catholique in Paris, however, he began to raise critical questions about the historicity of the Book of Genesis and to engender suspicions about his orthodoxy. In an article on "La Question biblique" published in the French liberal Catholic periodical Le Correspondant in January 1893, Mgr. d'Hulst, the liberal rector of the Institut, attempted to remove suspicion from Loisy's critical work and from use of the new scientific methods of Biblical criticism. He argued that there were three wings in Biblical criticism: a right wing which held that the inspiration of Scripture meant that there was no error of any kind; a left wing which held that inspiration applied only to statements about faith and morals; and a center which adopted a via media between the other two wings. D'Hulst urged toleration within the Church for all three wings. His article had exactly the opposite effect from what he intended, for it aroused a storm of controversy within the French Church. Instead of securing Loisy's position, d'Hulst felt constrained to take Loisy's chair of Holy Scripture away from him and eventually dismissed him from the Institut Catholique.[48]

Although in France such liberal-minded churchmen as Duchesne and Bishop Meignan thought it unwise to become

involved in the issue of Biblical criticism,[49] Hügel's
interest in the issue was growing. The English liberal
Catholics followed his lead in hoping for toleration of
Loisy, whom they regarded as a Catholic pioneer in scientific Biblical criticism. Gasquet had written to Hügel in
November 1892: "Of course you know that I have always
agreed with you as to his [Loisy's] teaching. It is certainly a wonderful thing to find a man speaking out so
boldly and perhaps from what we know of the narrowness of
our teachers in England at least--to have a man who is
allowed to speak as he does."[50] In his reminiscences,
Wilfrid Ward wrote that "from my confidence in von Hügel I
was at that time anxious that Loisy should be tolerated,
and I had little sympathy for the attitude of his
enemies."[51]

          The agitated controversy in the French Church over
the Biblical question occasioned <u>Providentissimus Deus</u>
(1893), the encyclical of Pope Leo XIII on the study of
Scripture. The encyclical was intended to encourage
Biblical study but, more significantly, to guide it along
the right paths. It rejected the notion that the "higher
criticism," not the Church, was the ultimate authority in
judging the Bible, the notion that the agnostic James
Fitzjames Stephen had detected in Mivart's <u>Nineteenth
Century</u> article on Scripture. Besides upholding the
doctrines of Biblical revelation and inspiration, the
encyclical supported the authenticity of the books of the
New Testament and the possibility of miracles and prophecies. It pointed out that many of the conclusions of
Biblical criticism had not been firmly established and
were constantly changing. It tried to give assurance that
there could be no ultimate conflict between the true
results of Biblical criticism and the doctrine of the
Church. External evidence and the authority of the Church,

as well as internal criticism of the Biblical documents themselves, were witnesses to the truth. Critics who believed in nothing beyond the natural order could hardly be expected to interpret the Bible as believing Christians would interpret it. Nevertheless, the encyclical conceded that the sacred writers sometimes spoke figuratively or in the terms of their day, especially about physical phenomena. But it was particularly insistent that the traditional doctrines about the inerrancy of Scripture and the inspiration of Scripture in all its parts should not be denied.[52]

The English liberal Catholics were very much concerned about the impression that the encyclical would make in England. In an article in the Guardian, Gore looked upon it as setting up an impediment to the study of Scripture by Roman Catholic Biblical scholars and as a victory for those ultraconservative theologians who opposed liberal Catholic efforts. He inaccurately charged that it said that the original language of the books of the Bible was verbally inspired.[53] And in a very bitter vein, an anonymous Roman Catholic wrote a series of articles in the Contemporary Review charging that the encyclical was an obscurantist document and generally an attempt to make black seem white.[54]

The English liberal Catholics were especially concerned lest the encyclical continue to be misinterpreted by non-Catholics as Gore had misinterpreted it, and lest obscurantists within the Roman Church in England claim a victory. Consequently, Hügel wrote a series of articles on "The Church and the Bible" in the Dublin Review in which he accepted the encyclical and sought to offer a favorable interpretation of it.[55] He began by trying to distinguish between two stages of interpretation of the Bible. The first stage he assigned to reason and the second to faith. Viewing the Bible first as containing documents of human authority, "this human authority has to be established by human, historical means and methods--our first stage." But then, "The free act of Faith, acting, under the illumination and impulsion of grace, upon this and other cumulative evidence, brings us to the divine authority of the Church. And by the Church alone we are then conclusively taught the existence, nature, and range of the divine authority of the Bible--certain truths and facts above and additional to the legitimate operations and conclusions of Reason."[56] This particular view of Biblical interpretation seems to have corresponded to the distinction between the sphere of science and the sphere of religion that Hügel was making at the time. His view of Biblical interpretation was not, however, of major interest to the English liberal Catholics at the time, although it would become significant in later controversy. It was his treatment of the encyclical itself that primarily interested them. He said that the encyclical had legitimate claims to the obedience of all Catholics.[57] He thought the encyclical right when it warned against premature acceptance of conclusions of Biblical criticism or when it said that the dogmatic sense of Scripture could not be determined by internal criticism alone and could not be found uncorrupted among rationalist critics. He agreed, furthermore, that the question of the inspiration of Scripture in all its parts was a matter of faith and fell for decision to the authority of the Church. But he was careful to add that questions about dates, composition, adaptation, and development regarding the Bible remained unanswered. In any case, he agreed that a transcendent quality distinguished the Bible from other books.[58] Moreover, he argued that the Church had existed before the Bible and, consequently, that revelation was inconceivable without the Church.[59] In short, while he was willing to make concessions on many points to Biblical criticism,

50

Hügel indicated that he was not a liberal or modern Catholic if that term were taken to mean one who did not believe in the objective truth of Christian dogma or to denote one who accepted not the ultimate authority of the Church but of science or reason in matters of dogma.

Although the encyclical was not an obscurantist document, there was no doubt about its conservative nature, and it raised fears among the English liberal Catholics whether Biblical scholars using the new critical methods would be tolerated within the Roman Church. While their fundamental loyalties or acceptance of Catholic dogma were not hedged with mental reservations, the liberals expressed reservations to each other in private about the encyclical. Hügel, Ward, and Gasquet feared that in the wake of the encyclical the Holy Office would attempt to suppress the work of Loisy and other Biblical scholars. Bishop Mignot of Fréjus, later the Archbishop of Albi, wrote Hügel: "I have just written to the Sovereign Pontiff to beg him not to restrain further the freedom of action of Catholic savants . . . but will my letter be given to him?"[60] Even the nonintellectual and generally conservative Archbishop of Westminster, Cardinal Vaughan, who was on friendly personal terms with Hügel, wrote Rome warning against any attempt by the Holy Office to apply the teachings of the encyclical in a rigid manner.[61]

A very pessimistic note as to the future of the liberal Catholic cause was struck by Duchesne, who wrote to Hügel with bitterness and sarcasm:

> Again it is shown that the Church wants no widening of its ways. . . . Some blame Cardinal Mazella [a Jesuit who was a close theological adviser to Leo XIII], the Jesuits; others the particular disposition of the Pope. At bottom every one is responsible . . . neither princes nor peoples are interested in the conciliation of intelligence and religion. . . .

With regard to intellectual needs, there are none
here, and those who possess any are frowned upon
. . . looked upon as manifestations of an indiscreet
curiosity about progress, because an indirect
criticism of what exists. You are like those
troublesome monks who cannot stomach the refectory
fare, and take little secret meals. Therefore they
are suspect! Your little actions will be tolerated,
or rather ignored so long as you do not make too
much noise about them; or rather perhaps so long
as you have no enemy to denounce you.[62]

Among the English liberal Catholics, at least
Edmund Bishop was inclined to agree with Duchesne's pessimistic assessment of the future. Whereas Hügel, Ward, and
the other liberals tended to believe that with the reign of
Leo XIII the tide had turned in favor of their cause,
Bishop thought instead that the tide was still running
against them and that Leo's office would prevent him from
reversing the tide.[63] Bishop and Ward--who first corresponded with one another in 1893--did not get along well
personally, in part because of their conflicting interpretations of the recent history of the Roman Church. In
addition, Bishop emphasized the need "for facts--facts to
correct fancies."[64] Ward, on the other hand, had a more
speculative turn of mind. While Ward numbered philosophy
among his interests, Bishop had an aversion to philosophy,
which he regarded as a priori pretentiousness. Hügel later
was to comment unfavorably on Bishop's aversion to all
philosophy.[65]

In 1894, a small crack began to open in the ranks
of the English liberal Catholics who did hold hopes for the
future. Although Hügel accepted the teachings of the
encyclical and, in fact, had always held the plenary
inspiration of Scripture,[66] he thought the Pope had been
unwise in promulgating the encyclical. Moreover, he
pointed out in private that it said little about certain
problems confronting the Biblical scholars: "The real

question to my mind is whether there is or is not such a thing as a science of the Bible (as distinguished from its dogmatic and devotional use); and whether it is to be allowed to pursue its own methods (as distinct from proclaiming any and every conclusion), and whether suppression of labour, or even of publication (again as distinct from broadcast dissemination), is not a danger as great as any that is attempted to be met."[67] Ward, on the other hand, was inclined to think that a conservative attitude by the ecclesiastical authorities was at least inevitable under the circumstances, due to their governing rather than intellectual responsibilities. He thought the Roman authorities were uneasy about views of Loisy and other Catholic Biblical scholars, but expected that they would grant a cautious toleration to moderate Biblical work. While both Ward and Hügel thought that Biblical scholars should be free to accept certain or highly probable results of research, the encyclical had said nothing specific about this. In contrast to Ward, Hügel seemed to be of the opinion that almost complete freedom of speculation was needed for progress in Biblical study and that its excesses would gradually be pruned.[68] Thus, Hügel's position on Biblical criticism was beginning to bear some resemblance to the position of Döllinger and Acton on historical criticism in the 1860's.

This difference in judging the wisdom and appropriateness of the actions of the Roman authorities was smoothed over by the tentative agreement of Hügel, Ward, and other liberal Catholics on the immediate necessity for cautious and prudent action by themselves. Ward thought the encyclical reflected the ambiguity of Leo XIII's sympathies: he had encouraged historical research, but seemed to Ward to be inclined toward excessive scholasticism and conservatism.[69] Hügel reluctantly came to the

53

same conclusions. When Loisy suspended publication of his scholarly periodical, <u>L'Enseignement Biblique</u>, Hügel agreed with his decision to maintain silence temporarily.[70] Hügel wrote to Ward:

> I have not only been extra-busy, but my scripture interests, Encyclical, Loisy etc., have had to pass through a period of fog and suspense of judgment, not one bit on questions of principle or of doubt as to fundamental or as to the ultimate triumph of our views, but all on questions of immediate policy and practical bearing. . . . You will have noticed at once that I have gone, as far as possible to the right as to the documents and the encyclical's doctrinal importance, as far as possible to the left as to its liberal interpretation. This too I think the wiser course <u>with an eye to Rome</u>.[71]

Illustrative of the kind of vocal, public expression that the liberal Catholics feared would discredit their cause in the eyes of the ecclesiastical authorities was St. George Mivart's article, "Happiness in Hell," published in December 1892.[72] Mivart had become convinced that many non-believers were being repelled from Christianity and some Christians were abandoning their religion because of a modern distaste for the Christian teaching about a hell in which evildoers would endure everlasting suffering. With every intention again of doing the Church a service, he attempted to determine what the Christian theological tradition, and not popular preaching, actually did teach about hell. He concluded that it taught a hell without the characteristic of perpetual unhappiness and the image of hell-fire and generally in accord with what he took to be modern reason:

> Its teaching, as we understand it, may be briefly summed up as follows: God has with infinite benevolence, but with inscrutable purposes, created human beings the overwhelming majority of whom, being incapable of grave sin, attain to an eternity

of unimaginable natural happiness. . . . Another
multitude undergo a certain probation on earth and
attain to a future state exactly proportioned to
their merits or demerits which may equal or fall
short of the natural happiness of those incapable
of sin.

God has further endowed a certain number of mankind
with faculties whereby they are rendered capable of
a supernatural union with Him. . . .

This privilege carries with it a dread risk of
failure, resulting in the loss of such supernatural
happiness. . . . Yet for the very worst, in spite
of the positive and unceasing suffering before
referred to, existence is acceptable and is by them
preferred to non-existence; while we are permitted
to believe in an eternal upward progress, though
never attaining to the supernatural state which
would be most unwelcome and repugnant to such souls.

. . . .

Hell in its widest sense . . . must be considered as
. . . an abode of happiness transcending all our
most vivid anticipations, so that man's natural
capacity for happiness is there gratified to the
very utmost. . . .[73]

Mivart had gone further than his earlier attempts
to reconcile Christianity with biological evolution or even
with Biblical criticism. He was no longer standing on the
grounds of science or the contested middle ground between
science and theology but had now crossed over entirely
into the field of theology and proposed to show the true
meaning of theological teachings about hell. A barrage of
theological opinion came down against Mivart's articles on
hell[74] and, in a short time, they were placed on the Index.
His good intentions, however, were generally recognized, as
was his position as the leading Catholic biologist and a
scientist to whom Pius IX had granted a doctor's cap. By
Mivart's own account, Cardinal Vaughan treated him with the
utmost kindness in this affair. He found he was able, at
least for the next several years, to accept the placing of

his articles on the _Index_. He concluded that his views had
not been censured outright, but that their publication
might have been considered, perhaps rightly, inopportune.[75]

While the encyclical on the study of Scripture had
made the English liberal Catholics apprehensive, another
event on the English scene lent encouragement to their
still optimistic hopes. In the early months of 1895, the
hierarchy finally agreed to lift the ban against Roman
Catholics attending Oxford and Cambridge. Catholic laymen
had begun to press for general permission to attend the
English universities after the death of Cardinal Manning,
who would never hear of removing the ban. In July 1894,
the Duke of Norfolk, the highest titled Catholic layman,
led their representations to the ecclesiastical authorities.
Well-circumstanced Catholic laymen wanted their sons to be
able to enter important positions in public life, and
Oxford and Cambridge opened doors to such positions. Moreover, there was no English Roman Catholic university as an
alternative. Other Catholic laymen like the liberal
Wilfrid Ward were influenced by the hope that had earlier
been Newman's, the hope of seeing Catholics brought abreast
of modern thought and thereby removing fears that modern
thought was necessarily destructive to Christianity.[76]

At length, Cardinal Vaughan reluctantly agreed that
under the circumstances it would be the wisest course for
the hierarchy to remove the ban. Even in Manning's day,
individuals had been granted permission by their bishops
to attend the universities, and others had simply gone
without troubling themselves about permission. The ban,
while general, fell short of attaching moral censure to
the attendance of any individual Catholic. An inquiry con-
ducted by Vaughan came to the general conclusion that
Catholics who attended the universities were not losing
their faith. Furthermore, as Hügel pointed out, Catholics

on the Continent were already allowed to attend secular universities even where Catholic universities existed. After sounding out influential Catholic laymen on the possibility of a second attempt to found an English Catholic university as an alternative and receiving a negative reply, Vaughan concluded that the ban would have to be lifted. While hedging its removal with requirements for safeguarding the faith of Catholics attending Oxford and Cambridge, Vaughan secured permission from the Roman authorities to lift it.[77]

The situation of the English liberal Catholics was becoming fluid and their future was shrouded in uncertainty. The reign of Leo XIII had buoyed their hopes, but, after the encyclical on the study of Scripture, they could not be sure what they might ultimately expect from him. Cahtolic scholarship had been encouraged and was off to a good start in the use of the new scientific methods, but a cloud hung over its future. The English liberal Catholics were generally on good terms with the English ecclesiastical authorities, yet the latter were regarded as conservative and had little interest in scholarship and intellectual work. And within the English liberal Catholics' own ranks, there was general agreement on ends and means but some divisions were already beginning to appear.

CHAPTER II

ENGLISH LIBERAL CATHOLICS IN THE

MID- AND LATE 1890'S

During the middle years of the decade, an issue
arose that drove a wedge between the English liberal
Catholics themselves, and between some of them and Cardinal
Vaughan. This was the vexed question of Anglican orders
and the larger question of relations with the established
Church of England. In 1894, Lord Halifax, the leader of
that section of the High Church party interested in reunion
with Rome, entertained the French abbé Fernand Portal and
aroused in him high hopes for an Anglican reunion with
Rome. Halifax and Portal decided that a point of contact
was needed to bring Anglican and Roman Catholic theologians
together in conferences as a first step toward future
reunion. They chose the question of Anglican orders to
provide that point of contact. Portal then published under
the pseudonym "F. Dalbus" a sympathetic pamphlet, Les
Ordinations anglicanes. Interest in the question grew when
Duchesne reviewed the pamphlet in his Bulletin Critique and
pronounced an opinion in favor of the validity of Anglican
orders.

Cardinal Vaughan, Gasquet, and Bishop took a dim
view of the validity of Anglican orders and of prospects
for reunion. From their studies in English Reformation
history, Gasquet and Bishop had concluded that Anglican
orders were definitely invalid. Moreover, like Vaughan,
they thought that a decision in any way favorable toward

58

Anglican orders would be damaging to the position of the Roman Church in England. It might result in individuals being attracted to the Anglo-Catholic wing of the established Church of England instead of to Rome; it would certainly hold back Anglo-Catholic conversions to Rome. As for the prospects of reunion in the immediate future, they were non-existent. True, some of the Anglo-Catholics wanted reunion with Rome, but--Vaughan, Gasquet, and Bishop argued--only on their own terms. They meant to constitute themselves as an independent and equal branch of Catholicism, and would not accept the only terms that Rome as the one visible Catholic Church could offer: submission. Even if this estimate of Anglo-Catholic views were inaccurate, corporate reunion was completely impractical. The comprehensiveness of the Anglican Church had its definite advantages, but it was an insurmountable bar to reunion with Rome. Only a small portion of the Anglican Church could be considered in any sense Catholic. How then could the Anglican Church possibly submit as a body to Rome even if submission were favored by a sizable group within it?[1]

Vaughan, Gasquet, and Bishop did not want to see the question of Anglican orders raised, for they thought that the only new result would be embittered relations between English Roman Catholics and other Englishmen. Gasquet and Bishop tried to persuade Halifax and his French Catholic sympathizers from bringing the question to a head. They thought that conferences between Anglicans and Catholics might be useful, but not over the question of Anglican orders which, in their view, only Rome itself could decide.[2] This view coincided with that of the Archbishop of Canterbury, E. W. Benson, to the extent that he also believed the question was not for the other side (Roman Catholic, in this case) to decide; he refused to

sanction a joint conference.[3] Once raised, however, the
question of the validity of Anglican orders was not to be
put off. Realizing this, Vaughan, Gasquet, and Bishop on
the one hand and Halifax on the other agreed that a decision
based on a full new investigation of the question must be
made by the Roman authorities. Indeed, Vaughan and Gasquet
were opposed to any decision by the Holy Office without a
new investigation.[4] The rub was that each side expected
that the inquiry would turn out in its favor.

Ward and Hügel found that they could not fully agree
with either the position adopted by Vaughan and his supporters or by Halifax and his advocates. They agreed with
the former that Anglican orders would not be judged valid
by Rome and that, because the divergences between the Roman
and Anglican positions were extensive and deep, there was
little chance of any form of corporate reunion in the near
future. On the other hand, they hoped that Rome would not
definitely decide against Anglican orders. They thought
that either the validity of Anglican orders would be judged
doubtful or that no decision would be rendered. Moreover,
they feared that Vaughan and his supporters would adopt a
controversial tone which would have a bad effect in England.
Engaged in writing The Life and Times of Cardinal Wiseman
(1897), Ward was impressed by the sympathy that Wiseman had
shown toward the Oxford Movement and by the degree to which
this had been a factor in the conversions of Newman, his
father, and others in the 1840's. Ward thought that a
sympathetic attitude toward Anglo-Catholic claims was also
called for in the 1890's and that it would deepen the Anglo-
Catholic desire for reunion and attract souls to Rome. A
controversial tone, which he fully expected from some
English Catholic periodicals as well as from Vaughan, would
produce the opposite effect. Hügel agreed with this assessment.[5] In a letter to Halifax, Ward gave what was in the

1890's perhaps the typical liberal Catholic estimate of Cardinal Vaughan, irrespective of the Anglican orders question. Although he expressed his pride in Vaughan as a leader of single-minded good intentions, he thought the Cardinal was accustomed to speak in an old-fashioned controversial manner. But he optimistically added that Vaughan was emerging through sheer goodness from an early narrowness which had sometimes been excessive.[6]

In an article in the Nineteenth Century in November 1895, Ward elaborated on his views regarding the nature and prospects of the Roman Church and its relationship to the Anglican Church.[7] Some critics charged that the Roman Church was incapable of assimilating modern civilization. Paradoxically, Rome owed its present rigidity to its essential adaptability, specifically to the effects of its adapting to the state of seige brought about by the Reformation's challenge to the very constitution of the Church. The critics were right, however, if by the rigidity of Rome they meant that Rome would not modify dogma or essential principles in order to facilitate reunion or for any other purpose. Nevertheless, if Rome was not essentially rigid but assimilative, then assimilation of contemporary thought and the consequent reduction of prejudices against the Church should improve its relations with Englishmen. At present, corporate reunion between Rome and any large section of Englishmen was impossible. Divergences were too deep, especially over the conceptions of the church held by Englishmen at large and the Roman conception of the church as a single polity, international and universal, with the authority to determine its conditions of membership. The revival of sympathies toward Catholicism might gradually remove obstacles to reunion, but the tradition of three hundred years could not be cancelled in one generation. Fortunately, present reunion and controversial hostility were not the only alternatives. Rapprochement, not reunion, was called for at present. A temper of justice and kindness might gradually clear away existing prejudices: "it is the growth of this temper of fairness and sympathy on all sides, by mutual co-operation against our common foes, irreligion, vice, anarchy, infidelity, which will eventually lead to a real reunion if it is ever to be attained. Nothing else can give a true knowledge of the degree of union already existing, and the degree of divergence yet remaining. Nothing will tend more to increase the former and diminish the latter."[8]

There had been indications, however, that this sort of temper would not be easy to attain. In a provocative speech at Preston in autumn 1894, Vaughan had flatly declared that the Anglican Church was in schism and heresy and that submission was the condition of reunion. Irritation was increased shortly thereafter when The Times published a letter by Vaughan to the Archbishop of Toledo in which he termed Anglican orders null and void.[9] Although the Roman authorities at first seemed to take a more favorable view toward the prospects of reunion than Vaughan, they gradually became convinced that their hopes were too optimistic. In April 1895, the Pope addressed an apostolic letter to the English people. He invited them to pray for the reunion of Christendom, but in closing called upon Roman Catholics to pray the rosary to Mary for the conversion of England and granted indulgences for doing so. Although there were some complaints in the press, the apostolic letter was generally well received. Bishop and Gasquet had participated in drafting it, although the last section was not their work.[10] Archbishop Benson wrote Halifax that he thought the closing section of the letter indicated that the Pope was trying to be honest in holding out no hope for modification of Roman dogma.[11]

In September, it was announced in England that the Holy See was formally reopening the question of Anglican orders, and in March 1896, the Pope appointed a commission to report on the matter. The commission consisted of eight consultors. Gasquet, his liberal Franciscan friend David Fleming,[12] and two other consultors had expressed themselves against the validity of Anglican orders. However, the other four consultors, including Duchesne, favored a verdict that the validity of Anglican orders was at least doubtful. Gasquet, the only specialist in English Reformation history on the commission, discovered some important documents in the Roman archives that seemed to provide answers to the question why Rome had considered Anglican orders invalid in the first place. These documents included: letters concerning this matter that Cardinal Pole, papal legate to England, sent to Rome during the reign of Mary Tudor; a description of the rites under the Edwardine Ordinal; the papal bull Praeclara Charissimi (dated June 20, 1555) on the subject of reordination of Edwardine clergymen; a brief of Pope Paul IV explaining the bull; and, in the Douai archives, a copy of the bull in Pole's register with his attestation that he had received it for promulgation.[13] Gasquet was using the new historical methods to support Rome's traditional view of Anglican orders.

Meanwhile Ward, who was in frequent correspondence with Halifax, had been trying to represent Halifax's views sympathetically to Vaughan and vice versa. Hügel had also concerned himself with the Anglican orders question. In early 1895, he had gone to the extent of submitting a memorandum on the question to the Papal Secretary of State, Cardinal Rampolla--an action which Cardinal Ledochowski, the Prefect of Propaganda, referred to as an impertinence on the part of a layman. Ward, Hügel, and Halifax remained sanguine as the time for a decision on Anglican orders

approached. At the beginning of 1896, Ward wrote to
Halifax that he thought "things are moving very fast towards
a broad and sympathetic temper." Reporting from Rome,
Hügel had "never written so hopefully on this subject."
Even after the commission on Anglican orders had begun to
meet, Ward expected a verdict of doubtful.[14]

In June the commission submitted its report, and
the cardinals of the Holy Office began considering the
evidence produced. In the meantime, the encyclical De
Unitate (June 1896) was promulgated. It stated on what
terms the reunion of Christendom could be accomplished.
The first condition was acceptance of the Pope's divinely
appointed jurisdiction over the whole Church. It was clear
that Rome would not make modifications of doctrine or of
terms of communion. In July, the cardinals of the Holy
Office met under the presidency of the Pope for a decision
on Anglican orders, and concluded that Anglican orders were
definitely invalid. The Pope, however, reserved his
decision for several weeks. Then in September he promulgated the bull Apostolicae Curae declaring Anglican orders
invalid by the Roman standard.[15] Although the decision
came as a shock to Halifax, Ward and Hügel found little
difficulty in accepting it. Ward agreed with Hügel's
remark regarding the verdict: for the Anglican reformers
of the sixteenth century "to throw down altars and break
altar stones was a strange way of expressing that the
sacrifice [of the Mass] was impetratory and not propitia-
tory."[16]

Ward had not achieved the degree of success he had
hoped for in trying to dampen controversy over Anglican
orders and promote better ecclesiastical relations between
Anglicans and Roman Catholics; however, he succeeded with
another venture, more limited in scope, in which he participated at the same time. In the first months of 1896, he

was instrumental in founding the Synthetic Society in which well-known public figures of various hues of religious belief met periodically to discuss contemporary intellectual criticisms bearing on religion and to co-operate in working together toward a philosophy of theism. Ward was elected secretary of the Society, which continued to meet until 1910. Among its members, at one time or another, were: the Anglican clergymen Charles Gore, Henry Scott Holland, Hastings Rashdall, and Edward Talbot; Prime Minister Arthur Balfour; the exponent of the "New Theology," R. J. Campbell; Lord Haldane; Richard Hutton of the Spectator; the orientalist Sir Alfred Lyall; the Unitarian James Martineau; Cambridge Professor Henry Sidgwick; Oxford Professor Clement Webb; and Chief Secretary for Ireland George Wyndham.[17] Ward, Hügel, and the Jesuit George Tyrrell[18] were the leading Roman Catholic members.

In 1896, William Barry, a liberal Catholic priest who was conversant with both modern literature and ancient metaphysics, penned this comment to Ward on the intellectual condition of the Roman Church in England: "I never am present at one of our conferences, or in a clerical gathering, that I do not feel amazed at the isolation from the modern world in which our [clerical] friends live. They cannot judge it because they do not know it; their tactics are such as would follow upon this state of mind."[19] Gasquet added his opinion that "the state of the Church in no country can be satisfactory in which the secular clergy do not take a prominent part in the intellectual life and movements of the time."[20]

The division of the English liberal Catholic group over the Anglican orders controversy was, in any case, the beginning of their gradual loss of confidence in each other. Hügel began to lose confidence in Gasquet and Fleming, who was soon to become a figure in Rome as a Consultor of the

Holy Office. Moreover, Hügel thought that he had lost Vaughan's confidence, and that the Cardinal had become cold toward the Biblical question because he had not supported Vaughan adequately in the Anglican orders question. A new constitution for bringing the Index up-to-date seemed ominous to Hügel. Although Loisy had participated in the formation of an editorless review, Revue d'Histoire et de Littérature Religieuses, approved of by Bishop Mignot, Hügel reacted with terror to a plan of an article on the Prologue of St. John's Gospel. He thought the freedom of Biblical studies could now best be maintained by not raising new questions or proposals in Rome. He counselled prudence.[21]

Although the liberals had become wary of what the immediate future might bring, they did not expect the developments in the late 1890's that led Hügel, Mivart, and some lesser English liberals to lose confidence in the highest ecclesiastical authorities in Rome. The first of these developments occurred in January 1897 when the Holy Office decided that the authenticity of the Comma Johanneum,[22] a verse referring explicitly to the Trinity, should not be denied or called into question. Since practically all critical Biblical scholars were agreed that the verse was a later addition into the New Testament, Hügel was very disturbed. He wrote to Ward:

> I of course know all about that truly phenomenal decision of the H. Office. As there is no doubt that Cardinal Mazella is somehow at the bottom of it, and as he enjoys an ever-increasing ascendancy over the Pope's mind, . . . and as there is not the slightest chance of that neo-scholastic [Mazella] acquiring either special knowledge, or the instinct of the complexity of critical questions and of the wisdom of either studying them carefully or letting them alone--we must, I think, be prepared if His Holiness lives on, for, if that be possible, even bigger things in this kind of line. . . .

Hügel was convinced that the Holy Office decree was completely wrong, and, therefore, that he could not say one
word in defense of it. Consequently, three courses seemed
open to him: "silence, or frank and unqualified admission
of a blunder, or brisk though, of course, carefully limited
attack." Although he chose silence, this seems to have
been the first decree issuing from Rome that he found
impossible to accept.[23]

The Comma Johanneum decision put Cardinal Vaughan
in an embarrassing position. The Anglican orders question
had been referred to the Holy Office for decision, and now
that same Holy Office had given a decision rejected by
nearly all critical Biblical scholars. This could make the
former decision seem worthy of little respect also,
especially in the eyes of Anglicans. Vaughan took up the
matter in Rome, and ascertained "from an excellent source"
there that the Comma Johanneum decision related to the
theological value of the verse in question and not to its
critical value. Vaughan wrote Ward to this effect, and
gave Ward permission to publish his letter.[24] To Hügel,
the Holy Office's extreme decision seemed to produce for a
time a sobering effect in Rome as well as with Cardinal
Vaughan. Hügel was glad to repeat to his friends Duchesne's
quip: "There are three persons that are doing most useful
work in Rome ever since last winter: Pater et Filius et
Spiritus Sanctus."[25]

Nevertheless, the decision on the Comma Johanneum
continued to bother Hügel. At the end of the century, he
was still writing to Ward about it: "for quite a quarter
of a century Catholic Exegetes have, with full Episcopal
approbation, fully and formally not simply doubted, but
rejected it--in Germany, in France--in Italy even, I
think. . . ." To him the decision had signified in regard
to the Roman authorities "not a question of pace, but a

question of <u>direction of movement</u>, distinct and serious
retrogression." While he believed that the future of
Christianity depended on understanding and wide tolerance,
he feared that narrow scholastic officials who had no
policy except condemnation and intolerance were gaining
decisive influence with the Pope.[26] As the century drew
to a close, some other English liberals came to the same
general conclusions as a result of further developments
issuing from Rome.

Deeply concerned with the task of reconciling
Catholicism to the fact of biological evolution, St. George
Mivart had advanced a thesis that the body of man had not
been formed directly by God from the dust of the earth but
had evolved from the body of a lower animal, although God
subsequently infused man's rational soul. Mivart's lead
was followed and his view defended by the French priest
M. D. Leroy in <u>L'Evolution restreinte aux espèces organiques</u>
(1891) and by the American priest J. A. Zahm in <u>Evolution
and Dogma</u> (1897). In an article in the <u>Dublin Review</u> in
October 1898,[27] Bishop Hedley reviewed some of the problems
involved in the reconciliation of Roman Catholic theology
with evolution, problems raised by Zahm's recent work. He
said that a majority of educated Catholics had already
accepted in a general way the hypothesis of evolution, but
could not accept the naturalistic philosophies of Herbert
Spencer and Ernst Haeckel which absolutely rejected the
idea of creation and denied the existence of God. Hedley
noted that Zahm had advocated no particular theory of
evolution, but had supported the fact of evolution. Even
Darwin's biological theories, however, were completely
compatible with an original creative act of God. Hedley
pointed out that many English scientists agreed that
Darwin's theory of evolution as such was neither theistic
nor anti-theistic but, as Huxley said, had no more to do
with theism than the books of Euclid.[28]

Hedley maintained that Christians and theists must hold that God created everything that is and gave laws and tendencies to primordial matter. They must insist that God intervened "in the instance of the rational soul, and also (as seems most probable) when animal life first appeared, and when the body of the first man was formed." Because these questions were not subject to research or experiment, biology could say nothing about them. Hedley conceded that Catholic dogma did not hold that the soul or vital principle of an animal was created directly by God, and that Catholic philosophy left room for the possibility that God at the creation of things could have once for all given the non-living the potency to develop life later. In bringing his article to a conclusion, he optimistically wrote: "It appears to me that the Catholic student who carefully studies the pages of Dr. Zahm will have no hesitation in dismissing all fear that to accept organic evolution is in any degree to endanger the faith. What is more, he will probably conclude that he would be shutting his eyes to scientific truth if he did not admit evolution as a useful and probable explanation and co-ordination of facts." As a final note, Hedley suggested that young English Catholics could do much for religion if they studied biology, geology, or Biblical criticism.[29]

But Hügel had already heard a report conflicting with Hedley's optimism: the Holy Office was said to be considering a condemnation of evolution. Hügel went to see Vaughan about the matter only to be told by the Cardinal that he should be thankful if the Holy Office furnished light on it.[30]

In January 1899, an article entitled "Evoluzione e domma" appeared in the Civiltà Cattolica, the Jesuit organ in Rome. It spoke unfavorably of Zahm's work and Hedley's article. Whether the Civiltà Cattolica article altogether

rejected evolution in the physical world was unclear, but
the article let it be known publicly that Père Leroy, who
had defended Mivart's view of man's bodily evolution, had
been called to Rome in February 1895 and had learnt from
"competent authority" that his thesis was untenable--"being
incompatible with the text of Holy Scripture and with the
principles of sound philosophy." A letter of retraction
by Leroy, dated February 26, 1895, was appended to the
Civiltà Cattolica article.[31] In response to this development, Bishop Hedley wrote a letter to the Tablet in which
he concluded that the "competent authority" was the Holy
Office,[32] that it had apparently decided against Mivart's
thesis, and, therefore, that this thesis now must be considered at least rash. Hedley was careful to point out
that his Dublin Review article had cautiously refrained
from saying anything specifically in favor of this theory.[33]

Soon other retractions were made known in England.
In June 1899, the Tablet reprinted a letter by Zahm to the
Italian translator of his Evolution and Dogma.[34] Zahm
wrote that he had learnt "from unquestionable authority
that the Holy See is adverse to the further distribution
of Evolution and Dogma, and I therefore beg you to use all
your influence to have the work withdrawn from sale. . . .
As for myself it will cause me no pain to see the fruit of
so much toil consigned to oblivion. God rewards the intention, and our intentions were good. . . ." Also reprinted
by the Tablet was a letter of retraction by Bishop Jeremiah
Bonomelli of Cremona, whose Seguiamo la Ragione (1898) had
contained an appendix giving a synopsis of Zahm's Evolution
and Dogma.[35] These retractions became another factor at
work in undermining the confidence of some English liberals
in the Roman authorities.

The third major event that shook their confidence
was an action taken by the Pope himself. In January 1899,

70

Pope Leo addressed to James Cardinal Gibbons, the titular leader of the American hierarchy, an apostolic letter censuring certain ideas and practices grouped together under the heading "Americanism." The American Church under the leadership of Gibbons, John Ireland, and other liberal-minded prelates had been trying to adapt itself to the democratic, pluralistic, non-Catholic society in which it existed. The efforts of these prelates met with opposition from conservative-minded American bishops. Under a different set of conditions than existed in America, liberal French churchmen were advocating adaptation of the Church to the public life of the secularist Third Republic, and were meeting with strong opposition from conservative churchmen. In 1897, the liberal abbé Félix Klein edited a French version of the life of Isaac Hecker, the founder of the liberal American Paulist order. Klein's work was the catalyst that produced an agitated controversy in the French Church between "Americanists" and their conservative opponents. While the controversy in the American Church was generally fought over issues at the pastoral or practical level, the controversy in France reached the theological level of argument. These controversies occasioned Leo XIII's letter on "Americanism."[36]

Although the issues involved in the Americanist controversy did not directly concern the intellectual work of the English liberal Catholics, the conservative drift of the Holy See's policy was a matter of concern to them. William Barry, who had a strong interest in the problems of democracy and the Church, was the best informed English liberal Catholic on America and the background of the Americanist controversy. In several articles published in popular periodicals in 1899,[37] he sought to unravel the knots of the controversy and to interpret the meaning of the papal letter.

Barry argued that the example of liberal American churchmen attracted young liberal French Catholics because of their own hope for reconciling French Catholicism with the democracy of the Third Republic.[38] The conservative charges of heresy against the French "Americanists" were put in summary form in the book of the anti-democratic abbé Charles Maignen, Études sur l'Américanisme, le père Hecker est-il un saint? (1898). Maignen contended that Hecker and the Americanizers fell into heresy in regard to the inward life and the relations of individuals to the Church. Furthermore, he charged that they advocated with-holding essential articles of Catholic faith in order to win converts, valued the natural virtues above the super-natural, supported the principle of separation of church and state, looked down upon religious vows, and considered religious orders useless and ill suited to the age. Maignen's book claimed to represent anti-democratic and orthodox France against democratic and heretical America. But in fact the Americans had advocated, Barry argued, no dogmatic or mystical novelties.[39] They had nothing in common with these heretical opinions, and never meddled with dogma.[40] Hecker himself believed in evolution only as regards the way in which the Christian message must be preached to bring it home under new social conditions; he was not concerned with the development of dogma as such.[41] But the Italian Curia and the French could not understand the non-metaphysical language or plane of thought of the Americans, and looked upon it as heretical. This reflected, Barry suggested, the need for the Curia itself to become more representative by including more non-Italians.[42]

As for the significance of the apostolic letter itself, Barry said that it censured certain opinions as erroneous, but he noted that it did not mention who had formed them. It affirmed "the unity of Church and doctrine;

72

the privileges and services of the religious orders; the supernatural as above the natural; obedience to authority; the need of wise direction; and the claim of Catholicism to be recognized as the one Divine Revelation by individuals and society."[43] Democracy was the wave of the future, and Leo's encyclicals taken as a whole continued to offer hope of reconciliation between democracy and the Roman Church. The apostolic letter had, Barry argued, the good effect of making it impossible for anyone to continue charging the American bishops with heresy. They had been able to accept the letter only because they had never held the heretical opinions censured therein. The Pope himself recognized their orthodoxy when he wrote in the letter that if "Americanism" was taken to mean the heretical opinions he had censured, the American bishops would condemn them also as an insult to themselves and their people.[44] But there was an American demand--not for the revolutionizing of dogma but for more democracy within the Church. How could the Church be reconciled with modern society if it used the methods and displayed the temper of the Reformation era?[45]

In spite of Barry's explanations and optimism, the English liberal Catholics could not help but fear that after the recent Roman censures the apostolic letter might be an indication that the Pope himself had opted for the restriction of freedom and even for repression in the immediate future. In his diary, Hügel numbered the "Americanist" letter among the trials he had suffered in 1899.[46]

Besides boding ill for the future of the liberal Catholic cause, the censures of the late 1890's initiated a further series of developments that eventually split the English liberal Catholics into two different camps. The main lines of this division were already foreshadowed shortly after the promulgation of the Americanist letter by

two articles by English liberal Catholics in the Nineteenth
Century. The first article was a vehement criticism of the
Church by William Gibson (later Lord Ashbourne), the author
of The Abbé de Lamennais and the Liberal Catholic Movement
in France (1896); the second article was a reply by Wilfrid
Ward in support of a more moderate position.[47] As a result
of the controversies involving the Vatican in the late
1890's, English liberal Catholic writers were now beginning
to divide into moderate and radical wings. Gibson's article
proved to be only the first of a succession of radical
criticisms that the controversies provoked in the English
periodical press.

     Gibson began his article by connecting the American-
ist letter with other acts of the latter part of Leo's
pontificate. These acts included the encyclical on the
study of Scripture, the Comma Johanneum decision, and the
Index's recent censure of all the works of Hermann Schell,
a German professor who had attempted to modernize Catholic
apologetics. Taken together, they indicated an attempt
"to consolidate the system, to ensure unity of teaching,
and to silence all discordant notes." Another case in
point was the recent condemnations of Catholic supporters
of evolution. A biologist teaching in a Catholic institution must now beware of concluding that man is descended
from the lower animals. Catholic apologetics at present
made little appeal to non-Catholics or to Catholics experiencing mental doubt and uncertainty in the modern world.
The average Catholic theologian thought he could find all
the answers in his text-book, but his text-book knowledge
was irrelevant to actual life in the modern world. Public
opinion was drawing the conclusion "that serious scientific
investigation in any of the higher branches is impossible,
in any Catholic .faculty, in cases where the subject matter
is likely to be of interest to the ecclesiastical

74

authorities." In regard to apologetics, "most of us have already realised that we must settle the matter for ourselves, doing what we can for others when the occasion presents itself." The outburst of activity in the Roman congregations would accelerate the transition toward a highly organized official body of apologists, trained on the Jesuit model, on one hand, and on the other, the public, to whom apologists should appeal, "living its own life, answering its own questions, and speaking a language which, to the authorised apologists, is utterly incomprehensible." Much friction and unpleasantness might be forthcoming. There was, at present, an aged and infirm pope with a Jesuit cardinal (Mazella) as his confidential theological adviser and a second Jesuit cardinal (Steinhuber) as prefect of the Index. Few persons would be surprised if there were extraordinary activity and new condemnations in the Roman congregations in the next few months.[48]

Ward's reply to Gibson's article began by questioning the wisdom of discussing in the periodical press the attitude of the ecclesiastical authorities toward Catholic apologetics, Biblical criticism, and scientific inquiry, for the English public was already too inclined to judge the shortcomings of the Roman authorities harshly. Ward declared himself to be "one among many to whom a reasonable measure of liberty does seem essential if Catholic thinkers and critics are to hold their own intellectually in the modern world. . . ." But he warned that the ecclesiastical authorities, having to maintain principles more vital than the advancement of secular learning, would not allow that requisite intellectual liberty to Catholic thinkers and critics if other Catholics published writings like Gibson's, and in his tone. Ward then took up the recent censures to which Gibson had referred. He regretted the effect of the Comma Johanneum decision on the public but, as Cardinal

75

Vaughan had written to Ward, the decision pertained to the theological value of the text rather than its historical authenticity. Teachers in Catholic institutions were still free to form their own scholarly judgments on its historical authenticity. On the other hand, the exaggerated statements made by scientific scholars on the evolution of man's body and in Biblical criticism were also to be regretted because of their unfortunate effect on the Roman theologians, whose views naturally influenced the Roman congregations' decisions. The theologians might be attentive "to consolidated and moderate expositions of highly probable conclusions in science and criticism, though they may have simply rejected the first exaggerated statements of the pioneers." Such statements discredit the scientific methods employed. This was all the more reason to believe that writings like Gibson's would have the opposite effect from that intended. They would hold back, not stimulate, theological progress, and render most difficult a crucially important understanding between the theologians and the scientists.[49]

Ward concluded his article by referring to Newman's ideas. He recalled Newman's recognition that the student of science must be free in his own discipline, but that ecclesiastical authority had the right to intervene when the scientist encroached on theology. Such encroachments, which occurred often because the scientist despised and liked to bully the theologian, were responsible for having provoked intrusions of ecclesiastical authority on science. Ward suggested that "at the present time, authoritative condemnations which would have been wise and valuable when such censures were effectual--when they really checked the reckless diffusion of new lines of secular thought which were dangerous to the faith of the multitude--might now bear the aspect of useless and obscurantist protests against the free exercise of a trustworthy method of

76

inquiry. For critical and scientific hypotheses are already public property." Each side concerned with the issues, he concluded, should keep in mind the "general fact urged by the Cardinal [Newman] . . . that all sciences are progressive; that the application of theological principles to secular science is also progressive; and that, at a given stage, sciences, theological or secular, may therefore appear to point to contending conclusions." The dawn of all new scientific discoveries was "like the dawn of day—a streak of light visible amid darkness. Both sides, the theological and the scientific, are unable to see clearly in the dark; and fighting in the dark often ends in killing your own friends."[50]

Gibson had arrived at just the opposite conclusion: that the theological side, the Roman authorities, were presently the aggressors and that liberals should begin to protest publicly lest the authorities unwittingly go on in the dark to slay their friends. Nevertheless, Gibson wrote to Ward privately saying he had no disagreement with the Church or Catholic apologetics per se, but he had felt that he should publicly raise the question of the recent drift of the Vatican's policy since the situation was becoming serious. He was pleased with Ward's article because, though critical of his, it was a striking protest against unwise interferences by Church officials.[51] In addition to Ward, George Tyrrell was critical of Gibson. Writing to Hügel, he suggested that Gibson was inadvertently playing into the hands of the liberals' opponents and discrediting the whole liberal group. Camp-followers ruin every good cause, he remarked.[52]

Ward considered a project of informing the Pope that the recent repressive policy of the Vatican was doing a good deal of harm in the English intellectual world. This message might be conveyed to the Pope through Ward's

wife's uncle, the Duke of Norfolk. Ward, however, abandoned
his project when he became convinced of its impracticality.
It was objected that laymen would only be heard on political
or social matters. To this objection, Hügel added his
opinion that if anything like this were to be attempted it
would be best to wait for more propitious days under a new
pope.[53]

Before the century ended, one more event further
shook the confidence of some liberals in the Roman authorities. The close of the century saw a major act in the
Dreyfus Affair in France. When in September 1899 the Rennes
verdict again found Dreyfus guilty of treason, censures of
the French Catholic Church's role in the Affair and of the
Pope's lack of protest against a travesty of justice began
to appear in the English press.

In reply, Cardinal Vaughan wrote to The Times
expressing his indignation at the Rennes verdict which he
deemed unjust. He held that the Catholic Church had
incurred no guilt in the Dreyfus Affair. He maintained
that the Church condemned persecution of the Jews or any
other race, but that the Pope had declined to intervene
because it was purely an affair of the French state.[54]

The Times answered Vaughan's letter in a leading
article claiming that he had not met the charges brought
against the Roman Church. All the French bishops and the
Pope had remained silent while a part of the French Catholic
press roused nationalist and anti-Semitic passions against
Dreyfus, and they continued to maintain their silence even
after Dreyfus was again denied justice. Moreover, Catholic
anti-Dreyfusards hoped to overthrow the Republic and to
restore the influence of the Church over the French nation.
Truth and justice weighed little with the Church in this
affair. One result of the Dreyfus case would be, The Times
believed, "to repel men yet further from her [the Church's]

embrace, and to deepen the sense of incompatibility between the Jesuit principle of absolute subordination of the individual will to the authority of the Church and the vigorous independence, in matters religious as well as secular, of the Anglo-Saxon temper." The Times referred to "the Jesuit wire-pullers of the HOLY SEE" and asked: "How long can such a system of uncompromising and reactionary discipline, which sets the so-called welfare of the Church above even the 'eternal verities' of truth and justice, keep its hold upon the consciences of men?"[55]

This vehement indictment by The Times drew a reply from Wilfrid Ward. He complained against ascribing the worst motives to the Roman Church as well as to the anti-Dreyfusard French Catholics. He argued that if Dreyfus was condemned on insufficient and hearsay evidence the Roman Church was being condemned on a similar basis. Moveover, the charges in The Times were a blanket indictment against the whole French Church and the whole Roman Church without making any distinctions. Ward concluded that "we are now witnessing the curious spectacle of a self-righteous condemnation of unjust and irrational anti-Semiticism [sic] among our neighbours, under the not very persuasive form of an unjust and irrational 'No Popery' agitation among ourselves."[56]

The defensive letters of Vaughan and Ward were followed by a number of other letters by Roman Catholics. Most of these censured the role of the anti-Dreyfusard French Catholic press, and many regretted the Roman Catholic hierarchy's silence on the injustice involved in the Dreyfus Affair. In an article on October 17, 1899, The Times wrote: "The most striking, and we beg leave to think the most hopeful, feature of this controversy has been that it is from the ranks of English Roman Catholics themselves that the most earnest protests have proceeded against the excesses of their French co-religionists."[57]

On the same day, there appeared in The Times a letter by St. George Mivart censuring the French Catholic press and the silence of the Catholic hierarchy. It was by far the strongest censure written by an English Catholic. Mivart began his letter by condemning "the mendacity and cruelty" of the entire French Catholic press. Further, the great majority of French Catholics were to be reprobated, especially the French bishops who had disgraced themselves by tolerating and even giving their imprimatur to anti-Dreyfusard publications. It was wrong, however, to accuse the whole Catholic Church of injustice. Catholics generally had been on the side of Dreyfus. Nevertheless, the Pope's silence over the injustices being done was "amazing and appalling." Leo XIII had not only failed to speak out, but he had also given scandal by receiving with commendation the French priest Bailly, editor of the anti-Dreyfusard, anti-Semitic newspaper, La Croix. While silent about Dreyfus, the Pope had disparaged "the 'National virtues' in his American letter--i.e., truth, honour, justice, and fair play." Dreyfus was the Galileo of the nineteenth century. In the case of Galileo the papacy and Curia had misled the world in a matter of belief, the interpretation of Scripture, and thus rendered futile any such scriptural decrees in the future; in the case of Dreyfus, the Pope had now misled the world in a matter of morals.[58]

Mivart was not content to stop with this censure of the Pope's conduct. How was the Pope's conduct to be explained? he asked. Leo XIII surely wanted to see justice done, but how could "he condemn flagrant injustice when his mouth is closed by the flagrant injustice of his own special agents, the 'Roman congregations,'" particularly the Holy Office? "The Roman congregations consist of men who have obtained more or less of what most men care for--influence, power, and some 'ways and means.'" Consequently, "it is only natural that, as a body, the Curialists should try to move heaven and earth to keep the advantages they have obtained." The forced retractions of Leroy and Zahm were futile efforts by the Curia to dissipate the growing belief in evolution. The Curia's indifference to truth, justice, and even religion was matched by its stupidity. The curial system was abhorrent to the entire civilized world. Mivart concluded by saying that, however painful, it was now necessary to speak out energetically and immediately in public to bring about reform, for "the evils at Rome, here pointed out, will also cease only when reprobation by the universal judgment of civilized mankind has been brought to bear upon them."[59]

Mivart's outburst raised a number of questions pertaining to the liberals' attitudes and future course of action. Would they retain confidence in the Roman authorities after the scriptural decisions, the retractations of Catholic evolutionists, the Americanist letter, and the Church's role in the Dreyfus Affair? Mivart did not. To what extent were obedience and respect owed to the ecclesiastical authorities? Had Leo XIII really adopted a policy of repression? What should the liberals' response be to censures of intellectual work? Should they continue to pursue a policy of moderation and caution or, like Mivart, should they try to force reforms from the ecclesiastical authorities by bold, public statements? In essence, they were being made to come to terms with practical problems involved in the larger problem of the role of the intellectual and that of authority within the Church. They were reaching the threshold of a critical period.

The division in their ranks was beginning to open wide over these questions. Looking back on Mivart's letter to The Times, Ward wrote to Hügel:

> Do you remember that when I read Mivart's letter
> to the _Times_ (before his later developments) you
> hailed it as in the right direction though exag-
> gerated and in bad taste. To me it seemed not at
> all in the right direction. . . . I think much
> the greatest practical difference between us is
> that you more or less welcome anything on the left
> side though you yourself may not agree with it,
> while I feel that there is a species of agitation
> so indiscriminate and unintelligent that it simply
> injures the cause of progress and justifies the
> reactionaries.[60]

Gasquet and Bishop had already concluded that it was best
to stick strictly to one's own scholarly work and to refrain
from publishing controversial views that went beyond this.
In July 1899, Gasquet wrote to Bishop that Vaughan had told
him that hints of his "advanced Liberal views" had been
given to Roman authorities by the Abbot Primate of his
order. Gasquet suggested, "At present all our ends are
best served by work not talk." Commenting on Mivart's
letter to The Times, he wrote again to Bishop, "What a
pity it is that Mivart can't stick to his 'biology.'"[61]

Bishop had all along advised a policy of sticking
strictly to one's scientific work, and had been pessimistic
about the hopes of the other English liberal Catholics. At
the turn of the century, however, even he diverged from
this policy. In the New Era[62] of December 2, 1899, he
reviewed Abbé Pichot's La Conscience chrétienne et l'affaire
de Dreyfus. Bishop looked upon the Dreyfus Affair as
involving fundamental Christian moral principles, yet the
French clergy were nearly all on the wrong side. Why?
Bishop agreed with Pichot that it was unjust to ascribe
the worst motives to them and accepted his explanation that
they had been duped by newspapers in which they had a priori
put their confidence. But how could they be so misled?
This was, Bishop suggested, a product of the history of the
French clergy in the nineteenth century. The remedy was,

he believed, to be found in frank unprejudiced inquiry.
In reply to a letter to the New Era sharply criticizing
his views, Bishop wrote:

> Whatever the sub-varieties, crossings or particular
> manifestations, minds in this world may be roughly
> reduced to two main types. As it is in the world,
> so it is in the Church. There is, for instance,
> on one side the admirer of the thesis, the adept
> in a priori methods; on the other the man who pro-
> ceeds by way of investigation and hypothesis.
> There is the man with the spirit of the lawgiver,
> the man with the spirit of the enquirer. There is
> the votary of absolutism, the devotee of liberty.
> There is the lion and there is the lamb, and we
> have good grounds for thinking that in the Catholic
> Church at any rate they will have to lie down
> together till the end, whatever violence may have
> thereby to be done to the natural instincts of the
> nobler creature.[63]

The problem in the eyes of other English liberal
Catholics, however, was that ecclesiastical authority
"lions" were not allowing some liberal Catholic "lambs"
to go about their work in peace. Gasquet and Bishop could
freely pursue their researches into monastic history and
the history of liturgy, two relatively noncontroversial
areas within the Church. But Hügel was interested in
Biblical criticism, and the Jesuit George Tyrrell was soon
to encounter problems with ecclesiastical authorities in
publishing theological writings related to his pastoral
work. The authorities, on the other hand, had a problem
also. They were responsible for their domain and, in their
view, some liberal "lambs" were chewing at the roots of its
heartland and even claiming lordship over it. A critical
time lay ahead for both the liberal Catholics and the
ecclesiastical authorities.

CHAPTER III

THE JOINT PASTORAL CENSURING

LIBERAL CATHOLICISM

The twentieth century opened with a face-to-face
confrontation between one of the liberal Catholics and the
English ecclesiastical authorities. In January 1900, St.
George Mivart published two articles challenging a number
of Catholic doctrines.[1] In addition to the recent events
involving Rome, personal factors occasioned his outburst.
In 1899 the Index had been reissued with his earlier
articles on hell remaining under censure. Moreover, he was
suffering from diabetes. In the face of death, Mivart,
having written works of Catholic apologetics before, felt
obliged to make his latest convictions known to his readers.
He thought science would bring about radical alterations in
Christian belief in the future, and hoped to prepare the
way for these changes. He wished to encourage broad open-
mindedness and scrupulous honesty and candor in the Church,
which he recognized as still possessing enormous power and
influence as a moral agent.[2] Most significantly, his two
articles were an attempt to discover whether he and other
persons arriving at the same conclusions regarding Catholic
belief could remain within the Roman Communion.

In an article entitled "The Continuity of Catholicism" in the Nineteenth Century, Mivart attempted to facilitate conformity by allowing for a radical interpretation of
doctrinal development. Asking whether there was any real
continuity in the development of doctrine, he began by

answering that "no such sudden and considerable changes have simultaneously occurred within it as would constitute 'a breach of continuity.'" He went on to state the essence of his position: "Dogmas cannot be explicitly called in question, though sometimes they may be so explained (as we shall shortly see) that they thereby become (practically) explained away or even reversed." Mivart then attempted to illustrate this position. He made a preparatory reference to changes of belief in regard to the teachings on usury and on the possibility of salvation outside the Church. His position really unfolded when he took up Scripture. Referring to the belief in the plenary inspiration and inerrancy of Scripture as affirmed in Leo XIII's _Providentissimus Deus_, he wrote: "The pope's declaration that the Bible can 'contain no errors' is but a matter of formal parade, only saved from falsehood by a more ingenious than honest distinction between 'errors' and 'untruths,' whereby theologians are able to declare that statements 'utterly untrue' are entirely 'free from error.'" Scripture "is of course still regarded as 'inspired,' but the meaning given to that term is rapidly changing. . . . Can we venture to deny that Homer and Plato, Æschylus and Aristotle, Virgil and Tacitus, Dante and Shakespeare, were in various degrees inspired?" Moreover, a transformation had also taken place in regard to the right and power of churchly authority to interpret Scripture. The Galileo case demonstrated once and for all the futility of that claim.[3]

Having disposed of the Church's claims regarding Scripture and ecclesiastical authority, Mivart moved on to other matters of belief. Taking up original sin, he maintained: "No man of education now regards the Biblical account of 'the fall' as more than 'a myth intended to symbolize some moral lapse of the earliest races of mankind,' or, possibly, 'the first awakening of the human conscience

to a perception of right and wrong.' This is the utmost
which such a man would admit. . . ." Although many persons
considered the redemptive value of Christ's crucifixion to
be the essence of the Christian religion, radical change
was going on in regard to that doctrine also. Many "modern
Catholics as orthodox as learned" held that "Christ's life
and death have served to set before us a great 'object
lesson.' Such Catholics affirm that, beyond this, they
know not, and that no one knows 'how' man was benefited by
the passion of Christ Jesus." As to Christ's bodily resurrection, the four gospels conspicuously disagreed in their
accounts of it. This, as well as other reasons, suggested
that these accounts might be wholly legendary. The accounts
of Mary's perpetual virginity and the virgin birth of Christ
might also be wholly legendary. Some Catholics already
believed these doctrines to be true only in a figurative
sense and untrue if virginity was taken in a physical sense.
Mivart brought his illustrations to an end with a reference
to earlier beliefs in the imminent coming of Christ and in
witchcraft and demonic possession. The former had passed
away in early times; the latter in modern times.[4]

At the same time, he published in the Fortnightly
Review another article entitled "Some Recent Catholic
Apologists." It was designed to advocate the legitimacy of
his radical approach to the development of doctrine. He
began by recalling his former apologetic work aimed at
mitigating misunderstanding between Christianity and biological and Biblical science. Recalling also his articles
on hell, he announced that he still held the propositions
advanced therein and was withdrawing his submission to the
Index. Then he referred to a recent apologetic article
entitled "The Ethics of Religious Conformity," which had
appeared in the Quarterly Review (January, 1899).[5] It had
concluded that religion's utility could not justify

conformity for those who regarded the theory of doctrinal development as tantamount to simple denial of the creeds or who rejected development while having no other theory but a negative position. Mivart disagreed and concluded: "It seems to me better, instead of professing reverence for incomprehensible formulae, to patiently await their disappearance." They might disappear by transformation or by being explained away or by simply being dropped altogether. In replying to some other recent works by Catholic apologists, Mivart elaborated on points related to those made in his article in the Nineteenth Century. To scientists, not to ecclesiastical authorities, was given the elucidation of all scientific questions whatever. This applied "to Scripture criticism, to biology, and to all questions concerning evolution, the antiquity of man, and the origin of either his body or his soul, or of both." In regard to the interpretation of Scripture, "church authorities have continuously misled the Christian world concerning it for eighteen hundred years; which world has only recently been delivered from such delusion through the labors of non-Catholic scientific men of Holland, Germany, and France." Leo XIII had recently reaffirmed the inerrancy as well as the plenary inspiration of Scripture. But for Mivart, the scientist, truth meant simply: "Did it or did it not agree with objective fact?" Of course, Pope Leo could not have spoken much differently, "being bound hand and foot by the declarations of the Councils of the Vatican and of Trent." But why had Leo not simply let the matter die out gradually as the early belief in the imminent coming of Christ had been allowed to die out?[6]

Although Mivart received support nowhere in the Catholic press for his conclusions, the Tablet went beyond criticism of his opinions to make a personal attack; it used the words "lie," "slander," and "cowardly."[7] Consequently, he wrote to Cardinal Vaughan, the owner of the _Tablet_, complaining of that paper's charges. Putting aside the question of what the _Tablet_ had written, Vaughan wrote back in his official capacity as guardian of the faith in England and Mivart's bishop requesting him to sign an attached profession of faith. This included belief in the physical virginity of Mary, bodily resurrection of Christ, original sin and its transmission through Adam to mankind, redemptive value of Christ's crucifixion, everlasting punishment in hell, inerrancy and plenary inspiration of Scripture, the right of the Church to interpret Scripture with authority, and the Church's perpetual retention of the original sense of dogma.[8]

After a fruitless exchange of letters between the two,[9] Vaughan replied that he was obliged to ask Mivart for a last time to sign the profession of faith, and that he could not allow him to evade this duty because of anything that the _Tablet_ had written. In reply to a subsequent letter from Mivart which put aside the question of what had appeared in the _Tablet_ but did not include a profession of faith, Vaughan went to the core of the matter:

> . . . the church, being the divine teacher established by Christ in the world, rightly claims from her disciples a hearty and intellectual acceptance of all that she authoritatively teaches. . . .

> But, if you are going to give the assent of faith only to such doctrines as present no difficulties beyond the power of your finite intelligence to see through and solve by direct answer, you must put aside at once all the mysteries of faith, and you must frankly own yourself to be a rationalist pure and simple. . . .

> This is to return to the old Protestant system of private judgment, or to open rationalism and unbelief.

Vaughan suggested that a talk with the liberal Catholic priest George Tyrrell might be useful. Meanwhile, in the absence of a profession of faith from Mivart, Vaughan excommunicated him.[10]

Mivart's excommunication proved to be permanent. His position rested on the ground that the highest authority in questions of religious belief was the reason of the individual. The position of Vaughan rested on the ground that in questions of religious belief the authority of the Church was supreme. Holding his basic position, Mivart could continue to accept traditional Catholic teaching only if he were allowed to interpret it as he wanted, in particular, to adjust it to scientific knowledge as he saw fit. When this claim was disallowed, he found himself carried outside the Church. His rationalism, like Renan's earlier, led him to reject doctrines in conflict with his own reason. He too was certain that the conclusions being drawn by nineteenth-century scientific criticism were right. His faith in science, which seemed to him in accord with reason itself, thus prevailed over his belief in traditional Christian teaching. Thinking the correspondence between Vaughan and himself ended, he sent it to The Times for publication. In a final letter to Vaughan, he wrote: "As to the old, worn-out saying, 'There can be no discrepancy between science and religion,' it is quite true if religion is always careful to change its teaching in obedience to science, but not otherwise."[11] Two months later, Mivart died and was buried outside the Church.

Although they could sympathize to some degree with his outburst, the English liberal Catholics accepted neither his basic position nor his conclusions. At the outset of the affair, Vaughan had asked Edmund Bishop, who was on friendly terms with Mivart, to see if he could help him. Writing to Bishop, Mivart flatly stated: "It then was, and

now is, <u>disgusting</u> to me that children should be taught or
men have preached to them a parcel of fairy tales and pre-
tend that there are not gross falsehoods in the Bible, e.g.
the tower of Babel business is no myth, no lesson of any
kind, but simply a baseless, barbarous fiction devoid of
any value in any way save as a sign of the absurd ideas
prevailing in early times." On the letter, Bishop underlined "<u>disgusting</u>," "a parcel of fairy tales," "gross falsehoods," "simply a baseless, barbarous fiction," and "ideas
prevailing in early times," and commented in antipathy to
such conclusions, "I harden." A few days later he had a
final fruitless meeting with Mivart: "A short conversation
sufficed to shew that it was too late; that things just now
must take their course, whatever that may be."[12]

     Like Bishop, Gasquet too had been personally con-
cerned with the Mivart Affair. Knowing Mivart to be ill
and in danger of death, he had persuaded him before his
excommunication to see a priest and receive the last sacra-
ment. Writing to Fleming, still a Consultor of the Holy
Office, Gasquet said that what Mivart had written was
indefensible. But like Bishop who regarded the <u>Tablet</u>'s
attitude as "damnable,"[13] he disapproved of that journal's
role in the affair. "It would add to the terrors of
Catholic life, if there was to be excommunication by
<u>leading article</u>."[14]

     The English liberal Catholics feared that the Mivart
Affair would make advocacy of their cause much more difficult with the ecclesiastical authorities. Tyrrell wrote to
Wilfrid Ward: "How horrid all this about Mivart. It will
throw everything back a decade and leave the Ark of God in
the hands of the Philistines." Ward wrote to Hügel that
such affairs would result in the ecclesiastical authorities
tending to identify extreme liberalism with moderate
liberalism and responding with "sheer intolerance."[15] Hügel

was struck by two things in regard to the Mivart Affair: how the lack of work by Catholics in Biblical criticism occasioned difficulties like Mivart's and how Mivart and his neo-scholastic opponents resembled each other in their rationalistic tone and method. Although Hügel disliked the Tablet's actions in the affair and although he wished Vaughan had been slower in excommunicating Mivart, he thought the Tablet was right in protesting and Vaughan in taking action. He too feared "that the reaction from all this affair will last long, and may go far."[16]

Some English Catholics were taking the Mivart Affair to illustrate that only very rigid attention and submission to curial congregations would keep Catholics straight. Instead, it proved to Hügel "that without an active, carefully fostered spiritual, mystical life and habit of mind, a hungering and thirsting after what is above and beyond the power of all the natural or indeed any sciences to awaken or to supply,--a man remains or becomes but half a man, uninteresting and vulgar (even simply intellectually), and of course ceases to have all patience with the imperfect administration, and even all tenderness for the real requirements and duties of a religion which has ceased to stimulate and to supply a faculty and want of his nature." Hügel took Mivart's rationalist tendency of mind as an illustration of the weaknesses of a temper of mind given to natural science only. He said that he clearly saw that Mivart and his neo-scholastic opponents, similar in their tone and mental habit, though not in their conclusions, could not cure each other.[17]

At about the same time as the Mivart Affair, the Jesuit Tyrrell fell into trouble with his order over an article he had published in the Weekly Register criticizing attempts of neo-scholastics to rationalize the doctrine of hell.[18] His article appeared at the worst possible time, for the Mivart Affair naturally brought back memories of Mivart's censured articles on hell.

Although like Mivart's articles in objecting to some of the ways in which the nature of the eternal pains of hell and the proportion of mankind going there were being popularly presented, Tyrrell's article was essentially different in its protest against all attempts to rationalize the doctrine of hell. "But when faint illustrative analogies from reason are put forward as satisfactory and adequate explanations of a difficulty which is only aggravated by such futile alleviations, we at once resent this intrusion of pert rationalism into the arcana fidei, and send the would-be theologian about his business." Rationalism was the contemporary opponent of belief, but Mivart was not the only guilty person; scholastic theologians were also guilty of the attempt to rationalize dogma. Tyrrell hoped that "rationalism would cease its elucidations. God will save His word in all things; no particle of the Church's accredited teaching but shall be found true in some higher and grander sense than our poor muddled wits ever dreamt of; and yet all shall be well." He concluded that the Church could and should move forward "by purging out of our midst any remnant of the leaven of rationalism that we may have carried with us from earlier and cruder days, when faith needed the rein more than the spur."[19]

Had Tyrrell's article not appeared coincidentally with the Mivart Affair, it might have avoided becoming controversial. Although it met with no censure from Jesuit theologians of his own English province, it did not escape reprobation from Jesuit headquarters in Rome. Tyrrell was surprised to receive a command from the Superior General of the Jesuit order forbidding him to publish articles in any journal save the Month, the English Jesuit organ, until his article had been examined.[20]

This dispute was Tyrrell's first major conflict with the authorities of his order, and it upset him and other liberal Catholics as well. Tyrrell told Hügel that he was afraid Mivart's outburst had thrown things back at least ten years and that ultramontane opponents of liberals now possessed the ark of God--he hoped they would not upset it into the mud. In a temper, he went on to say that he was convinced Christ's message to man was lodged in the Roman Church as gold in ore; since he could not separate them he took them together. Using hyperbole he compared Christ to a savant giving a set of scientific lectures to bushmen and bequeathing them a synopsis of the lectures. Christianity in the Roman Church's hands was like the synopsis in the bushmen's hands. In the course of time they might understand some of it and, though savages, only they possessed the authentic record.[21] Wilfrid Ward told Hügel that Tyrrell had been treated "abominably" by the Jesuit authorities in Rome and had mentioned to him the possibility of going into schism. Ward had placed his hopes for toleration from the authorities in moderate work by liberal Catholics. Since he thought Tyrrell particularly agreed with him in this, he considered Tyrrell's case the biggest blow that his hopes had yet encountered. Tyrrell was "in an Irish temper" over the treatment he had received, but Ward thought that he would get over it. He suggested, however, that Hügel write a sympathetic letter to Tyrrell encouraging him to do nothing rash.[22] Hügel, who had become Tyrrell's close friend since making his acquaintance in 1897, did write to him and found high praise for his article: "I do not think you have ever written anything finer, perhaps never anything quite so fine. It is so deep and tender too, so full of the mystery of Faith and of the world unseen. . . ." He told Tyrrell that he still thought there was reason for confidence and initiative, and suggested that the check to Tyrrell was more trying than destructive.[23]

In an encouraging reply, Tyrrell said that the recent Mivart Affair was a useful lesson to him on the need to keep his temper. He had now received, however, written censures of his article from two Jesuit theologians in Rome. He informed Hügel that the censures contained, in addition to personal remarks, objections based on an ignorance of the English language and a complete failure to grasp the article as a whole. He said he was identified with T. H. Huxley, Herbert Spencer, and Mivart, and reproached coarsely with many theological epithets.[24]

Over and above personal remarks, Tyrrell's treatment of reason was an issue. The two censors defended the use and cogency of reason in elucidating dogma and denied that its analogies could serve to aggravate rather than to lessen difficulties. Moreover, they warned against attempting to overcome difficulties by appeals to the mysteriousness of dogma. In reply to the censors, Tyrrell admitted that perhaps the strongest charge against him was his treatment of reason. But he pointed out that in his article he had distinguished between the use and the abuse of rational analogy, which was, he argued, necessarily inadequate. For it to be useful its inadequacy had to be remembered, for it was an attempt to achieve some understanding of the "spiritual and eternal" by conceptions borrowed from "sensible and temporal" things. If one forgot this inadequacy, the doctrine of hell seemed not only negatively but also positively repugnant to one's sense of justice. Tyrrell summarized his position in the following words: "In fine, I cordially accept the sentiment of the Vatican Council, which I am supposed to contradict, where it says: 'Reason, illumined by faith, when it earnestly, devoutly and soberly seeks a certain God-given--Deo dante--

94

understanding of mysteries can attain thereto.' But I would lay emphasis on the word 'soberly' and would also point out that it is not of pure reason, but of reason illumined by faith, that the Council speaks."[25] His article was a pastoral attempt to minister to troubled souls bothered by difficulties concerning the doctrine of hell. But he was beginning to raise epistemological questions, which would later play an important part in the modernist controversy.[26]

Tyrrell's dispute with the Jesuit General dragged on until two occurrences apparently precipitated a decision. The first was Robert Edward Dell's article, "A Liberal Catholic View of the Case of Dr. Mivart," in the April issue of the Nineteenth Century. In the article, Dell criticized the Jesuit system while paying a compliment to Tyrrell as "an English Jesuit father, whose views seem to be as much out of harmony with the spirit of his Society as his abilities are superior to those of his confrères." Tyrrell's friend Maude Petre wrote to Wilfrid Ward that the compliment only compounded his difficulties with his order; she asked Ward, as someone known to be influential and moderate, if he could help to show that Tyrrell's works could be taken as a bulwark against both extreme liberalism and ultra-conservatism.[27] The second occurrence was the aggravation that the dispute was causing the General, who recently had fallen seriously ill. Tyrrell now was ordered by the General to restate the meaning of his article on hell. When he sent back two unsatisfactory replies to this order, the General dictated a statement which he suggested Tyrrell should publish in the Weekly Register. It said that "three things must be distinguished--dogmas of faith, Catholic truth, and theological opinion." Regarding the first two there could be no doubt as to Tyrrell's position, "all loyal sons of the Church are bound to accept them"; concerning the third, he "subscribes to the common opinion

of Catholic theologians; and that his article must be thus
interpreted, _i.e._ he only meant to say that we must not
require more than the Church requires through her recognised
spokesmen." Tyrrell accordingly sent to the Weekly Register
a letter which was published on June 1, 1900. Writing to
Hügel, he remarked: "An absolutely fatuous and unmeaning
letter to the Editor of the Weekly Register, which appeared
last week, is the mouse of which the labouring mountain has
at last been delivered."[28]

Writing to Ward, Tyrrell gave his own assessment of
the situation confronting the liberal Catholics. Still
identifying himself as a moderate with Ward, he commented:
"The Extreme Right hopes weakly in violent methods of repression; and strives to pitchfork back the incoming tide. The
Extreme Left calls on them to surrender and cry peccavimus;
or demands what is not so much reform as a revolution, a
breaking down, preparatory to building up; nor has it any
very definite plan of reconstruction. If there is not a
mediating party, these two will tug till the rope breaks
and each is thrown backwards with disaster." The policy of
the mediating or moderate party was one of adaptation: "the
new matter to be sorted and accepted so far as it will in
any wise consist with the old forms; the old forms to be
interpreted so far as they can be made honestly and consistently to cover and inform the new matter." "Instead of
first destroying and then rebuilding, it renews brick by
brick as renewal is required. But its characteristic note
is noiselessness." Consequently, the moderates were not,
Tyrrell thought, distinct from the more radical liberals
simply in wanting less or in being less strident; they were
totally different in principle and aim. If one had to apply
a label, mediatorial was preferable to moderate, for the
latter term might suggest "a definite programme (e.g., with
regard to the Index, Inquisition, Higher Criticism, Church

Government), whereas all I want is a conciliatory spirit on both sides, each wishing to yield all that can rightly be yielded to the other in a spirit of true liberty."[29]

The rebuke that Tyrrell received for his article was his first major personal encounter with the problem of the roles of the intellectual and of authority within the Church, a problem that was to hold his attention during the next several years. For the time being, however, his role and that of authority within the Jesuit order was the more immediate problem. Although inward questionings as to his position in the order had been with him since his days as a Jesuit novice, the problem became acute with the publication of his article on hell. Tyrrell's role had been that of a spiritual adviser through his pastoral work and writings directed to those suffering intellectual difficulties regarding faith, and he felt a loyalty to those who depended on him for such guidance. Therefore, when he was ordered to cease publishing articles except in the Month and his rights as a retreat-master and confessor were curtailed, he was forced, in effect, to reduce or even abandon the role and responsibilities he had taken on. Moreover, the rebuke came just at the time when his influence was widening: Vaughan had referred Mivart to him, and he had membership in the Synthetic Society. Secondly, in his view, loyalty to the Church had higher claims on his obedience than loyalty to the order, for the Jesuits existed solely to serve the Church. Consequently when he moved to a small Jesuit mission in Richmond, Yorkshire, where, as it turned out, he spent the next five years, he continued publishing articles and letters pseudonymously and anonymously in disobedience to the orders of the Jesuit authorities.[30]

Why then did Tyrrell not leave the Jesuits and carry on his work elsewhere in the Church? Many considerations compelled him to decide to remain within the order.

97

He was apprehensive that his leaving would hurt those who depended on him for guidance, and he was fearful that it would mean a triumph of the ultra-conservatives. Moreover, he did not conceal from members of his English province the fact that he was publishing articles disobediently, and since his actions were plainly unlawful he did not feel he was compromising the order. Furthermore, he thought the Jesuit authorities in Rome would not allow him dispensation to leave the order; therefore, to leave would be to go into schism. He was also afraid that he might go to extremes when released from checks. Lastly, he continued to entertain a faint hope that things might change for the better within the order.[31]

Still he anguished at times over his position with the Jesuits. In her diary, Maude Petre, a close friend, noted in October, 1900: "I prayed a long while last night-- begging that he [Tyrrell] might not leave the Church." Further entries in her diary are illuminating: "Oh, if only he were less bitter: if he would not be so hard when the [English Jesuit] provincial and others make advances. I do believe that, at bottom, he still loves the Society, and that that is one reason of his bitterness." "He is suffering and has been, I am convinced, more deeply wounded in his feelings and affections than he would own or recognize himself."[32]

Affection and intimacy developed between Petre and him. However, it must be added that they apparently never knew each other "in the Biblical sense"--that is, they apparently were not sexually intimate. Petre's diary entry, October 3, 1900, reads (in part): "I believe God means us to help one another, and that our affection is to be for mutual good. I feel life has grown more serious, that not a step must be taken without God now . . . ." In a letter in November, Tyrrell addressed Petre as Maude for the first

time and signed: "Affectionately yours G. Tyrrell." In
December, his signature reads: "Yours, I know not how
GT."[33] Many of his later letters to Maude Petre are not
signed at all.

Beyond its effect on Tyrrell's situation, the Mivart
Affair produced a whole series of repercussions that eventually affected the entire English liberal Catholic group.
In his article in the April issue of the Nineteenth Century,
Robert Dell had viewed the Mivart Affair as a result of the
existing situation in the Church.[34] He argued that the
Church had been dominated for the previous half century by
a party which had succeeded all too well in stifling
originality and independent intellectual activity and in
getting an ever firmer hold on the government of the Church.
The present Archbishop of Westminster, Cardinal Vaughan,
had once been an active member of this ultramontane party.
The motive-power of this party, however, was the Jesuit
order. The ultramontanes were attempting to force an
acceptance of scholastic philosophy and methods on all
Catholics and to brand modern philosophy as incompatible
with Catholicism. Because of their adherence to scholastic
ideas which had long been abandoned by the modern mind,
they were hopelessly out of touch with modern thought. Their
policy was one of despair, for they only sought to keep
modern thought from seeping into the Church through the
walls they had erected. The neo-scholastics never wearied
of denouncing rationalism, but they were inveterate rationalists themselves. Only the ecclesiastical authorities had
the right to decide what must or must not be believed, but
the neo-scholastics were trying to impose their own deductions as necessary conclusions from dogma.[35]

Dell suggested that some of the indignation spent
on Mivart should be directed against the neo-scholastics
who had made him fall. It was not surprising that a

scientist should react the way he did, for the neo-
scholastics had intruded their deductions into the field of
science and had sought to impose scientific theories proven
false. They had asserted that doctrine had not undergone
modification, a false assertion that would not stand the
test of facts if modification be "taken in its ordinary and
natural sense." Mivart had failed to distinguish between
matters of dogma and the contemporary opinions or consentient teaching of theologians, but the neo-scholastics were
again responsible for this, for they attributed practically
the same value to dogma, non-infallible papal statements,
curial decisions, and theologians' consentient teaching.
As for the future, political considerations would be important. Much would depend on whether Italians, who were
unable to understand the Anglo-Saxon mind, would continue
to dominate the offices of the central government of the
Church.[36]

Steadfast in his advocacy of a moderate position by
liberals lest their cause be ruined, Wilfrid Ward was loath
to let Dell's remarks pass as those of a typical liberal.
In an article entitled "Liberalism and Intransigeance," he
replied to Dell in the pages of the Nineteenth Century.[37]
The past year had seen, Ward remarked, a display of
hostility by some English Catholics toward the ecclesiastical authorities. The Curia, the Jesuit order, the ultramontane party, scholasticism, the temporal power, the Index,
and the Inquisition had all been denounced as corrupt.
Except for Mivart, these denunciations were not the work of
liberal scholars or thinkers, of experts, but the work of
agitators. Both the left-wing agitators and their extreme
right-wing opponents had tried to identify the agitators'
views with those of the experts. The left-wing hoped to
cloak their excesses with respectability; the right-wing
opposed all change and wished to discredit as excessive the

plea of the experts for moderate change and for "reality and
life." This presented a great danger since it would be disastrous if the ecclesiastical authorities also mistakenly
identified the moderate experts with the left-wing agitators.
Ward detailed his own overall view of the present situation:

> In an age which is pre-eminently one of transition--
> when new lights on matters scientific, historical,
> critical; new points of view and new overmastering
> impulses on matters social, political, philosophical
> are making their appearance year by year, it is only
> those few who have made these subjects specially
> their own, and who, at the same time, have the
> interests of the Church at heart, who can be, in
> the nature of the case, equal to the situation.
> They alone have the perceptions and knowledge
> needed to see how Catholic thought can deal with
> and assimilate what is sound or true, can effec-
> tively resist what is dangerous. They are the
> natural eyes of those in power, in matters where
> only specialists have the training and knowledge
> to see accurately. And when the ruling power is
> really alive to the situation, its first wish is
> to find such assistants. If on the other hand it
> is not alive to the situation, if the experts are
> set aside and such matters are left to those who
> have no sympathy with or understanding of the
> modern world, whose minds move only in the tradi-
> tional groove, the Church loses for the time the
> active principle of intellectual progress. Cathol-
> icism may lose touch with the age, and forfeit much
> of its influence. And this may happen although the
> Church is not internally corrupt. Zeal may still
> abound. True religion--which is after all the
> Church's first concern--may still flourish. But
> Catholic thought may no longer hold its own with
> the thought of the day; and Catholicism may fail
> to win, or even in some cases to keep, those who
> are intellectually the children of their time,
> being in their eyes identified with antiquated
> scientific or critical positions which are now
> untenable.

Appealing to the past history of the Church, Ward argued
that authority has discharged the responsibility of guarding
the tradition and checking too startling innovations, but

only the "men of insight" (intellectuals) have been able to adapt "the expression of Christian thought to the conditions and culture of the times." In the long run authority was too aware of its own interests to reject the help of the experts. But it might do so in the short run, especially in countries like England where Catholics were in a position of intellectual isolation from their neighbors.[38]

As to the future, Ward thought that improvement could not be expected overnight, for it might take some time for the authorities to separate the experts from the grumblers when many people were offering criticisms and proposing reforms. It was necessary to place oneself mentally in the position of the authorities, and ask oneself what would it be practical for them to grant. If all the institutions of the Church were abused by agitators, it would no longer be safe for the authorities to permit free discussion on behalf of reform. Agitation might then provoke from them a really repressive policy which would make the moderates useless to the Church, even if it did not embitter them and turn them against the authorities. The right-wing extremists were not the ultramontane or the Jesuit or the neo-scholastic party; they were a motley phalanx including certain types of human nature more than certain types of Catholicism. They were those who opposed any novelty and who could not see beyond their own limited horizons. At present, there was no proof that the ecclesiastical authorities had already accepted the extreme right's calls for a policy of repression; nevertheless, "Rulers do not choose a time of mutiny as the moment for far-reaching concessions." And the left-wing extremists were wantonly insulting the authorities by calling them devoid of both sense and high motive. Many Catholics already acknowledged that priests whose minds had been formed only on scholasticism would become more unsuited to deal intellectually with the present age, that the Index's rules needed to be altered further, that the Inquisition's procedure was designed to suit a much earlier period, that a complete sifting of the "higher criticism" was imperative and should not be impeded by theological presumptions, that nationalities should be more fully represented at Rome, that there was a deplorable "recent tendency in some influential quarters towards a conservatism which refuses even to consider facts which are patent to so many thinking Catholics. . . ." But this was something different from demanding a revolutionary abolition of these institutions or complete freedom to accept any and all conclusions put forward in the name of science. In short, there was a need for reform, but reform could not come if its advocates acted like disloyal revolutionaries.[39]

The next issue of the Nineteenth Century found Dell having the last word with an article entitled "Mr. Wilfrid Ward's Apologetics."[40] Dell began by saying that since Ward was one of the few English Catholics whose views carried any weight among non-Catholics in England, he was almost expected to express his views whenever a matter involving the Roman Church was in question. But it was unclear where Ward stood, and perhaps he himself did not know. What he said in his recent article might be true in the abstract, but he seemed to shrink from candidly recognizing the relevant facts. In this, he was like many other Catholic apologists. The Jesuit Society might not be composed of reactionaries, but the facts indicated that those who were directing the order in Rome were following a reactionary policy. The Roman ecclesiastical authorities might not be following a repressive policy--indeed, Leo XIII's early policy was in the opposite direction--but what was Leo's recent policy? And if there was agitation by liberals, what had caused it? Ward spoke of repression following agitation, but the present agitation resulted

from repression. Dell recalled the repression of the French
Biblical scholar Loisy, the German apologist Schell, the
American evolutionist Zahm, and the "Americanists." "There
is, in fact, no important country in Europe where the intellectual life of Catholics is not paralysed." This was not
surprising in view of the facts that the late Cardinal
Mazella, S.J., had been the decisive influence at the
Vatican in recent years and Cardinal Steinhuber, another
Jesuit, was Prefect of the Index. If further proof were
needed that the ecclesiastical authorities had accepted the
call of the extreme right for repression, it was to be
found in the fact that all those censured of late were men
alive to modern ideas.[41]

Those whom Ward called disloyal were not, Dell continued, in fact so, although they might differ with Ward
over what constituted loyalty. If criticism of the authorities necessarily constituted disloyalty, then some of the
greatest saints of the Church had been disloyal. Actually
those whom Ward called the extreme left agreed with him
when he spoke of the need for reforming, not overthrowing,
ecclesiastical institutions, but it was doubtful whether
the authorities would agree with him. They would not like
to read that they were inclined toward a conservatism that
refused to consider facts, that the present training of
clergy, the rules of the Index, and the procedure of the
Holy Office were out of date, and that the pursuit of Biblical criticism should be permitted without its being impeded
by theological presumptions. Ward's moderate ultramontanism
seemed indistinguishable from what Dell would call liberal
Catholicism. In any case, it was wrong to allow ecclesiastics to claim exemption from criticism for their official
actions. Reform could only come about if those who pleaded
for it were united in spite of minor differences. Unfortunately Ward's article was inclined, Dell concluded, in the
opposite direction.[42]

The exchange between Ward and Dell occasioned a baring of differences between Ward and Hügel. Before reading Ward's article, Hügel had written to him with some anticipation of disagreement. He thought Ward tended to judge views by their orthodoxy, whereas he preferred to "leave the question of true orthodoxy to God and the Church authorities." After reading Ward's article he remarked that he particularly liked Ward's treatment of the leading Roman Catholic specialists of the day as men not only to be tolerated but also to be consulted. He thought Dell's article was the work of a journalist with the faults of one, but did not think it as extreme as the writings of the intransigent right. Moreover, he considered it the work of a well-intentioned and concerned Catholic. He was aware that it would irritate the authorities and do some harm, but thought it might also accomplish some good unattainable by more moderate methods. In conclusion, he recognized that Ward disagreed with him on these points, but he believed that the difference was small compared with their measure of agreement.[43]

Ward replied to Hügel that it was absurd for Dell to connect his views with those of the experts and that Dell had failed to put his finger on the real weaknesses or trouble spots in the Church. Moreover, Ward thought Dell was somewhat fond of grumbling. Hügel was "ready to believe in a maximum of intelligent disapproval and a minimum of sheer 'cussedness' and I should reverse the proportions." In any case, Cardinal Vaughan was angry even with Ward for his moderate "Liberalism and Intransigeance" article. Highly indiscriminate and unintelligent agitation simply injured the cause of the liberals.[44]

Hügel was not so aware as Ward of the danger of immoderation for the liberal Catholic cause, but it was not only on the practicality of irritating the ecclesiastical

authorities that they differed. Hügel noted that Ward's
writing was becoming so involved in arranging and balancing
facts that it was coming to be unduly apologetical. Hügel
privately told Tyrrell that he thought the main difference
between Ward and himself was not over policy and diplomacy,
what to say or how, but over their evaluation and practice
of religion's driving forces. He commented that the constituents of religion lay not in external arrangements,
policies and politics, no matter how wise or necessary,
but in spiritual forces, experiences and genuinely willed
mortifications, purifications, and elaborations.[45] He
remarked to Tyrrell that there was an unconscious dash of
impertinence towards the height and depth of God's truth
when the soul becomes directly and predominantly occupied
with arranging, balancing, and trimming in apologetics.[46]
Ward, on the other hand, following the ideas of Newman, saw
a certain wisdom which Hügel did not see in restrictions
placed on Catholic intellectuals by the authorities. In
the view of Newman and Ward, it was a psychological fact
that a variety of popular traditional beliefs were often
bound up with matters of faith in the popular imagination.
Consequently, if religious faith were really vitally important, it was dangerous for Catholic intellectuals to venti-
late most freely all the conclusions put forward by Biblical
criticism or other sciences, for this was likely to upset
the faith as well as popular traditional beliefs of undiscerning people. Moreover, there was a tendency for human
reason in matters of religious belief to outstrip its legitimate competence. Scientific hypotheses which seemed true
in one generation commonly met with rejection later; consequently, a scientific conclusion had to become clearly
established before change could be admitted by the ecclesiastical authorities. The preservation of the Christian
faith was entrusted to the Church, not to the individual

thinker, and the authorities had the responsibility of determining what was or was not to be believed.[47]

The last of the major articles by English Catholics in 1900 calling for reform appeared in the _Contemporary Review_ under the pseudonym "Fidelis."[48] In a first article in June, Fidelis described himself simply as a recent convert to Catholicism. Although his faith had not been shaken, he had experienced a perhaps typical convert reaction of surprise at abuses existing within the Roman Church. There were instances of abuses regarding the raising of money and popular devotions; moreover, the ecclesiastical authorities had remained silent in the Dreyfus Affair. All Catholics were agreed on essential matters of faith, but Fidelis found that in regard to the modification of non-essentials where the faith met the natural sciences some of the views he had been accustomed to take for granted were considered "liberal." The Holy Office's decision on the _Comma Johanneum_ and its harassment of Catholic supporters of evolution seemed to reflect a tendency toward obscurantism. Fidelis recognized that there was something to be said for the curial position: that the Curia was charged with preserving and reaffirming the faith, that it was simply putting a check on too hasty acceptance of modern ideas, and that it was protecting the faith of the undiscerning. But to many educated Catholics, the main reason for the Curia's decisions appeared to be its total ignorance of modern thought and its loss of contact with the cultivated lay intellect even within the Church. Fidelis did not like the term "liberal Catholic" because it connoted a difference in essential belief not permissible to Catholics. But some Catholics rightly wanted to accommodate antiquated non-essentials of the faith with modern knowledge; they continued to recognize the Church as the guardian and

107

interpreter of the faith, a revelation which had been given
to the Church and could not be changed in its essence.[49]

In November, Fidelis' second and last article
appeared in the Contemporary Review. If he had not discovered that some broad views bounded by necessary limits
existed in the Roman Church, Fidelis thought he might have
left. As it was, one could be completely convinced that
the Roman Catholic Church was the true church and, consequently, that its dogmatic definitions were true, and yet
want reform in its non-essential features. Some Catholics
wrongly charged disloyalty if one bared facts about, or
criticized, the actions of ecclesiastical authorities.
Fidelis thought some Catholic journals would probably attack
him for his "plain speaking," but public opinion and criticism were presently the only hope for a strong stimulus to
reform. Parties could not exist within the Church because
there could be no divisions on the essential matters of
faith; moreover, party implied program, policy, and organization. Thus there could be no liberal party within the
Church, but there was a group, "simply a number of Catholics,
lay and cleric, independent of each other and of any
organisation, not necessarily known to each other, who, in
different degrees and ways, according to the personal element, mental constitution and experience of each, have
become conscious of certain separable defects which hinder
the Church's mission in the world." They were critical and
concerned because they loved true religion and the Church,
although the present policy of ecclesiastical authority
encouraged an uncritical and apathetic attitude. Extreme
conservatives were now at work trying to force Catholics to
accept mere theological opinions as the Church's official
teaching, and to make accountable to ecclesiastical authority matters remotely connected with faith. They sought to
impose conformity to something they called the Catholic

position in such departments of intellectual activity as history, textual criticism, politics, political economy, natural science, and, in particular, philosophy. Those who favored reforms stood opposed to these attempts. The Jesuit order and the Curia, however, opposed reform, even though the Curia itself needed some reform. All those who advocated reform did not agree in detail but were agreed in principle. The spontaneous, unorganized nature of their call justified the reform movement. Reform would have to come from above. What was needed at present was a call for it from below that might be partly responsible for stimulating necessary reforms by the ecclesiastical authorities. Reform would take time. However, if his articles did nothing else, Fidelis hoped they might let in fresh air where the doors and windows had been closed and the atmosphere had become laden with properties inducing sleep.[50]

Even before the Mivart Affair, some calls for reform had appeared in certain English Catholic periodicals. The Weekly Register and the short-lived New Era had begun to support reform. From August 26 to September 16, 1899, the Weekly Register had carried on a spirited discussion on the Roman congregations' secret methods and actions;[51] in December, it had published Tyrrell's "A Perverted Devotion" article. Robert Dell edited the Weekly Register in 1899-1900. And from October 30, 1899 to January 19, 1900, he edited the New Era.[52] That journal was completely suppressed in January 1900, seemingly for lack of funds but also because of pressure from ecclesiastical authority, and the Weekly Register was "carpeted."[53] The intervention of ecclesiastical authorities in the Catholic press, however, had not kept Dell, Ward, and Fidelis from publishing articles in the secular press in the wake of the Mivart Affair.

Before the year 1900 was out, the English Catholic episcopacy took the rather drastic action of promulgating a pastoral letter in which all sixteen bishops joined in censuring what they termed liberal Catholicism.[54] At the outset of their letter, they identified the rejection of the authority of the Church as the source of many evils. They noted that some Catholics had felt free in private speech or in the press to put forward their own opinions on the Church's doctrine, theology, government, practice, and discipline without referring to the mind of the Church or to ecclesiastical authorities. This characterized, the bishops said, the habit of mind of the liberal Catholic. Among English Catholics, it was generally due to ignorance of the nature of the Church and of the place and duty of individual members or due to ignorance of the continuity and indefectibility of the Church's belief. Although this liberal Catholic habit of mind existed among only a few English Catholics, it might infect and unsettle many other minds. To keep it from spreading if unnoticed, the joint pastoral had been issued as a warning and a statement of certain doctrines to guide the faithful.[55]

The pastoral directed the attention of Catholics to the existence of two different orders within the visible Church: the small body of men who represented the authority of Christ and the large body of the faithful. The former, the Ecclesia docens, was charged with teaching doctrine and consisted of the pope and the bishops, the successors of Peter and the Apostles. The Church's proclamation of doctrine did not result from consultation with specialists in divinity, philosophy, or natural sciences, and the Ecclesia docens needed no dictation from outside itself to determine how to guard the truth or condemn errors. The large body of faithful was the Ecclesia discens; it consisted of the laity, ecclesiastics, and bishops as private individuals.

110

It was taught doctrine. No matter how learned, members of the Ecclesia discens had no right to teach in the Church, although even the laity might be encouraged to write or lecture on matters concerning religion--but only in strict subordination to the Church's authority. Some disloyal and disobedient Catholics, however, "itch to have their hand in the government of the Church and in her teaching: or if this cannot be, they vainly strive to enforce their views by appeals to the press and to public opinion." Moreover, some of these liberal Catholics would preach another Gospel that included one or more of the following recently advanced errors:

> . . . that in the past, the Episcopate or Ecclesia docens, was not competent to define doctrinal truths with accuracy, because recent discoveries were then unknown; that the dogmas of Catholic faith are not immutable but tentative efforts after truth, to be reformed under the inspiration of modern science; that the Church's teaching should be limited to the articles or definitions of Catholic faith; that it is permissible to reject her other decisions; to set aside her censures; to criticise her devotions; to belittle her authority, and especially that of the Roman Congregations; to distrust her ability in dealing with intellectual and scientific objections; to place her character as nearly as possible on the level of that of a human institution--that the constitution as well as the teaching of the Church ought to be brought into harmony with, what is styled, modern thought and the progress of the world; that the government of the Church should be largely shared by the laity, as a right; and that men of science and broad-minded culture should employ themselves in devising means to bring this about: that the distinctions of Shepherd and Sheep should be blended by entitling the more learned among the laity to rank no longer as disciples, but as teachers and masters in Israel; that the growth of popular interest in ecclesiastical affairs and the spread of education render it right and expedient to appeal from ecclesiastical authority to public opinion; and that it is permissible to the faithful to correct abuses and scandals by recourse to the people and to the powers of the world, rather

than to the Authorities of the Church; . . . that
they [Catholics] may retain the name of Catholic
and receive the Sacraments, while disbelieving one,
or more of the truths of Faith; and that they are
in these respects subjects to no ecclesiastical
authority, or Episcopal correction.[56]

All Catholics were bound, the pastoral continued, to give "a firm assent to all revealed doctrines that are defined or universally held by the Church as of 'Catholic Faith;'. . ." They were obliged to "assent also to the decisions of the Church concerning matters appertaining to or affecting revelation, though these matters be not found, strictly speaking, within the deposit of Faith." In addition, Catholics were bound to give a second kind of assent, one "elicited by virtue of 'religious obedience,'" to the teaching of the Church that fell under the exercise of its ordinary authority or magisterium. This included "Pastoral Letters of Bishops, diocesan and provincial decrees, and (though standing respectively on higher ground, as being of a superior order and covering the whole Church), many Acts of the Supreme Pontiff, and all the decisions of the Roman Congregations." The pastoral noted, however, that as "points of discipline may be decreed at one time and modified or set aside at another, so may novel theories and opinions, advanced even by learned men, be at one time censured by the Roman Congregations, and at a later time tolerated and even accepted." For instance, the Holy Office might later change its decision on a disputed Biblical text; in the meantime while accepting the decision as one to be observed for the present, Catholics may continue their research on the disputed text. Moreover, they should distinguish between decisions by Roman congregations and definitions of faith. But the liberal Catholic spirit would not be satisfied because it "strips itself of all the instincts of faith and religious obedience, till scarcely

112

any sentiment survives beyond a desire to avoid actual heresy." Heresies and schisms arose from seeds like those the liberal Catholic would plant.[57]

The pastoral censured two errors in particular: the belief that the Church had departed from Christianity's original doctrines and the belief that it possessed less authority now than in the first centuries after Christ's coming. On the contrary, the pastoral argued: "The Church is continuous and indefectible in her existence and constitution; so also in her doctrine. But her continuity and indefectibility is that of a living organic being, animated by the Holy Ghost." A true theory of development existed: the faith itself grows, but does not change essentially. Moreover, the doctrines of faith had been entrusted not to mankind generally but to the teaching Church alone--"to guard faithfully, and to develop and explain, with divine and infallible authority"--and this teaching authority was particularly needed to guard the minds of Catholics in the present confusing times. The continued progress of all knowledge and science, within their own proper sphere, was to be welcomed and not indiscriminately rejected. But the false theory of development of dogma, approved by some writers in England, made its development to consist in real change; certain dogmas were to die out or be supplanted in accordance with the progress of natural science. There were even Catholics who imagined they could remain within the Church by holding dogma not in the Church's sense but in their own, and who maintained that the traditional sense given by the Church to dogma would give way under illumination from science to other senses partially or wholly different. Besides this belief, another erroneous belief in regard to the relationship between the Church and science was the opinion that decrees of the Holy See were an encumbrance on science and an obstacle to progress. This was especially true concerning decrees prohibiting certain books or censuring certain erroneous doctrines. However, Roman congregations were not, the pastoral again noted, infallible; it should be remembered that, as with civil courts, their authority was not to be rejected if a miscarriage of justice occurred. The mistake could be corrected only by further legal action. The Holy See and the Roman congregations acted primarily to protect faith and morals, but persons who were ignorant of the actual procedures of the congregations had been decrying them. The pastoral concluded with an appeal for unswerving loyalty to the Church. It asked English Catholics to remember that in this earthly life "we must live in the midst of mysteries. Mysteries of the natural order are all around us, so also mysteries of the supernatural order." It was dated December 29, 1900, was signed by all sixteen English bishops, and was to be read at Sunday Mass to the Catholics of England.[58]

Coming as it did from all the English bishops, the joint pastoral was a formidable warning against certain opinions recently voiced by English Catholics in the periodical press and against a continuation of their publishing articles critical of ecclesiastical authorities. Moreover, Cardinal Merry del Val in Rome had encouraged Vaughan to issue a forceful pastoral, and he had assured Vaughan of the Pope's support in advance.[59]

After the joint pastoral was issued, it was made more formidable by a letter from Pope Leo XIII congratulating the English bishops on the pastoral. In his letter, the Pope wrote:

> Too well known is the actual and threatening mischief of that body of fallacious opinions which is commonly designated as Liberal Catholicism. Without in any way exaggerating the danger which menaces the Catholics of England, you show wherein that danger lies;

114

and your letter, based on the teaching and precepts of the Church, contains nothing but truth. . . .

You have done most wisely in issuing a solemn warning against the subtle and insidious spread of Rationalism, than which no poison is more fatal to Divine faith.[60]

A commentary on the pastoral by the Tablet, Cardinal Vaughan's own paper, suggested that the pastoral was not, however, a wholesale condemnation of the views and efforts of the entire English liberal Catholic group. The Tablet thought that anyone who had followed the periodical literature in recent years could see the need for the pastoral and would recognize the type of liberal Catholic writer against whom it was directed. Liberal Catholicism in the joint pastoral as in the contemporary practical vocabulary of the Church connoted an unsound and undutiful frame of mind. But the pastoral was not intended as a "censure for Catholics who are lovers of light and learning and true progress, nor yet for men who are filled with zeal to help the hands of the Church in any work of wise and orderly reform carried out, as any Catholic reform must be, under the sanction and aegis of authority." "If these in a true sense be liberal, as well as soundly Catholic, they are no more censured by our bishops than America and the love of things American was condemned by the Holy See when 'Americanism' was reprobated in the errors which had sheltered themselves under that name." In summary, the Tablet said the pastoral did not condemn "that truer and loyal liberalism of the Catholic mind" which was fired by a passion for reconciling faith and science and for smoothing the way of the outsider into the Church.[61]

Still the liberal Catholic group could not help but be worried by the pastoral and its possible implications for the future. Gasquet complained to Fleming in Rome that

Vaughan seemed completely out of touch with everyone, that the general outlook in England was very depressing, and that the position made for Catholics by Manning had been lowered. Bishop saw in the pastoral confirmation of his long-held personal conviction that the ecclesiastical authorities were in the wrong on most of the important contemporary questions, of which they lacked understanding.[62] Hügel seemed somewhat less critical of the pastoral than other liberal Catholics. In his view, the pastoral spoke in two voices, one absolutist, the other liberal, with the second correcting the first. But he, too, had apprehensions about the future and, writing to Loisy, he again implored him to be prudent lest the work of the liberal Catholics be undone.[63] Even James Britten, the founder of the Catholic Truth Society, was critical of the pastoral. He related how it had been called "the joint" upon its issuance, "the cold joint" upon reception, and "the hash" after it had been discussed.[64] There were rumors that even some English bishops, namely, Hedley of Newport and Brownlow of Clifton, both of whom had shown some sympathy to the work of the liberals, had not quite liked the pastoral although they had felt obliged to sign it.[65]

English liberal Catholics were able to continue their efforts at reconciling the Church with contemporary thought and scientific criticism since distinctions could be made between the liberal Catholicism censured by the pastoral and permissible forms that represented a tendency of mind recurring in the Church. Nevertheless, the pastoral touched off a hot debate among liberal Catholics. At a meeting of the Rota dining club in April, 1901, Robert Dell, the author of two of the articles that had provoked the pastoral, registered his critical reaction in a paper entitled "Liberal Catholicism." He maintained that the problem was not mainly intellectual but one of ecclesiastical politics: clericalism was the enemy. At the _Rota_ dinner in June, Ward replied again to Dell. In a paper entitled "Liberalism as a Temper of Mind," he used the term "liberal Catholic" as the pastoral had used it--as a technical term of censure. He argued that the "liberal" temper of mind was characterized by "an absence of the sense of proportion" and "a disregard for the effect of words or actions on the community and its rulers." At the next dinner in July, Edmund Bishop retorted that the temper of mind castigated by Ward had been especially common among the opponents of liberal Catholics in the mid-nineteenth century. He singled out Ward's own father, William George Ward, as having particularly exhibited that temper. After this, Ward apparently ceased attending _Rota_ dinners.[66] Writing to Ward, the Newman scholar W. J. Williams, also a liberal Catholic, said Bishop seemed to have taken in only a few sentences of Ward's paper. Williams agreed with Ward that they ought to exercise caution but he said they had to remember that the bishops were the revolutionaries who were introducing destructive novelties into the Church's constitution.[67]

Writing to both Ward and Bishop, the liberal Catholic William Barry commented on the differences between the two men. To Bishop, he said that he took Ward's use of the term "liberal Catholic" almost as a move on a chessboard: it allowed for acceptance of the joint pastoral while making room for a less objectionable term to describe the efforts of liberals not censured by the pastoral. He observed that the temper of mind disturbing both Ward and Bishop was not the monopoly of either the liberal Catholic side or their opponents but had appeared in both. Briefly listing those English Catholics whom he judged to have displayed this immoderate temper in their recent articles, he remarked: "Look at the whole Mivart episode. If Cardinal Vaughan managed badly, did not Mivart manage worse, from his friends' point of view? And this was, largely, 'tone and temper'. Again, Dell and the Weekly Register, in their undergraduate mood of 'making hay' with all sorts of Catholic prejudices. And would anyone trust his cause to William Gibson who aimed at winning it?"[68] Barry told Ward he had tried to point out to Bishop that Ward was not censuring the "Liberal method" but dangerous excesses of persons acting as liberals. He agreed with Ward that intemperate language was dangerous in the present critical times. But he noted that Bishop thought it wrong to charge liberals with faults that were at least as common among extremists who opposed them. "No doubt, it is irritating to mark a licence among the very persons that are hindering the truth which truth itself must not claim." Barry concluded by saying that the ecclesiastical authorities could not ban the scientific method, and that what was wanted was study and acquaintance with the facts instead of a journalism that only brought down censures.[69] Bishop agreed that study and acquaintance with facts were wanted. Writing to Everard Green, he implied that English Catholics constituted a sect alienated from contemporary culture. He told Green that the only thing he saw of use was solid work.[70]

The strongest reaction to the joint pastoral came from Tyrrell. He told F. Rooke Ley, the editor of the Weekly Register, that he had been making himself ill over the pastoral, perhaps more because of its "felt spirit" than because of anything stated.[71] In his view, the pastoral was of basic importance because it concerned a question of the Church's constitution--the relationship of the Ecclesia docens to the Ecclesia discens. What was the legitimate relationship of the papacy and episcopacy to the Church as a whole? Writing to Ward, Tyrrell said the pastoral implied a conception of church authority that cut the Church clean in two: "on one side a living, active Ecclesia docens

118

(reducible to the Pope, for the Bishops have no assignable raison d'etre save as papal delegates)"; on the other, a passive, lifeless Ecclesia discens with no participation in the thought, will, and action of the Church, "its duty being to contribute money, obey blindly, and ask no questions." The pope became "an alter Christus, a personality distinct from that of the Church, outside and above her"--he was no longer the inherent head of the Church, a part (albeit principal) of the whole body or moral persona, of which "Christ is the Spouse." The practical corollary of the pastoral was unqualified papal absolutism.[72]

Tyrrell became even more upset when Pope Leo XIII congratulated the English bishops on the pastoral. He vehemently wrote to Hügel that Leo XIII had approved of an absurd and heretical document, for the pastoral implied a completely new conception of the Church's constitution. Tyrrell remarked that the pastoral had misused the metaphor of the Divine Teacher. Beginning with the point that Christ was God, it went on to maintain that Peter was Christ, the Pope was Peter, and that, therefore, the Pope was, not God of course, but a Divine Teacher. It made no attempt to qualify or limit papal power. Tyrrell hotly blurted out what he considered to be logical conclusions of the principles of the pastoral: why then did the Pope not also perform miracles and bring the dead back to life? Why was he too not worshipped on the altar? Was he really present with Christ in the Eucharist? Referring to rabid nonsense and the drunkenness of absolutism, Tyrrell said no one among them had the freedom or the authority necessary to protest against it. If these things were true, he added, then every-thing John Henry Newman had written was false. He felt Wilfrid Ward, who had a great admiration for Newman, was now being too apologetical for the pastoral. He remarked that while Ward claimed the bishops had merely failed in

119

analyzing facts, their false analysis had become a false doctrine since it had been acted upon and officially approved.[73]

In a pseudonymous letter to the editor of the Anglo-
Catholic Pilot, Tyrrell registered a protest against the
pastoral. He argued that the current teaching of the Roman
theological schools, with which the pastoral coincided, and
the teaching of history disagreed. The current theory of
the schools concerning the Ecclesia docens' functions was a
heretical innovation which could not even be defended as a
valid deduction from the decrees of the Vatican Council:

> It would cleave the Church into two bodies, the one
> all active, the other all passive, related literally
> as sheep and shepards--as beings of a different
> order with conflicting interests; it would destroy
> the organic unity of the Church by putting the Pope
> (or the Ecclesia docens) outside and over the
> Church, not a part of her, but her partner, spouse,
> and Lord, in a sense proper to Christ alone; it
> would shear the bishops of their inherent preroga-
> tives while restoring to them a tenfold power as
> the delegates and plenipotentiaries of the infallible
> and unlimited authority claimed for the Pope.

This scholastic theory purported to analyze the way in which
the Church's life had been historically governed, although
the predominance of a priori methods in the schools practically excluded the study of ecclesiastical history. One who
had faith both in the Church and in history would believe
that this theory could not survive the test of criticism.
Although it was now imposed by the English bishops and
approved in some vague sense by the pope, it would not
daunt those who remembered that the Ecclesia docens was
once half Arian while the Ecclesia discens remained orthodox; the pope was no less infallible then and no less
obedience was owed to the "Arianising" bishops of that age.
The pastoral might be decisive for those who already
accepted the absolutism of which it spoke but not for those

who looked to the history of the Church. The pastoral, moreover, was directed against the rationalist views of Mivart who hardly typified the so-called liberal school, for its principles, if not all its conclusions, were found in Newman. Furthermore, this liberal school was the truly conservative school since it stood for antiquity against innovation and, like the true conservative, was ready to jettison superfluous burdens if these endangered the ship-- its method was liberal but its motive conservative.[74]

The joint pastoral remained on Tyrrell's mind during the first half of 1901. In the Weekly Register, he published an anonymous leading article in which he now maintained that either of two opposite views of the constitution of the Church might be consistent with the decrees of the Vatican Council. The view which he saw in the joint pastoral he ironically called the "badge of orthodoxy": as he described it, the pope headed the Church as "a distinct personality with a distinct mind, will and action; or like a shepherd who is not part of his flock but stands outside and over." In Tyrrell's own view which he called "amended Gallicanism" because it was opposed to the "absolutist" view, the pope was the Church's organic head, not a distinct personality but "an internal part of the Church's single personality." Although Wilfrid Ward and Father Ignatius Ryder, Newman's old friend at the Birmingham Oratory, maintained that there was a tenable middle position between these two views, Tyrrell saw no room for it.[75] In a pseudonymous letter to the Weekly Register, he elaborated on his own view. "Amended Gallicanism" held: "It is in the collective mind of the Church, not in the separate mind of the Pontiff, that the truth is elaborated; he is final and infallible in inter- preting and imposing his interpretation." The pope could speak infallibly only when he professedly investigated the mind of the Church. This was not the cause of an infallible

decision but it was the conditio sine qua non. The "badge
of orthodoxy," on the other hand, maintained that truth was
elaborated under the guidance of the Holy Spirit in the
separate mind of the pope. The Church's mind was "infallible, not actively in its independent operation, but
passively and receptively because it is the mirror of his."
If the "badge of orthodoxy" were correct, the motive power
of doctrinal development in the Church would reside in the
pope. Writing to Rooke Ley, Tyrrell put this view in epigrammatic form: "L'Église c'est moi is literally the Pope's
attitude. He is the steam-engine; the episcopate is the
carriages; the faithful are passengers."[76]

Tyrrell told Hügel that Ward and Ryder were unclear
about their own position and were attempting to blow hot and
cold simultaneously. In addition, he called Hügel's attention to what he regarded as a very offensive article on the
pastoral in the Month, the English Jesuit organ.[77] He said
that its author, Joseph Rickaby, S.J., sought to show how the
root of liberalism was worldliness and irreligion. Tyrrell
wrote to Rickaby and asked him why the liberals were so few
if it was worldliness that gave birth to liberalism.[78]

Although agreeing with some of what Tyrrell had
written, Ward found Tyrrell's view of the joint pastoral
unacceptable. In an article entitled "Doctores Ecclesiæ,"
in the Pilot, Ward presented what he regarded as the representative and correct view among Catholics. He argued that
the pastoral denounced a form of liberal Catholicism that
had to be denounced and insisted on truths which such liberal
Catholics were neglecting. It was wrong to take the pastoral
as a document standing by itself or as an exhaustive theological treatise. The function of a pastoral should be
understood correctly: "It may omit qualifications which
are needed to make its treatment exhaustive, because it is
concerned with only one aspect of the case; and such

omissions are not necessarily misleading, because Catholics know that all the bishops are bound to accept and endorse such portions of the universally received theology as are needed to fill in the lacunæ in question, and to interpret the text of the document." Ward went on to argue that the Ecclesia docens, who were bound to protect the faith of the flock, must be distinguished from the doctors of the Church, or "individual Catholic thinkers of genius or learning," who elucidated that faith theologically in light of the circumstances of the times. For the most part, these doctors had historically done their work as members of the Ecclesia discens, sometimes in spite of opposition from some unworthier members of the Ecclesia docens. Just as those who sought intellectual support against the rationalism of the thirteenth century turned to Aquinas rather than to a pope or bishop, persons wanting similar support at present were more likely to turn to Newman than to a pastoral. This did not imply disrespect to authority but simply recognized the division of parts in the Church. Since the Reformation, emphasis had been placed on the ecclesiastical authorities and the obedience owed to them but the principle of division of parts had not been forgotten. Indeed, "individual initiative on the part of those best qualified for their special tasks has been the providential instrument whereby the greatest glories of the Church have been won, in its religious orders and in its theological schools."[79]

Hügel thought Ward's article was, as usual with Ward, well-intentioned and well-written; however, it only confirmed the contention that authorities and interpretations limiting papal authority were practically non-existent in the eyes of the pastoral and its theory. Hügel remarked that since Ward had not shown even the stems of such limitations to be in the pastoral, his defense of it was a failure. On the other hand, Hügel was delighted with

Tyrrell's writings in the Weekly Register on the pastoral.
He remarked that Tyrrell had thought the matter out with an
unusual freshness and easy mastery while avoiding ambiguities
still enmeshing intellects as able and well-informed as
Ryder and Ward. His writings, moreover, were not spoiled by
being primarily apologetical as theirs were; his works
sprang directly from within the subject matter. Hügel went
on to say that Tyrrell had forwarded the philosophy of the
question by his distinction between the Pope's independence
in actually defining doctrine and his dependence on the
mind of the Church for the subject matter of his definitions.
Hügel felt that this was Tyrrell's greatest service yet to
the cause of the Church.[80] Tyrrell was very much encouraged
by his friend's evaluation. He had been working privately
without advice or consultation, and felt that he was probably wrong somewhere when Ryder as well as Ward opposed his
views.[81]

Writing to Ward shortly after the publication of
his article, Tyrrell predicted that a radical change of view
regarding the sphere of papal infallibility would occur in
the future. This would happen not through analyzing theories
or sharpening definitions but simply through historical
research into the past: it would be impossible to hold that
the Church or the pope was infallible in areas in which they
erred again and again. In addition, Tyrrell thought that
while the present sense of the Church was the living rule
of faith for all Catholics, the active-minded would read it
with individual variations; the masses who only wanted to be
taught would take the official formulation literally. The
forward-minded would sympathize more with the Church of the
future than of the present. If there were no forward minds,
he argued, there could be no development of doctrine since
it demanded a principle of variation that selection could
work upon.[82] Tyrrell explained to Maude Petre that he

thought "the _official_ teaching Church is a divinely
appointed instrument." But "the active-minded few while
acknowledging the same rule of faith as the many"--the
consensus of the living Church at present--"may and do go
ahead of the official exponents of that mind."[83]

Besides Tyrrell, James Britten also wrote to Ward.
After congratulating him on his article, Britten added:
"It is an ungrateful task to be continually protecting
those in authority from the consequences of their own
utterances--and, after all, _they_ do mean what they say,
and the average man knows they do. . . . It is matter of
fact that the 'Joint' and its subsequent endorsement at
Rome has troubled many folk who might not be supposed to
have concerned themselves about it. I have been surprised
at the extent to which this is true, both among clergy and
laity (men and women)."[84]

The joint pastoral had suppressed for the time
being the publication of strident articles like those that
had appeared during the previous year. But tempers among
English liberal Catholics were beginning to run high over
issues treated in the pastoral, and basic questions were
beginning to be put in pointed form. Articles appearing
in the press had provoked the pastoral, and for the present
those liberals who urged moderation could believe that only
some journalists among the liberal group were immoderate.
But what would happen when liberal scholars and thinkers
also confronted ecclesiastical authorities?

CHAPTER IV

THE PARTING OF THE WAYS

By the turn of the century, Biblical criticism had
centered on the Christological problem and the question of
Christ's relationship to the Church. In the front ranks of
Catholic exegesis was Loisy, whose forthcoming works were
to meet with censure by the ecclesiastical authorities. A
whole new situation would then develop for the English
liberal Catholics. With a leading Catholic scholar advancing his scholarly criticisms of the origins and nature of
the Church and its beliefs, and suggesting basic changes,
the general problem of the relationship of Catholic intellectual work and ecclesiastical authority was raised in a
pointed form. Most of the English liberals had little
specialized knowledge of Biblical criticism, and until the
specific issues were clarified in vehement controversy they
looked at the question of Loisy's scholarship in the broad
perspective of the problem of free sciencific inquiry and
the role of the Catholic intellectual vis-a-vis that of
ecclesiastical authority. At first sight, they took the
Loisy case to be a decisive test case; consequently, most
of them initially sympathized with him.

A sign that the Roman Church was becoming particularly concerned with Biblical criticism was the appointment
of a special Biblical Commission by the Pope, an appointment announced in English newspapers in January 1902. Hügel
was pleased with this development and thought it augured
well for the future. Writing to Ward, he commented that

126

nearly all the twelve men appointed as Consultors were not narrow-minded; he felt sure that David Fleming, who had been appointed Secretary of the Commission, was still a liberal at heart.   Furthermore, the appointment of the Commission took the Biblical question out of the hands of the Curia and thus seemed to replace curial condemnations and restrictions. Since the Commission was permanent, Hügel thought it would allow a slow threshing out of the Biblical question, while Catholic scholars continued their research and provided the Commission with the results of their work.   Hügel noted, however, that the Commission was not representative of the views of the majority of the ecclesiastical authorities and that the future remained uncertain.[1]   Ward was much more apprehensive about the Commission than Hügel, for he thought it might make more or less premature reports on which unfavorable decisions would be based, and thus make matters worse rather than better.[2]   Nevertheless, the English liberals were generally pleased with the appointment of the Commission.   Gasquet wrote Edmund Bishop expressing his satisfaction, and remarked: "The great point is to get the Romans to realise there is a question."[3]

The publication of Loisy's L'Évangile et l'Église in November 1902 proved to be the decisive new factor. Based on scientific Biblical criticism, the work was a Catholic reply to Adolf von Harnack's Das Wesen des Christentums (1900).   Reducing doctrine to a minimum, stressing Christianity's ethical side, and interpreting Jesus through historical criticism, Harnack seemed to typify contemporary liberal Protestantism.   He had contended that a historical view must divorce Christ from the Church. According to him, Christ had preached essentially a simple gospel proclaiming the Kingdom of God which persons could enter by recognizing the Fatherhood of God and leading righteous lives.   The Church's organization, dogma, and

127

ritual were entirely new developments, influenced by Greek sources and constituting a break with Christ's gospel. Like Albert Schweitzer and Johannes Weiss, Loisy countered Harnack by arguing that the Gospels could not be reduced to his simple elements and that, in fact, Christ had not preached an immanent Kingdom of God to be realized by moral endeavor but the coming of an eschatological Kingdom. Nor, Loisy maintained, could the Gospels be divorced from the Church, for they had been written by and for the Church. Harnack regarded the development of doctrine and of the Church as a husk obscuring what he took to be the kernal, or essence, of Christianity in the Gospels; Loisy replied that the essence of Christianity should be sought in the totality and fullness of its life, not only in its beginnings. Using the historical method, he then tried to show how the Church's organization, dogma, and worship had necessarily resulted from Christ's ministry.[4]

The English liberals were pleased with Loisy's work as a historical vindication of Catholicism and an effective criticism of liberal Protestantism. While Tyrrell thought Loisy's work too conservative and lacking a criterion to distinguish true from false developments, Ward told Hügel that Loisy had grasped Newman's lead and had put wide and wise limitations on Catholic development. Apparently not realizing that Loisy might have difficulty in obtaining an imprimatur for his work, Barry suggested to Hügel that he should get one.[5] Hügel wrote to Loisy: "It is just simply superb. . . . They will find it very difficult to condemn this, since it will show itself to be the only effective reply to Harnack; and these people are even more business men than men of narrow views."[6] Even Giuseppe Cardinal Sarto, soon to become Pope Pius X, had read the book and "expressed great satisfaction with it with the exception of certain passages he found obscure."[7]

Some leading French Catholic scholars familiar with
the specific questions involved were not so satisfied. Both
the Dominican Biblical scholar Marie-Joseph Lagrange and the
historian of the early Church Mgr. Pierre Batiffol were displeased. The historian Duchesne wrote to Loisy that he had
better hope Catholics would not understand his work, for
only in that way could he avoid condemnation.[8] To forestall
any possible Roman condemnation, Hügel wrote to a Consultor
of the Biblical Commission, the Italian Jesuit Enrico
Gismondi, saying that the work had made a very good impression in England.[9] But Paris rather than Rome proved to be
the source of immediate danger to Loisy. In January 1903,
Cardinal Richard, the Archbishop of Paris, condemned the
book on the ground that it had been published without an
imprimatur and was likely to disturb the faith of the flock
concerning the basic doctrines of the Church: especially
the authority of the Bible and tradition, Christ's divinity
and infallible knowledge, the redemption wrought by Christ's
death, his resurrection, the Eucharist, and the divine
institution of the pontificate and the episcopacy.[10]

To the English liberals, Loisy seemed to use the
historical methods to defend Catholicism and to show how
the Church was a legitimate development from the Gospels.
In Loisy's own view, he was doing more. He regarded historical methodology as the one and only means by which the
development of Catholicism was to be explained and judged.
In his view, modern thought could accept as true only what
the historical methods could prove conclusively; implicitly,
therefore, Catholicism eventually would have to reject or
transform radically many of its basic beliefs and institutions. Loisy was suggesting a revolution in Catholic
ideas of dogma and the Church, although he did not draw this
consequence in L'Évangile et l'Église itself. As he later
wrote: "Historically speaking, I did not admit that Christ

129

founded the Church or the Sacraments; I professed that dogmas formed themselves gradually and that they were not unchangeable; and it was the same for ecclesiastical authority which I conceived of as a ministry of human education. . . ."[11] Therefore:

> . . . my defense of the Roman Church against certain judgments of the learned author [Harnack] implied at the same time the abandonment of those absolute theses which are professed by the Scholastic theology touching the formal institution of the Church and its sacraments by Christ, the immutability of its dogmas, and the nature of its ecclesiastical authority. Thus I did not confine myself to a criticism of Professor Harnack, but paved the way, discreetly yet definitely, for an essential reform in Biblical exegesis, in the whole of theology, and even in Catholicism generally.[12]

Soon there was talk of an imminent condemnation of Loisy by Rome on top of that by the Archbishop of Paris. To the English liberals who still saw Loisy's book as a scholarly line of defense against Harnack and had not yet realized its extensive theological implications, its condemnation would mean a defeat for scientific work by Catholics. Barry asked Gasquet: "I write as hoping you have access to the Bible Commission and would be listened to. If Father David [Fleming] is as strong as some think, he might get them to accept a _via media_. I put it in one word, Correction not suppression. The time is short."[13] Fleming himself was still hopeful, and Hügel compared him "to the Abyssinian heroes who at the battle of Adowa penetrated into the midst of the Italian ranks and inflicted on the invaders a final victory." Evidence indicated that Leo XIII was reluctant to take action in the hope that Loisy would give no further trouble.[14]

Three new developments changed the situation. First, the Biblical Commission was enlarged in February 1903 to forty members; the new appointees were more conservative than the original members. Secondly, the aged Leo XIII died in July and the more conservative Cardinal Sarto became Pope Pius X; in addition, Cardinal Rampolla was replaced as Papal Secretary of State by Cardinal Merry del Val, who was also more conservative. Lastly, in October Loisy published Autour d'un petit livre which sought to defend and explain L'Évangile et l'Église.

Archbishop Mignot of Albi, Hügel, and Tyrrell had advised Loisy to write a defense and explanation of L'Évangile et l'Église. They got it but, as Loisy later remarked, it was not quite what they expected.[15] He also said that the propositions he put forward about Christ and the Church in Autour d'un petit livre "were wholly incompatible with the Scholastic conception of dogma, and with the personal and absolute divinity of Jesus. They were intelligible only in relation to a theory, more or less 'symbolist' in character, of religious belief and of the universal immanence of God in humanity."[16] Looking back from the position that he eventually embraced, Loisy drew out the consequences to which his line of thought could be carried:

> While perceiving with perfect clearness the impossibility of retaining the traditional beliefs, I indulged the illusion that it was possible to continue the use of the ancient creedal forms, merely putting into them a more or less symbolical interpretation. But that meant running into the additional and dangerous complication of having a set of symbols suggestive of false ideas rather than of true ones. I should then have had to urge the Church to abandon preaching its God, creator of the world some thousands of years ago, its God-Man Christ, and its own infallibility, and to place the emphasis solely on the high ideal of justice and of goodness which is the true heart of its tradition. The Pope and the bishops would not have failed to respond: Non possumus. In fact, they could not.17

131

Although there was a good deal of confusion as to
just what Loisy meant when his books appeared, there
was little doubt that he had called into question doctrines
generally prevailing among orthodox Catholics. Even though
Ward credited Loisy with being more orthodox than he really
was, he was upset by Autour d'un petit livre.[18] Moreover,
there were fears that Loisy's boldness would discredit
scientific Biblical criticism in the eyes of the ecclesiastical authorities in Rome, especially since the new Pope,
Secretary of State, and Biblical Commission were all of a
more conservative tendency of mind. Gasquet wrote to
Fleming in Rome: "I quite agree with you about poor Loisy
and am more than sorry. Would it not be possible to condemn him for the reasons of inexpediency without going into
the merits? . . . It is very curious that you say what I
have also felt that Merry del Val [a Spaniard and an
acclimated Englishman] cannot be relied on as a friend."[19]
William Barry remarked that Cardinal Richard and his friends
thought that "censures are enough. Clearly they are no
such thing." Barry saw much excitement, and even more misunderstanding in the situation. He could not "at all accept
Loisy's general position. But will it be defined and set
apart by authority from others more or less tenable?" If
not, he concluded, it was the beginning of sorrows.[20]

Even Hügel, while sympathizing with Loisy, feared
suppression of Catholic Biblical scholarship as a result of
his boldness. He wrote to Merry del Val, a family friend,
congratulating him on his appointment as Papal Secretary of
State, and took the occasion to emphasize that Biblical
questions were entirely independent of any individual, that
Loisy's views could not be mistaken for more than his own,
and that his work had won some persons "from an individualist Protestant conception of religion to the Catholic social,
unbroken-growth idea of it. . . ." Hügel was disappointed

to receive only a post card reply from Merry del Val thanking him for his letter. Writing also to Cardinal Rampolla, now president of the enlarged Biblical Commission, Hügel, like Gasquet, asked that if action need be taken against Loisy it should be merely disciplinary in character.[21]

In December, 1903, the Roman censure came in the form of a Holy Office decree placing Loisy's works on the Index. Loisy credited in part to Hügel's efforts the fact that the censure did not take the form of a condemnation of a list of doctrinal errors.[22] It was accompanied, however, by a letter from Merry del Val to the Archbishop of Paris which said that Loisy's works were filled with grave errors concerning "the primitive revelation, the authenticity of the facts and teachings of the gospels, the divinity and perfect knowledge of Christ, the resurrection, the divine institution of the Church, and the sacraments."[23] The ensuing months saw Loisy, Archbishop Richard, and Merry del Val involved in exchanges of notes in which Loisy professed his willingness to submit to the decree as a disciplinary decision but refused to retract the opinions he put forward as a historian, while the authorities pressed for a full and unqualified submission. In the meantime, it was uncertain whether Loisy would be excommunicated or not. At length he wrote a simple submission in which he declared that he condemned the errors that the Holy Office had censured in his writings, a statement he regarded as meaningless and later regretted. The Roman authorities, perhaps wanting to avoid the scandal that Loisy's excommunication might give, decided to press the matter no further.

In an attempt to clarify the reasons for the censure of Loisy's books and to place the affair into perspective for the English public, David Fleming, over the pseudonym "Catholicus," wrote a letter to the editor of The Times; the letter drew a reply from Hügel, writing over the pseudonym "Romanus."[24] Fleming pointed out that no side in the Loisy controversy had a monopoly on sincerity, courage, and faith, and argued that a Christian church should surely be allowed to hesitate before accepting the latest most advanced critical conclusions without its love of historic truth being questioned. He ventured to say that for some time past six propositions advanced by Biblical critics in one form or another had been a part of the contemporary permissible teaching in the Church, that they were held by several members of the Biblical Commission, and that they were not, therefore, at issue in the Loisy affair as some persons thought:

> That the Pentateuch in its present form may not have been the actual or original work of Moses; that the first chapters of Genesis are not exact history as to the origin of mankind; that all books of the Old Testament have not the same historical value; that many books of the Scripture, including those of the New Testament, were written with more free-dom than modern historical works; that the history of Biblical religious doctrine has undergone development in the idea of God, of human destiny, and the moral law; that the Bible teaching on natural science does not rise above the current notions of antiquity, and that such notions affected Biblical religious doctrine are all propositions which many amongst the authorities at Rome hold to be susceptible of a perfectly orthodox meaning. No doubt Catholics would insist upon a real develop-ment--viz., one which includes a fuller and clearer grasp of the sense of doctrine, from age to age, and not a mere transition from sense to sense, which evacuates and discards that which has gone before in favour of a sense which is substantially new and different. No doubt they would hold that the notions of natural science current in antiquity affected the accidental, and not the essential, or dogmatic sense of Biblical doctrine.[25]

Regarding the six positions mentioned by Fleming as having been permitted by the Church in its contemporary teaching, Hügel pointed out that the knowledge and toleration of them

was due to Loisy more than to any other man. Moreover, the
very occasion for the Biblical Commission owed more to him
than to anyone else.[26]

As to the real issue between Loisy and the Church,
Fleming said it involved the following questions:

> (a) Is it true that M. Loisy holds that Christ
>   was not conscious that He was true God and
>   consubstantial to God the Father?
>
> (b) Is it true that M. Loisy holds that Christ
>   did not personally teach the doctrine of
>   the Atonement?
>
> (c) Is it true that M. Loisy holds that the
>   Catholic Church as an organized body had
>   no place in the consciousness, or personal
>   teaching, or design of Christ?
>
> (d) Is it true that M. Loisy holds that Christ
>   did not actually institute the Holy Communion
>   as an ordinance of the new Law to be observed
>   for all time?
>
> (e) Is it true that M. Loisy denies the historic
>   truth of the Resurrection?

These were, Fleming remarked, the points which underlay
Merry del Val's letter to Archbishop Richard.[27] In regard
to these five censured positions of Loisy, Hügel thought
that the debate in each case should not turn on apparent
novelties in his intellectual presentation of the faith;
rather it should center on whether as historian he presented
these positions according to sound historical method and
whether as apologist "he sufficiently retains, whilst
reinterpreting under pressure of these facts, that substance
of the faith which necessarily transcends and interprets,
but may not contradict or ignore them." If "Catholicus"
rejected Loisy's critical conclusions, on what critical
grounds did he do so? Hügel asked. If he accepted them,
what more orthodox interpretation than Loisy's had he to

offer? Hügel himself accepted Loisy's critical positions,
but with a difference, for he held the objective reality of
each doctrine involved. The words of consecration of the
Eucharistic bread were, he wrote, "words so profoundly expres-
sive of the reality." About the Atonement, he asked: "Is
it really so important, except, perhaps, for Bible
Protestants, that our Lord should have personally proclaimed
the Atonement, if He is in very deed our Atoner?" Concerning the institution of the Church: "He [Christ] indeed
founds an organized preaching and healing fraternity, with
Simon Peter at their head; and His own teaching, life,
death, and resurrection are the direct source and cause of
that immense stream of spiritual renovation which soon
found its full expression in the world-wide Apostolate and
the completely separate organization of the Church."
Regarding the Resurrection: "What are the critical facts
as to 'the historic truth of the Resurrection'?--i.e., I
suppose, the determining cogency of the purely historical
evidence, since as to the actual reality there is no dispute." Finally, of Christ's consciousness of being God,
Hügel wrote:

> Nowhere, however, has the Abbé declared that Jesus'
> humanity had no consciousness of being God and
> consubstantial with the Father, but only that
> the mere historian had no constraining motive for
> affirming that this, rather than His Messianic
> character, was the psychological form of His
> human consciousness as to His deepest nature.
> The traditional dogma is for him the legitimate
> interpretation of the mystery contained in the
> relation between Christ and God; and he has but
> tried to enunciate in what terms the problem of
> this abiding truth and mystery seems to front us
> now.28

Thus, in his letter to The Times in reply to Fleming's
letter, Hügel outlined the position he had reached.

The censure of Loisy had put Hügel in a difficult situation. He had to balance three things: his faith and loyalty to the Church, his conviction that science and history could not be disregarded by the ecclesiastical authorities and were a source of discipline for the Christian, and his loyalty to Loisy as a personal friend.[29] Having outlined what he thought to be both his and Loisy's position, Hügel went on in his letter to state what he regarded as their conscientious obligations. As members of the Church, they sincerely accepted the disciplinary decree of the Index, even though this protection of the majority of the faithful may have resulted in great part from "the mental inertia and neglect" of generations. They sincerely accepted the decree of the Holy Office checking Loisy's apologetics since the ecclesiastical authorities were the official spokesmen for the Church. But they could not submit to this decree to the extent of rejecting the historical method or its immediate concerns, even if these were the records of the primitive Church. Here lay the crux of the matter for Hügel. He had always regarded Biblical criticism as an autonomous science, and demanded what amounted to complete freedom for it. What Biblical criticism concluded, only further Biblical criticism could alter or correct as to matters of historical fact and interpretation:

> Our historico-critical "facts" and methods may
> indeed demand emendation, but this can only come
> from the presence of and according to the laws
> intrinsic to these subject-matters. Our attempted
> synthesis of this historical science and the
> defined intellectual presentations of the faith
> may be wrong. Here Church authority has got a
> clear right to hesitate or to refuse, provided
> it does not insist upon our rejecting or ignoring
> that scientific method and its general results,
> a complexus which will even then still remain to
> be held by us, not as a mere hypothesis, but as
> something to ameliorate from within its own domain,
> and to reconcile with the faith from without it.

Hügel concluded his letter to The Times by emphasizing his own persistent theme of simultaneous and sincere belief in the truths of Catholic faith and the truths of science while embracing the present necessary tension between them as a means of deepening the spiritual life of the individual:

> And in this her [the Roman Church's] central
> life of deepest and divinely impelled, infal-
> lible instinct of sanctity and love, and in
> her supreme teaching office and final decisions,
> divinely protected as necessary and true, but
> inadequate and improvable, intellectual presenta-
> tions of the spiritual realities, we find what
> we find nowhere else, in anything like the same
> and necessary quality and degree. . . .   May
> we . . . trust that our poor labours, battlings,
> and sufferings may, at whatever cost to our-
> selves, help on that uniquely great cause,
> sincere Science linked hand in hand with the
> sincerest Faith?[30]

On the one hand, Hügel adhered to a critical view of the historic Christ; on the other, he retained a deep faith in Christ and the Church.[31]   In 1904, he gave an address on "Official Authority and Living Religion,"[32] and wrote an article entitled "Du Christ Éternal et de nos christologies successives," published in the French periodical Quinzaine in June.   In these papers, he elaborated on his views concerning the Christ of history and the Christ of faith, but he had already conveyed their essence in his "Romanus" letter to The Times.   Hügel, as well as Loisy, tended to divorce criticism from faith.[33] Maurice Blondel, a philosopher and a friend, publicly dis- agreed with them on this matter.   Blondel told Hügel: "The celestial Christ could not have been what you say He was unless the earthly Christ was more than you say." Ward wrote to Hügel: "I fancy that I have much less confidence than you as to the reliableness of the conclusions which claim to be scientific."[34]

Although Hügel agreed with Loisy on a number of points of criticism, his mysticism and absorbing interest in the spiritual life essentially distinguished him from Loisy. Indeed, he was at this time writing his first major work, The Mystical Element of Religion as Studied in St. Catherine of Genoa and her Friends.[35] Believing that religion and science would inevitably conflict in one's earthly life and that by bracing up to this tension one could deepen his spiritual life, he was able to maintain his confidence in both religion and science whereas Loisy chose science. Besides the spiritual life, Hügel's other great concern was advancement of what he regarded as the great cause, "sincere Science linked hand in hand with the sincerest Faith." To him, Biblical criticism had become the touchstone for determining the progress of this cause, and Loisy's work had become the test case. Beyond the demands of personal loyalty, he supported Loisy as strenuously as he could. The semi-mystical Hügel was not primarily interested in considering from the point of view of their orthodoxy the inferences of Loisy, Tyrrell, or anyone else. In contrast, the logical-minded Loisy was far more disposed to draw conclusions regarding doctrinal belief from his critical studies. Hügel had suggested to Loisy that he write the Pope a letter declaring his belief in the divinity of Christ and all the Church's dogmas. But, as Loisy commented later, that "was not as easy for me as those who took the trouble to recommend it imagined."[36] "M. von Hügel who defends me so bravely believes very differently from me in the divinity of Jesus Christ. Setting aside metaphysical phraseology,

I do not believe in the divinity of Jesus any more than
Harnack or Jean Reville, and I look on the personal Incarnation of God as a philosophic myth."[37]

The publication of Loisy's L'Évangile et l'Église
may be regarded as marking the onset of the modernist crisis
in the Roman Church. Hügel was a leader in the modernist
movement--as a friend of Loisy, as a pioneer among Roman
Catholics in the new methods of Biblical criticism and a
disseminator of its results and opinions among modernists,
as a point of contact among the modernists, and as an advocate of complete autonomy for science and scholarship within
the Roman Church. But Hügel rejected immanentism and,
ultimately, subjectivism in theology and philosophy.[38]

Joseph P. Whelan was right in noting that Hügel's
opposition to immanentism was early and constant, and that
his God was both transcendent and immanent.[39] To Tyrrell
he wrote in 1903 that for years he had an increasing sense
of the copious range of man's ethical, and other, capacities,
and of the value of their exercise, but "of all this not
being God, not one bit . . . . God is emphatically not
simply our Highest Selves."[40] Later, his rejection of
immanentism was to become an anxiety. Hügel had also
rejected--by the time the modernist movement was really
under way--what he called the "No Metaphysics" error,[41]
though not until years later did his mind move to a position
of critical realism in philosophy. He told Tyrrell in 1902
that religion "does not presuppose any explicit metaphysic,
but it does imply certain metaphysical realities and metaphysical affirmations. An absolute impossibility of all
metaphysical apprehension would be equivalent to the denial
of the possibility of any true religion."[42] He deplored the
indifference to, or neglect of, all philosophy by some of
his friends and acquaintances.[43] For example, he spoke dis-
approvingly of Edmund Bishop's gibes "at all philosophy as

140

so much _a priori_ pretentiousness; and yet (of course) the good man is talking _a_ philosophy of his own all the time!"[44]

Hügel's strenuous support of Loisy seems to have driven him to adopt more radical positions which he was to hold for the next several years. Although he continued to respect their offices, he was coming to have a low view of the ecclesiastical authorities.[45] Moreover, his opinion of those whom he formerly regarded as liberal friends and who now stood opposed to Loisy became unfavorable. He suspected Fleming of treachery for writing his "Catholicus" letter to The Times,[46] and felt alienated from Wilfrid Ward after the Loisy affair. He could never forgive Lagrange for writing against Loisy, and thought Mgr. Batiffol had dissociated himself from Loisy only to protect his own ecclesiastical position.[47] Hügel told Maude Petre that--"alas, alas, for poor, human nature"--Batiffol "hurried forward to prove his perfect orthodoxy at the expense of other people,--of souls deeper and greater indefinitely than himself. This is regrettable too for the reason that there seem to be no certain limits to what, in this kind of action, that poor man might not allow himself to do . . . ."[48] Tyrrell shared Hügel's aversion to Batiffol, Lagrange, and Fleming after the Loisy affair, and once commented that it was "foolish for Jackals to betray the Lion."[49] Under the strain of his involvement in the Loisy affair, Hügel became seriously fatigued and told Tyrrell that he was on the verge of a breakdown. He mentioned that he had not only himself but his wife and three daughters to think of, that he had taken a risk in writing to Merry del Val in favor of Loisy, and that, short of cowardice, he would have to cease prodding the ecclesiastical authorities.[50]

With the censure of Loisy, the question of Catholic Biblical criticism hung in suspense for the next few years. Meanwhile, rumors about the imminence of a new papal

syllabus of errors began to circulate,[51] and by 1905-1906
some signs of impending action by the central government of
the Church were appearing. In September, 1905, the conservative Belgian theologian Laurent Janssens had replaced
Fleming as Secretary of the Biblical Commission. In June,
1906, the Biblical Commission decided that critical arguments had not disproved the Mosaic authorship of the
Pentateuch. Although it conceded that Moses may not have
written the Pentateuch by his own hand or dictated all of
it, it intimated that perhaps he used oral or written documents or that possibly he suggested the thoughts to secre-
taries who may have composed it.[52] In April, 1906, moreover,
two works by the French Catholic philosopher Père Lucien
Laberthonnière and the novel Il Santo by the Italian liberal
Catholic Antonio Fogazzaro were placed on the Index.
Laberthonnière emphasized the attainment of truth not
through an intellectual process but through "action" or the
activity of the whole man--through thinking, willing, feeling, etc.; Fogazzaro called for a comprehensive reform of
the Roman Church from within.[53] Laberthonnière's work, however, seems not to have been censured merely for advocating
the philosophy of action, for the works of Blondel, its
leading French exponent, remained off the Index. A
general issue involved in the Loisy affair appears to have
been the primary factor in Laberthonnière's censure: he
was thought to have implied a need to reinterpret the idea
of dogma.[54] Were the traditional dogmatic formulations not
representative of objective realities? Were they merely
symbols of practical spiritual value to man and the Church--
or symbols that had been necessary or useful in the past?
In brief, were they true symbols only if taken in a subjectivist or immanentist sense? Reacting to the placing of
the books of Laberthonnière and Fogazzaro on the Index,
Hügel told Maude Petre that he thought a reactionary

entourage was influencing the Pope and that Rome was
embarking on a policy of condemning not only unusually
bold intellectuals like Loisy but the entire trend and
temper of modern thought.[55] Nevertheless, Hügel, who
believed unflinchingly in the objective reality of a
transcendent God, the divinity of Christ, and a divinely
commissioned Church, had begun to suspect inclinations
toward immanentism in some intellectual acquaintances.
He had already expressed this fear in a letter to Loisy,
who was quick to apply Hügel's comments to himself:
"Evidently the good baron is beginning to fear that I
shall fall into the abyss of immanentism."[56]

The intellectual trend toward immanentism had
deepened during the nineteenth century; it reinforced the
impact of Biblical and historical criticism on religion
and conditioned the response of some radical liberals.
The idea of evolution was probably the most far-reaching
intellectual influence promoting immanentism. Taken as
a _Weltanschauung_, evolution "seemed, at any rate to some
minds, to explain by processes going on _within_ the universe
what it had previously been commonly maintained that an
intelligent Power _beyond_ and _above_ the universe was
required to account for."[57] To reconcile religion with
this purported explanation of the universe, the idea of a
transcendent God had to be replaced by some idea of divine
immanence. Moreover, if, as evolutionism taught, all
things were subject to radical change, then the dogmas
and authority of the Church would also have to be given
some kind of immanentist interpretation. Closely related
to the growth of the idea of evolution, the rise of a
sense of history emphasizing change and relativity had
the same immanentist effect on religious thought.[58]

In philosophy, the impact of Kant's "Copernican
Revolution" was still being felt in the denial that reason

could know anything whatsoever about a transcendent God or
a supernatural order beyond the realm of phenomena. There
was now, however, some reaction against the anti-religious
positivism and materialism formerly prevalent in the intellectual atmosphere. In the early twentieth century, William
James and Henri Bergson were perhaps the two most popular
philosophers. Both men were interested in religious experience and defended a belief in God. Some of the modernists
found James' pragmatism and Bergson's vitalism appealing
since they seemed to represent a favorable change in attitude toward religion. In retrospect, however, there was
even a "practical" danger in adopting either as the only
philosophical basis for justifying belief in God and religious experience: as it turned out, both philosophies
declined in popularity in the twentieth century.[59] Moreover, the thought of the early twentieth century was in an
unstable condition. At that time there was a need for
theology to be willing to face new issues, but it also had
to exercise caution in embracing new conclusions.[60]

          In the first decade of this century, pragmatism was
probably the most popular form of philosophical subjectivism
holding that conceptions of things bear no likenesses
to things-in-themselves or that truth need not imply the
conformity of conceptions to objective reality. Instead,
pragmatism suggested that an idea leading to useful concrete
results, or working in practice, was true--at least for the
time being. In the pragmatist view, the value of religious
belief in concrete life was not one factor in determining
the truth of religious belief, but it was the sole factor.
James' empirical study of religion supported a belief in
God but only to the extent that it supported a belief in
something greater than ourselves.[61] Moreover, by considering the religious experience of man as experience within a
wholly natural order, pragmatism dismissed the possibility

of a special revelation or of dogma representing realities
of a supernatural order.

Unwilling to admit that truth was merely subjective,
some philosophers sought sources of objective truth other
than the reason. While fundamentally accepting the Kantian
criticism of reason, Henri Bergson believed that man could
know reality beyond the realm of phenomena but only by
experiencing it through "intuition." Blondel and
Laberthonnière emphasized "action" as a means of knowing
reality beyond phenomena. For a time, Hügel's philosophy
was under their influence. Also influenced by them and
Bergson, Tyrrell's thought bore an additional affinity
to the pragmatism of James. The thought of Edouard LeRoy, a
French Catholic modernist philosopher, was heavily pragmatic;
in addition, he was influenced by Bergson. More important
than any specific intellectual influences on the thought of
the leading modernists[62] was the general pervasiveness of
immanentism and subjectivism in the intellectual atmosphere
at the turn of the century. Alive to contemporary thought,
some modernists imbibed immanentist and subjectivist ideas
through various sources.

Tyrrell became perhaps the most striking figure
among the modernists. After the censuring of his article
on hell and the joint pastoral, he had moved away from the
position of moderate liberal Catholicism that Wilfrid Ward
so staunchly advocated. Both Maude Petre and Maisie Ward
have suggested that Hügel may have unintentionally deflected
him from his natural bent of writing on the spiritual life
by directing his studies to Biblical and historical criticism.[63] So, too, the vehemence of Tyrrell's reaction to
the joint pastoral, of his controversies with ecclesiastical
authorities, and of the difficulties he had with the Jesuits
may have deflected him. But was he really turned aside from
his bent? Maude Petre acknowledged that he had ability as a

theologian dealing with modern critical thought, although
she believed that it was not his natural inclination. This
question is debatable, as are many other questions concerning Tyrrell. It is clear, however, that after the turn of
the century he began to devote much attention to reconciling
Catholic dogma with "scientific" Biblical and historical
criticism. In that area especially he developed modernist
views. At the beginning of 1902, Tyrrell, who had been
reading and studying Loisy, told Hügel that he had taken heed
of the manner in which, Loisy excepted, churchmen evade the
inevitable difficulty that arises from the data of Biblical
criticism.[64] Whereas Hügel had acquired his knowledge of
Biblical criticism gradually, however, Tyrrell's acquisition
of knowledge was rapid. Two passages from their letters
will bring out the contrast. First, Hügel: "I am deeply
conscious how that, in my own case, it has been the merciful
condescension of God, which has generally given me my spiritual and mental food so piece-meal in such manageable and
far-between fragments, which has also, by this, enabled me
to keep and improve and add to, I hope and think, my convictions and their . . . life-giving power, as to Him, and our
Lord, and His Church. But, of course, even so, there have
been crises and trials, sometimes acute, and rarely altogether absent." In contrast, Tyrrell: "We get our food in
blocks and periodically like the lions in the zoo . . . and
I am not sure that I don't sometimes long for a good tough
block and rejoice when it comes." Tyrrell added that he
could not bear to think that there were faith or moral difficulties bothering others of which he knew nothing, and
that he owed his own stability "to any sort of ignorance or
half-view."[65]

At the beginning of 1904, Tyrrell privately circulated among friends a "Confidential Letter to a Friend Who
is a Professor of Anthropology"--a letter which would

eventually lead to his dismissal from the Jesuit order. It
seems to have been written to quiet the intellectual difficulties of no particular person, but of a type: those educated English Catholics who could not reconcile their faith
with the advances of science and who were experiencing
doubts whether to remain within the Roman Church. Tyrrell
may have particularly had in mind the difficulties of
Mivart, but he himself was also experiencing difficulties.[66]

Maude Petre's diary is revealing as to how much he
was experiencing difficulties. On June 19, 1902: "Am
suffering much depression--his loss of definite faith is
affecting me a good deal." And at about the time that
Tyrrell wrote his "Letter to a Professor of Anthropology,"
she expressed perplexity: "I have got into a state of
utter vagueness as to what cause I am working for at all.
Is it, the Church? or what is it? Then I have a distress-
ing feeling that he [Tyrrell] is almost anxious to undermine me in these things--and even moral truths grow
shakey" (December 21, 1903).[67]

In the "Letter to a Professor of Anthropology,"
Tyrrell sought to overcome difficulties regarding Catholic
belief by adopting a radical approach to dogma; he now
thought that the conflict of science and religion could be
resolved only along such lines. In the letter, he pointed
out that Catholic theologians had fallen down on their job
for generations. They had allowed difficulties to accumu-
late while trusting to authority, but had forgotten that
the claims to authority would also be questioned once the
reasons for them had been rejected. Tyrrell said that the
professor was alive to the consequences of scientific
Biblical criticism, especially of the gospels, and its bearing on the Church's claims to infallibility. He feared that
historical investigation of Christian origins and developments would undermine many basic assumptions regarding dogma

and ecclesiastical institutions. He saw how the sphere of the miraculous was becoming more limited due to the increasing difficulty of verifying miracles and to the increasing ease of reducing them, or belief in them, to natural causes. Taking the professor's objections as a whole against the orthodox theological positions, Tyrrell concluded that he was unable to solve them. If the orthodox theological positions were absolutely necessary, the professor, who maintained that intellectual assent to Catholicism was impossible for him, should separate himself from the Church. He should not, however, leave the Church "if Catholicism be primarily a life, and the Church a spiritual organism in whose life we participate, and if theology be but an attempt of that life to formulate and understand itself--an attempt which may fail wholly or in part without affecting the value and reality of the said life."[68]

Influenced by the Biblical and historical criticism of his times, Tyrrell's new theological position also reflected his sensitivity to contemporary trends in thought. He applied the psychological distinction between the conscious and the unconscious to the Church and its dogmas. Just as the individual must sometimes reconstruct his whole theory of himself and readjust the entire system of his aims and purposes due to a discovery about his unconscious, the Church must do the same, Tyrrell suggested, in regard to its dogmas:

> Analogously, it seems to me that a man might have great faith in the Church, in the people of God, in the unformulated ideas, sentiments and tendencies at work in the great body of the faithful, and constituting the Christian and Catholic "Spirit"; and yet regard the Church's consciously formulated ideas and intentions about herself as more or less untrue to her deepest nature; that he might refuse to believe her own account of herself as against his instinctive conviction of her true character. . . .[69]

148

More significant than Tyrrell's awareness of psychology was his sensitivity to the philosophical thought of his day--Bergson's vitalism, Blondel's philosophy of action, and, especially, James' pragmatism. For Tyrrell, the truth of the Church's creed was now to be tested by its practical value in promoting spiritual life and growth; dogmas might or might not correspond to objective realities or facts:

> "But," you will object--and this brings me to the main purpose of my letter--"this collapse of the intellectual position, this confusion and at least temporary agnosticism as to the true value of dogmas and sacraments, as to nearly all that theologians impose upon us under pain of anathema, does not stop with the brain, but strikes paralysis into all the members. Action may be in one sense prior to belief, and more important; but it is not wholly independent of it. . . . You [Tyrrell] say, 'Live the religion, test it experimentally, and you will come to see and feel its truth.' Yes, but to believe in it is an essential part of the very life in question, and one on which many of the other parts are dependent."

> [To this objection, Tyrrell replies] Here again I think you should be slow to take theology as seriously as theologians would have us take it. . . . This of course is at variance with reason and experience and with the whole character of that Gospel which was preached to the simple and hidden from the sophists. If in the Athanasian Creed the words "This is the Catholic Faith which except a man believe faithfully he cannot be saved" referred, as they seem, to the foregoing theological analysis, they would be ridiculous. Their only tolerable sense is: "This is the analysis of the Catholic Faith, of those facts and truths by which a man must live (or, of that supernatural world in which he must live) if he is to be saved."[70]

Tyrrell could not be charged with pure pragmatism, for he insisted that God and the supernatural order were objective realities which man could know through prayer and religious experience.[71] In his view, the religious

experience of man could not be reduced to experience within
a wholly natural order. Moreover, all the Church's dogmatic
formulations remained important to him:

> The Trinity, the Creation, the Fall, the Incarnation,
> the Atonement, the Resurrection, Heaven and Hell,
> Angels and Devils, the Madonna and the Saints, all
> are pieces of one mosaic, all, closer determinations
> of one and the same presentment of the Eternal Good-
> ness in the light of which man must shape his will
> and affections and actions if he is to live the life
> of religion, or self-adaptation to the ultimate
> realities. Doubtless, as an expression, it is full
> of distortions, excesses, defects; its truth lies
> inextricably mixed with error as gold in the ore;
> yet the ore may be richer than any yet given to
> man; and pure gold may be unattainable as long as
> man is man. [72]

Interpreted in this way, Christian belief was, Tyrrell
thought, beyond the reach of scientific criticism.

He advised the professor of anthropology to stay in
the Catholic Church in which "God's cause on earth, the
cause of Christianity, of Religion in its highest development, finds its visible embodiment and instrument." Summing
up, he wrote: "After all, your quarrel is not with the
Church, but with the theologians; not with ecclesiastical
authority, but with a certain theory as to the nature and
limits and grades of that authority, and of the value,
interpretation and obligation of its decisions. A breakdown
of theory and analysis does not do away with the reality
analysed." Tyrrell thought the dogmatic structure of
Catholicism would have to undergo a revolutionary transformation, and institutionalized Catholicism as it then
existed might have to die to allow a higher form of Catholicism to be born: "Wine-skins stretch, but only within
measure; for there comes at last a bursting-point when new
ones must be provided." [73]

At the same time that he began privately circulating his "Letter to a Professor of Anthropology," Tyrrell published in the Month an article entitled "Semper Eadem"[74] taking issue with Wilfrid Ward's moderate liberal Catholic hopes for a reconciliation of traditional Catholic theology with modern science. Ward looked forward to Catholic theology assimilating those elements of modern thought that it considered valid and could digest while rejecting invalid and indigestible ingredients, just as it had done with Aristotelianism in the thirteenth century. Tyrrell, on the other hand, took traditional Catholic theology and modern thought to be essentially incompatible. As a disciple of Newman, Ward expected that applications of his principle of development would gradually alleviate the conflict of science and religion but retain the substance of dogmatic belief; Tyrrell considered this reconciliation impossible since he thought that the principle of development necessarily implied substantial change in dogma as in science. Ward hoped to find a _via media_ between traditional theology and modern science; Tyrrell believed no _via media_ was possible. Ward had warned against pouring new wine indiscriminately into old bottles lest the bottles burst and both they and the wine be lost; Tyrrell hoped to allow for a future sponging up of the new wine which must, he now thought, eventually burst the old bottles.[75]

Tyrrell began his "Semper Eadem" article by noting that the problems Ward had dealt with in his periodical articles over the past years "are reducible to one, that, namely, of effecting a reconciliation between theology and science, meaning by science the rest of the field of knowledge so far as it has been unified and systematised by the labour of contemporary investigation and reflection." Tyrrell proposed to show that the basic principles of a wholly liberal or scientific theology, which had already been developed by religious thinkers outside the Church, were irreconcilable with traditional Catholic theology; in this fashion, he sought to dismiss Ward's hopes for a _via media_ between science and Catholic theology. Like Newman, Ward believed in Christian revelation and thought it a healthy check to the anti-theological extravagances of science; at the same time, he believed in the methods of modern science and regarded them as a healthy check to theologians who went beyond the province of theology. The principle of development in Catholic theology allowed for change in the form of doctrine but the substance remained always the same. Moreover, according to Ward, the Church's assimilation of Aristotelianism proved that it had already admitted the principle of development.[76]

Tyrrell questioned whether the principle of development could steer a course between Scylla, the rock of the old scholastic theology, and Charybdis, the whirlpool of the new liberal theology. The principal object of scholastic theology was the deposit of faith, which he defined as "a certain body of divine knowledge revealed supernaturally to the Apostles and delivered by them under the form of certain categories, ideas, and images, to their immediate successors." The Apostles transmitted to their followers what only they had seen and experienced; their followers possessed the record, not the direct vision or experience. This constituted, Tyrrell argued, an irreconcilable difference with liberal theology, which dealt with realities within the experience of all men:

> That which is _semper idem_, constantly the same
> under all developments and accretions, is in the
> case of scholastic theology a doctrine, a record
> of an experience gone, never to be repeated, pre-
> served for us only in and through that doctrine. . . .

> The "constant," the <u>semper idem</u> of liberal
> theology, on the other hand, is the reality dealt
> with, and not any doctrine, or representation of
> that reality. It deals with those ever-present
> evidences of God in Nature and in the universal
> religious experiences of mankind which are
> accessible to all, at all times. . . . It is
> the old "Natural Theology" enriched and improved
> by an application of the inductive historical
> and experimental method to the religions of
> mankind.[77]

Here Tyrrell neglected to mention that moderate liberal
Catholics like Ward, accepting the idea of a special revelation, would not identify themselves with the liberal
theology he was describing.

He went on to argue that an irreconcilable difference
regarding the principle of development followed from the difference in the ultimate objects of scholastic and liberal
theology. Like successive theories on a given subject in
science, developing doctrines in liberal theology were
about the same thing but were not the same doctrine: "the
latter does not contain the former as a constant nucleus
amid explanatory or decorative accretions, but simply sup-
plants and discards it." Again neglecting to mention that
the moderate liberal Catholics would reject this identification of development in science with that in dogma, he proceeded to contrast the scientific idea of development with
scholastic theology: "this comparative indifference to the
doctrinal forms and categories of the past is out of the
question in the case of Scholastic theology, whose principal
subject-matter is the record of an ancient and never-to-be-
repeated revelation of supernatural and inaccessible
realities . . . for they are known to us only representa-
tively; only in and through that record." Consequently, he
said, scholastic theology had "always and consistently
fought tooth and nail for those philosophical categories

and historical beliefs which it conceives to be involved in the very substance of the deposit of faith. . . ." In scholastic theology, moreover, the validity of doctrinal development was determined by the infallible criterion of the authority of the Church; in liberal theology, it was decided by the fallible standard of theological reasoning or of the experts' consensus. Indeed, on no other condition except the Church's infallibility "could the benefit of a revealed theology, final and universally valid, be secured to all generations to the end of the world against the obliterating influences of time and change." In contrast, liberal theology usually viewed Christianity as "the so far highest and fullest development of the religious spirit; but Christ's revelation was but one of many that have been and may yet be."[78]

Since scholastic theology and liberal theology contained irreconcilable principles, neither could compromise with the other without being absorbed by it. Identifying their conflict with that of religion and science, Tyrrell in closing suggested the lines along which he thought a solution might lie, although it would be no via media. The Church was to be considered only the guardian of the deposit of faith, which was an expression of supernatural experiences in natural terms. These experiences were beyond the world of ordinary experience, which was the only world that liberal theology dealt with. Catholic theology thus moved in an entirely different plane from liberal theology and modern science.[79] By these vaguely phrased suggestions, Tyrrell really meant the lines toward a solution of the conflict of religion and science that he had proposed in his "Letter to a Professor of Anthropology."[80]

In his "Semper Eadem" article, Tyrrell had criticized both liberal theology and scholastic theology—the former openly, the latter subtly and ironically. But some conservative theologians assumed that since he had criticized liberal theology and maintained the impossibility of reconciling it with scholastic theology, he must have intended to support the latter. Moreover, they drew the conclusion that he had identified Ward with liberal theology, and applauded what they took to be an attack. In reality, he thought Ward was in principle on the scholastic side which he rejected along with liberal theology.[81] In fact, he was attempting to advance his own revolutionary interpretation of Catholic dogma by criticizing what he regarded as the only other alternatives.

In a letter (January 4, 1904) to Ward, Tyrrell said he had received letters from ultra-conservative theologians congratulating him on an orthodox article: "Surely they are children in wisdom if not in malice; innocent as serpents, wise as doves." Scholastic theology, he asserted, had tied the Church to categories of the last twenty centuries. Therefore, "If Catholicism is to live, the school-theology must go." Even Ward could not believe at first that Tyrrell had been deliberately ironical in his "Semper Eadem" article. He had thought that the article tended to support scholastic theology and that it was largely true but too conservative.[82] When he became convinced of Tyrrell's irony, he attempted to print a reply. The editor of the English Jesuit Month told Ward that he had not understood Tyrrell's attitude: "He has never breathed a word to me as to his article having an ironical intention, on the contrary the letter in which he proposed it, quite conveyed the impression that he wanted to write because he thought you were going too far. Could I now examine it critically I should doubtless find that there were qualifications which I failed to perceive, and that construed literally his words were capable of quite a different sense." The editor added that Tyrrell's talk about Scylla and Charybdis was

"all very well but somewhat indefinite. Seemingly he has
an idea of his own which he prefers not to display as
yet."[83] In view of Tyrrell's shaky relations with his
order, Ward's attempt to publish a reply was abandoned. As
the Month's editor wrote to Ward: "Were your plain exposition of his meaning to appear now, which is sufficiently
cryptic to have escaped most eyes as well as mine, it would
I fear precipitate a catastrophe and complicate a situation
which is at the moment sufficiently delicate. He would certainly be required to disclaim the meaning attributed to
him, which, as certainly, he would not do,--and then, who
knows what would happen?"[84]

A letter from Tyrrell to Ward toward the end of
1904 frankly bared the growing alienation between the two
men and, by extension, between radical liberal Catholicism
and moderate liberal Catholicism. Tyrrell thought Ward
felt aggrieved over the "Semper Eadem" article because he
had dissented from Ward's moderate position without stating
his own radical position, and thereby had given the impression that he had become a conservative attacking Ward as a
proponent of an all too liberal theology. Tyrrell said
that if he had written the article otherwise, it would never
have been printed. The editor's "controversial greed made
him swallow the bait and the hook. He jumped at the idea
that it was an onslaught on liberalism all round and on you
in particular." But apart from these personal considerations, Tyrrell thought Ward might be aggrieved because he
had suggested that traditional Catholicism could not be
reconciled with modern thought. Since the moderate liberal
Catholics had hoped for and aimed at this reconciliation
from the beginning, his remark signified the deep gulf that
now lay between the moderate and radical positions. He said
he realized that their paths had already divided and were to
divide further. They were at odds not only on matters of

156

belief but also on their view of the persons of the present ecclesiastical authorities. Ward believed in the good faith of the officials; Tyrrell, like other radical liberals, did not. He realized that it was reasonable for Ward to want to be identified with him no longer; this was significant because with the publication of radical works, liberals of all shades were falling under suspicion in various quarters. Tyrrell concluded by noting that he had not offended Ward intentionally, but had at most been awkward in his article because his position in his order did not allow him to express his views freely.[85] Again his remark was significant because other modernists had also been unable to express their views freely; their consequent subtlety of expression would make heresy-hunters ever more willing to look for the same subtlety in moderate liberal works as well.

Hügel was not at all upset by his friend Tyrrell's writings and, in fact, had helped distribute his "Letter to a Professor of Anthropology." But writing to Tyrrell, he expressed his fear that many radical liberals of the "new school" would not be with him in regard to his book on The Mystical Element of Religion:

> For not in the least to get rid of all Metaphysic, all Transcendence, is my aim; but on the contrary to show how Metaphysics and Transcendence of some, indeed a definite, kind are in all religion: and how these are still imperative and possible. . . . In yourself I only sporadically feel the anti-metaphysical bias possessing you. I am never afraid of this, in the sense of feeling that perhaps, there too, you are right; but only afraid in the sense of not wishing that you should, for our times and in your way, become the exponent of the kind of trenchant anti-this or that, which one can study in the system of the Socini or of Calvin. Both these systems are through and through antitheses, and hence through and through dependent upon the systematic, full-blown scholasticism which they oppose step by step.

Where Hügel would hold back and sustain the tension of conflicting principles affecting religion, indeed where he believed this tension promoted spiritual growth, Tyrrell and Loisy drew conclusions; they were inclined to try to remove difficulties by advocating their own radical theological approaches. Hügel told Tyrrell that "mentally you apprehend, and more and more, the exceeding variety in unity of all reality, and the slow, ever incomplete, ever correction-begging character of all our apprehensions, still more of all our livings of them; whereas emotively, you are prime-sauteur, hic et nunc, neck or nothing to an equally rare degree." Putting this in epigrammatic form, Hügel said he believed that Tyrrell had a "German brain and Irish heart."[86]

Tyrrell's tendency toward immanentism and subjectivism in his theological and philosophical thought was restrained by his Christian mysticism. Both Hügel and Tyrrell were mystics who saw a need for balancing the mystical element with other elements in religion. In Lex Credendi (1906), Tyrrell attempted to balance it with the elements of feeling, or sentiment, and moral conduct. In his view, "the sentimentalism, or emotionalism rightly or wrongly associated with the name of Schleiermacher" had unduly emphasized feeling in religion. But a false mysticism, "mysticality," emphasized only the metaphysical. "Mysticality" was a perverse attempt to satisfy a real mystical need: "Every sense of contact with that mysterious Beyond lifts him [man] above earth and out of himself; and though his native materialism of thought and desire drag him down again and again, yet his restlessness and discontent with earth are incurable. Were it but a need of his intellect, we might call it his 'metaphysical need'; but it is primarily a need ·of his heart which earth is too small to satisfy, and, as such, let us call it his 'mystical need,'--

the need whose perverse cultivation leads to 'mysticality.'"
The true Christ satisfied the emotional, moral, and mystical
needs together, while the Christ of "sentimentalism" or of
"mysticality" satisfied only one or the other need. A third
error in religion was the "practicality" of Matthew Arnold,
who unduly emphasized moral conduct. It was "so much the
more dangerous because of its resemblance to the truth."
But it was blind to the mystical depth of Righteousness, to
the implication of supernatural reality beyond this world.
Tyrrell remarked about "practicality": "works without faith
are dead,--the mere corpse of conduct."[87]

It was advisable for Tyrrell to repudiate Schleiermacher and Arnold, for he himself was adopting an immanental
and pragmatic theological approach that he did not want
identified with them. Lex Credendi seems in part to have
been an attempt to reconcile his theological approach with
his mysticism. Tyrrell held that the spirit of the Lord's
Prayer defined "that spirit-life whose development is a test
of doctrinal truth just because doctrine is shaped by its
exigencies and is but a statement of its intellectual implications." There was insight in his view that the Church's
doctrines have been shaped less by metaphysical considerations than by religious needs.[88] But his suggestion that
the Christian Creed was primarily a rule of the spiritual
life and of prayer, a Lex Orandi, and that the Lord's Prayer
could be viewed as the rule of doctrine, the Lex Credendi,
went further.[89] He was trying to prepare the way for his
revolution in dogma, although he stated his intentions
obliquely:

> All we contend is that a Creed has representative
> truth so far as it constantly and universally
> fosters the spirit-life; that it is false so far
> as it is spiritually sterilizing and decadent.
> That takes us but a little way towards the apolo-
> gist's end. There are other kinds of truth which

159

the Creed claims to possess, and of which the
"Lex Orandi" can offer no criterion. Of these,
theology proper must undertake the defence. Thus,
the "Prayer-value" of certain historical beliefs
cannot demonstrably be shown to depend on the
historicity of the facts, which therefore must be
determined otherwise, namely, by the ordinary
apologetic methods. It is not however so much
in the interests of Theology as in those of Devotion that I have tried to make clear the relation
between the Church's spiritual life and her theological reflection, and to show their dependence
on one another.

The implication was that theology would be unable to defend
some of the "other kinds of truth which the Creed claims to
possess." Tyrrell, however, warned against attempts "to
sit down and sift every point of Catholic belief, with a
view to rejecting those that did not manifestly stand the
'Pragmatic' test," and against endeavors "to deduce a creed
a priori from the known exigencies of the spirit-life."
His aim was not to supply "a criterion for violent and arti-
ficial criticism, but to furnish a reason for trusting to
the natural criticism effected by Time and Experience; for
suffering Good and Evil to grow together till the harvest;
for quietly abiding the sure uprooting of every plant not
planted by the Father's hand; for living the Truth rather
than analysing it."[90]

Although Tyrrell continued to publish works in addition
to circulating pseudonymous and anonymous writings privately,[91] ecclesiastical censorship as well as his position
within the Jesuit order precluded a full and direct expression of his theological views. In a letter to Hügel in
February, 1907, he put these views more explicitly than
elsewhere in his writings.[92] Using the dogma of the Virgin
Birth as an illustration, he argued that the results of the
historical and critical method had led to its denial as a
historical fact and necessitated a complete revolution in

the conception of dogma. Tyrrell admitted that historical criticism in explaining how a belief might have arisen did not prove it false. But if one accepted the universal validity of the methods of historical criticism, the belief could no longer be accepted as historically true. Moreover, when the alleged fact was "miraculous or violently improbable," there was reason for saying it was historically false. "To take away the affirmative reasons for the Virgin Birth is to prove it false--as historic fact; as false as any alleged violation of the laws of Nature." In view of this conclusion, Tyrrell was forced to raise the question, in what sense was Christian dogma true if some dogmas were not historically true? In answering, he made a sharp distinction between the Christian revelation of the inspired Apostolic era and the theology that sought to explain it. He argued that revelation was prophetic in form and involved an idealized reading of history. No one could presently tell which elements of revelation were historic fact and of literal value and which were idealization and only of symbolic value. Nevertheless, revelation as a whole retained a vital truth. "All the elements conspire to express one thing--the Kingdom of God." "My faith is in the truth, shadowed by the whole creed; and in the direction it gives to spiritual life--in the Way, the Life, and the Truth. . . . It [the idealization of Jesus] is the inward truth of history, but it is not historic truth. That He was born of a Virgin and ascended into heaven may be but a 'visibilising' of the truth of His transcendence as divine. . . . But I do not feel bound to find how each bit of the creed helps to the one truth symbolised by the whole."[93]

As to the later dogmas of the Church, the Church's "authoritative uninspired statements as to the sense of revealed, or primary, dogmas, I am rather at a loss what to say." He maintained that faith was in revelation, not its translation by the Church: "Else we are driven to suppose that Aristotelian categories and exploded science and history are matters of faith." He said that he had first felt this dilemma in his "Semper Eadem" article and saw no way out of it but along the lines he proposed. He recognized that his evaluation of ecclesiastical definitions of dogma was revolutionary:

> More distinctly: I believe the Church is precisely and only the guardian of the deposit of revelation and that she cannot add to it in any way; and that her definitions are simply safeguards and protections of revealed truths. What she says is often absolutely wrong, but the truth in whose defence she says it is revealed, and to that truth alone we owe adhesion. . . . In all controversies the Church must instinctively take the side that best protects the spiritual life. . . . That a lie should be sometimes protective of truth is a consequence of the view of truth as relative to the mentality of a person or people. Hence, no definition of the historicity of the Virgin Birth could mean more than that the Virgin Birth was part of revelation. Because and so long as the denial of its historicity seems to destroy its religious value, she will and must affirm its historicity in order to affirm those values.

Nevertheless, Tyrrell admitted that certain religious values depended "not merely on ideas and symbols of truth, but on their realisation in history. The fiction of heroism can never stir or help me as can the fact. The value of the Gospel is not that it gives us an ideal life, but that that life was actually lived. The historicity of His [Christ's] passion is all-important, the factualness of His resurrection equally so. But the mode, not equally so." But the historicity of such dogmas as those concerning Mary was unimportant, he maintained, for their implicit assertion was Christ's glory and divinity which was expressed whether the Marian dogmas represented fact or idea and image. In concluding, he said that his symbolism could not square with the traditional conceptions of dogma, but he thought that scientific criticism was necessitating a revolutionary conception of dogma.[94]

Tyrrell's conceptions were perhaps even more revolutionary than he himself thought. He had accepted the historical methods and criteria as being of universal validity while he retained the Apostolic revelation as the norm of belief. But should not that to which scientific criteria are applied as of universal validity be regarded as of a wholly natural order? Yet revelation had been the traditionally accepted norm of belief because it was taken as having supernatural authority. Rejecting the idea of supernatural authority, liberal Protestantism consistently rejected the Apostolic revelation as the norm of belief. Could Tyrrell with intellectual consistency justify its retention as normative? Still drawing upon Catholic tradition for some of his conclusions, he too quickly accepted naturalistic presuppositions prevalent in nineteenth-century culture and thought. He did not seem to realize "that a theology or theory of religion, which is ultimately to satisfy the mind, must be coherent with a theory of the universe as a whole."[95]

The moderate liberals had less confidence than Tyrrell in some of the conclusions drawn from scientific criticism; in any case, they refused to abandon basic matters of belief in the face of its challenge. They persisted in their hopes of renewing the Church's teaching, making it intelligible to the modern world, and gradually sifting out many unessential accretions that were irreconcilable with scientific criticism. In contrast, Tyrrell, Loisy, and other modernists felt compelled by scientific criticism to abandon the liberals' original program aimed at reform; some of them now advocated subjectivist and immanentist conceptions aimed at revolutionizing the dogmas and institutions of the Church.

Ever since the controversy over his article on hell, Tyrrell's relationship with the Jesuit order had been shaky. His doubts about remaining a Jesuit were intensified as his theological position became more radical. By February, 1904, he had informed the Jesuit General in Rome that he was totally out of sympathy with the order, and sometime later, he finally applied to leave the Jesuits. His decision to withdraw was not easy. If he were dispensed from his vows as a Jesuit, he would still remain a priest and would have to attach himself to some diocese. What bishop would tolerate the publication or private circulation of his writings? Indeed, because Jesuit superiors had tacitly recognized as anomalous his position within the order, he feared that he would find far less toleration of his writings outside the order as a diocesan priest. He was, consequently, in no haste to leap from the frying pan of the order into the fire of an unsympathetic bishop. Moreover, he was having difficulty finding a bishop who would accept him. If he left the Jesuits without being able to attach himself to a diocese, he would have no priestly work, a serious consideration for a man who had no intention of abandoning his vocation as a priest. In view of these considerations, Hügel was advising him to try to remain a Jesuit as long as the circumstances remained what they were.[96] But he was experiencing more and more personal difficulty in staying.[97]

The timing and mode of Tyrrell's leaving the order were decided by events not of his own choosing. On January 1, 1906, some extracts from his "Letter to a Professor of Anthropology" were published without his knowledge or consent in the Corriere della Sera of Milan, and were ascribed to an English Jesuit. The Archbishop of Milan referred the matter to the Jesuit General who felt obliged

164

to take steps. He wrote Tyrrell asking him if he were the
author of the "Letter to a Professor of Anthropology"; when
Tyrrell replied affirmatively, the General demanded that he
publish a repudiation of what had appeared in the Corriere
della Sera. Since the extracts adequately represented his
real theological views, he could not repudiate them. Consequently, he was dismissed from the order in February,
1906. He now had no permission to say Mass. In the ensuing
months, negotiations were undertaken to attach him to a
diocese and to regularize his position. Only the Roman
Congregation of Bishops and Regulars, however, could remove
his suspension from priestly work, and its prefect made his
reinstatement conditional upon his consent to censorship of
some of his epistolary correspondence. Tyrrell rejected
this condition. As it turned out, his anomalous position
as a priest was never regularized.[98] Moreover, he, Loisy,
and others were soon to encounter a papal condemnation of
modernism and excommunication.

The election of Pius X in 1903 decisively influenced
the results of the intellectual crisis, but in that same
year a moderate liberal nearly occupied the see of Westminster, which lay vacant with the death of Cardinal Vaughan
in June. The Canons of Westminster nominated a list of
candidates including the liberal Gasquet and Bishop Hedley
of Newport, who had shown sympathy toward the liberals.[99]
Both Gasquet and Hedley were Benedictines. Gasquet had
been elected Abbot-President of the Anglo-Benedictine Congregation by its general chapter in 1900. Hedley, who was
already sixty-six years old, had long held the see of
Newport. The other two candidates on the list approved by
the English bishops and forwarded to Rome were Merry del Val
and Bishop Francis Bourne (1861-1935) of Southwark. After
the Duke of Norfolk had effectively vetoed Merry del Val's

candidature on the ground that he was a foreigner, the
English bishops had added Bourne's name to the list.[100]

Gasquet's close friend Edmund Bishop thought that
his appointment to Westminster would be best for the Roman
Church in England, but not for Gasquet.[101] Gasquet himself
came to think it likely that he would be appointed.[102]
Wilfrid Ward favored the appointment of Bishop Hedley, a
personal friend.[103] Hügel wanted either Gasquet or
Hedley.[104] In either case English liberals would have had
for the first time an Archbishop of Westminster sympathetic
to their cause. As it turned out, Rome appointed Bishop
Bourne. Gasquet wrote to Edmund Bishop that the final vote
of the cardinals who considered the appointment was:
Hedley 2, Gasquet 4, Bourne 5.[105]

The Daily Chronicle reported that Cardinal Gotti,
head of the group of cardinals that considered the appointment, had spoken unfavorably of the liberal sympathies of
Gasquet and Hedley. Gasquet was sufficiently concerned to
write Gotti to ask if the report were true. Gotti denied
it. Fleming wrote from Rome that he had heard from reliable
authority that Gotti had never said anything about Gasquet's
liberalism. Fleming reassured Gasquet that he did not have
the reputation of being a liberal in the bad sense in which
Roman officials took the term.[106]

Although not a liberal himself, the new Archbishop
of Westminster had been a pupil of the liberal priest J. B.
Hogan in the Sulpician seminary in Paris. Bourne's predecessor, Cardinal Vaughan, had been a family friend of Ward
and Hügel but had not understood their intellectual work,
although he apparently believed in their substantial orthodoxy. Bourne was not on terms of personal friendship with
Ward, Hügel, or the other English liberals, but he very
cautiously tried to support Catholic intellectual work in
England.[107] The English hierarchy in general, however, had

shown little interest in the liberals' efforts; in fact the
bishops were generally indifferent to them. The complex
intellectual questions which deeply concerned the liberals
and the Vatican did not engage the bishops; they were primarily administrators without intellectual or scholarly
interests. Bourne too was chiefly an administrator. He
too would leave the intellectual controversies to the
liberals and the Vatican. He could not be expected to support the liberals staunchly as the intellectual crisis
deepened; on the other hand, he would not welcome a policy
of repression by the Vatican. Hügel described Bourne as
possessing "the mind of an intelligent seminarist which was
still broadening," and thought that he would be an improvement over the nonintellectual Vaughan, whom Hügel regarded
as having fallen more and more under the influence of his
conservative entourage in his last years.[108]   Gasquet
accurately predicted to Edmund Bishop that Bourne would
never be a brilliant occupant of the see of Westminster but
that he certainly would not be narrow-minded.[109]

The liberals' hopes for Bourne were realized in
January 1906 when he approved Wilfrid Ward's appointment as
editor of the Dublin Review, the semi-official organ of the
Roman Church in England. By 1906, there were reports and
rumors of "heresy-hunters" at work, ultra-conservatives who
were now diligently on the lookout for heresy in the works
of liberals. The choice of an editor who could make the
periodical more appealing by raising its literary and intellectual level was in the hands of the publishers Burns and
Oates, but Bourne had to be concerned whether the editor
would also be able to steer a course between heresy and the
heresy-hunters. The previous editor, Canon Moyes, had disapproved of Ward as his successor. Ward told Bourne that
Moyes' objection reflected just that narrowness which had
made it impossible for Moyes' Dublin to command influence

167

or respect in the English intellectual world.[110] Ward's
Dublin got off to a very good start. Bishop Hedley wrote
Ward that he "read the [first] number through with very
great pleasure--and with a new hope for Catholic influence
in this country in the immediate future."[111]

Ward was well aware of taking a risk in becoming
editor of the Dublin, for if he were delated to Rome all
his work might come under a cloud. But the Dublin could
promote the invigoration of thought within the Roman Church
in England and improve relations between the Church and the
English intellectual world. Ward hoped to make the Dublin
represent both the unquestioned Catholic orthodoxy and
loyalty of his father's Dublin and the broad-mindedness and
brilliance of Acton's Rambler and Home and Foreign Review.
From Rome, Fleming alerted him to dangers. He told Ward
that certain people in Rome, though not officials, were
anxious to pounce on something of Ward's to criticize. For
some years he had followed with great interest Ward's treatment of various questions, and thought Ward had made no
serious mistakes. But in a letter that had reached Rome,
Mivart said that a passage in Ward's writings had given him
the lead for the articles that resulted in his excommunication. In addition to Fleming, Ward also heard from Cardinal
Merry del Val, who warned him against being identified in
the public mind with radicals. Ward informed Bourne that
Merry del Val had not committed himself to a definite
opinion about the Dublin but seemed satisfied with Ward's
proposed policy.[112] Nevertheless, besides left-wing
liberals like Tyrrell and Hügel, even very moderate liberals
like Ward were under suspicion in some quarters in Rome.
The papal condemnation of modernism would affect not only
the future of modernists.

CHAPTER V

THE CONDEMNATION OF MODERNISM

I have viewed Catholic "modernists" as a subgroup
that emerged among the larger liberal Catholic group as the
intellectual crisis unfolded. Two main issues in the crisis
were: the bearing of "scientific" criticism, especially
Biblical and historical criticism, on dogma and the question
of the nature and limits of authority in the Church. These
issues had confronted liberal Catholics since the middle of
the nineteenth century. Now, by 1906-1907, some of the more
extreme liberal Catholic intellectuals had raised them in a
pointed form and had returned radical answers. In contrast
to the more moderate liberal Catholics, some of these
"modernists" held that the meaning of dogma itself must be
radically reinterpreted so as to harmonize the dogmas with
the conclusions of modern scientific criticism; to provide
this reinterpretation, they drew upon immanentist theologies
and subjectivist philosophies. Tyrrell was the modernist
who dealt most fully with the related issue of authority in
the Church. He accepted the Church as the authoritative
custodian of revelation. However, he held that its authority in proclaiming dogma extended only to the protection of
revelation by condemning errors and not to the interpretation of revelation. The moderate liberal Catholics, on the
other hand, accepted the Church as the authoritative interpreter of revelation. Moreover, unlike Tyrrell, they
regarded the hierarchy as possessing the Church's authority.
They made a complete submission to infallible pronouncements

169

and were inclined to submit to non-infallible decisions con-ditionally, whereas modernists were far more disposed to circumvent or rebel against hierarchical verdicts.

Although each modernist scholar or thinker was par-ticularly concerned with his own set of problems, the lead-ing modernist figures recognized the immediate central issues in the crisis. Loisy, the leading modernist scholar, described modernism as "a somewhat diffuse, but for all that intense, endeavor . . . to moderate the rigor of Roman absolutism and of theological dogmatism."[1] Shortly before the papal condemnation of modernism, Tyrrell, the foremost modernist theologian, wrote in a personal letter: "The compatibility of freedom and authority, of science and revelation, is surely a most essential and fundamental Catholic principle. Its application is the perennial prob-lem. The Church which solves it first will sweep the world into its net."[2] Several months after the papal condemnation of modernism, he said in another letter: "I think the best description of 'Modernism' is, that it is the desire and effort to find a new theological synthesis consistent with the data of historico-critical research. The Modernist is not, as such, a critic or historian, but a philosopher or theologian; but he works upon data received from the critic and historian."[3] Writing to Tyrrell about the encyclical which condemned modernism, Hügel held that its most impor-tant point was its implication that the ecclesiastical authorities had direct and absolute--not merely indirect and disciplinary--jurisdiction in historical matters.[4] On the other hand, the Roman authorities were also aware of the immediate central issues at stake. In the decree Lamentabili which was promulgated shortly before the encyclical condemn-ing modernism, the following statement precedes the listing of sixty-five censured propositions: "It is to be greatly deplored that among Catholics also not a few writers are to

170

be found who, crossing the boundaries fixed by the Fathers and by the Church herself, seek out, on the plea of higher intelligence and in the name of historical considerations, that progress of dogmas which is in reality the corruption of the same."[5]

In the highly charged atmosphere that came to envelop the modernist controversy, an atmosphere reminiscent of that which surrounded Pius IX's condemnations in the 1860's, moderate liberals as well as modernists were liable to be struck without distinctions being made. The placing of the works of Fogazzaro and Laberthonnière on the Index and the Biblical Commission's decision on the Pentateuch seemed to indicate that Rome was beginning to think it would again have to resort to condemnation. By August 1906, Wilfrid Ward thought the same kind of anti-intellectual temper that had reigned in Rome in 1864-65 was returning. In both cases, he saw "a great dread of the excesses of Liberal Catholicism which, in the semi-educated Italian mind has no gradations but is in all forms an attack on the principle of authority in the Church." Ward did not think the state of affairs could be remedied by moderate Catholic intellectuals going over to the radical wing and agitating. They had the duty of submitting to the ecclesiastical authorities, and should hope their moderation would convince the authorities that a Catholic could be both devoted to thought and loyal to the Church. Ward regarded patience as the virtue presently called for, but he did not sympathize with a policy of intellectual repression.[6]

In accepting the position of editor of the Dublin Review, Ward recognized that he might become a target for charges of unorthodoxy. Indeed, after the first number of his Dublin appeared, William Barry told him that he heard of "some little breeze in Rome" over it. A priest who was "quite outside things" talked to Barry about one sentence

171

concerning Loisy that the priest interpreted in a bad sense--thus "showing how these troubles come up." In regard to the general situation at the time, Barry feared an increase of momentum on both sides--ultra-conservative and radical--that might bring about a catastrophe.[7]

Eventually Ward was threatened with delation to Rome. The elderly Mgr. Bagshawe, who had retired from his Nottingham bishopric, thought he discovered unsoundness in some of Ward's articles in the Dublin as well as in the epilogue of his reissued biography of Cardinal Wiseman; Bagshawe was reported to be preparing to delate Ward's writings to Rome.[8] Again the central questions involved the relationship of theology to scientific criticism and the problem of authority in the Church. Critics charged Ward with conceding too much to scientific criticism and with admonishing the Holy See and pretending to teach the Church rather than be taught by it.[9] Deploring the criticisms of Ward's writings, Basil Maturin, a liberal Catholic priest, suggested that if such writings met with disapproval from the ecclesiastical authorities, there could be no place for the Dublin Review "or indeed for a Catholic review of any intellectual standard in England." He praised Ward's Dublin highly saying that in just a few months Ward had raised it to a position in which it could hold its own among the leading reviews of the day. Before Ward became editor, it had been moribund. Maturin went on to say:

> In face of the strong and somewhat reckless things
> that are being said by a certain class amongst the
> most advanced school it seems to me little short
> of disastrous that a temperate effort like yours,
> to hold them in check should be met by disapproval.
> In dealing with converts and many others perplexed
> and harassed by the difficulty of reconciling cer-
> tain traditions with the conclusions arrived at by
> historical and critical science I have found your
> articles invaluable . . . . And I should feel it a

grave responsibility to receive people into the
Church who feel keenly the difficulties of the
day--which do not really affect faith or a firm
belief in the authority of the Church--if one is
prohibited from using such an argument as yours
. . . Are we to tell people that the Faith of
Catholics is wrapped up in traditions that they
know and can prove to be untrue, or that the condition of faith is, as so many of the Churchs [sic]
enemies insist, dependent upon ignorance and that
a Catholic cannot face facts.[10]

In a letter informing Ward that he had joined
Bagshawe in complaining to Archbishop Bourne about his
writings, Mgr. W. Croke-Robinson, while professing belief
in Ward's good intentions in attempting to champion the
Church, suggested that he should examine himself to see if
he had fallen into intellectual pride. Croke-Robinson's
letter was distinguished by its anti-intellectual tone:
"'How hardly shall "intellectuals" (as well as rich) enter
into the Kingdom of Heaven'! . . . Look at the wrecks of
the intellectuals strewing the path of Holy Church on either
side and all along the line." In reply to the letter, Ward
denied that he was trying to teach the Church when he should
be taught by it. He was dealing with detailed difficulties
which he himself had formerly felt and others were experiencing, problems which ecclesiastical authority naturally
could not be expected to treat. He hoped he would not be
silenced because he was constantly receiving evidence that
he was doing some good, but if silenced he would obey. He
added that it was hard to write so as to help those who saw
and felt strongly certain difficulties without offending
others who did not feel them and therefore did not understand what was really being said.[11]

Ward was very concerned about the possibility of
being delated to Rome. Since Archbishop Bourne's letters
informing him of the charges against his articles were stiff

in tone although non-committal, Ward incorrectly assumed
that Bourne was perturbed and had almost identified himself
with the charges.[12] Writing to Bourne, he asked him to
remember that in taking up the question of the relationship
of the Church's constitution to the new sciences, he was
venturing on ground unfamiliar to many Catholics just
because those sciences were new. Consequently, it was
inevitable that some critics would charge him with rashness
and unorthodoxy. Ward reminded Bourne that when Newman was
editor of the Rambler he had been delated to Rome for similar reasons and that his bishop had persuaded him to resign.
Later, Newman's orthodoxy while editor was proved, but his
resignation had prematurely ended his work. In reply to the
charge that he was admonishing the Holy See, Ward remarked
that he would not be admonishing the king if, in writing on
the British constitution, he said the monarch governed
according to law which he must not willfully supersede. So
too Ward was only expressing a principle of the Church's
constitution, one that Protestants who thought Rome could
act as capriciously and tyrannically as it chose in intellectual matters failed to recognize.[13]

     At Bourne's advice, Ward appealed to Bishop Hedley.
Ably summarizing the drift of Ward's articles, Hedley said
that they contained nothing contrary to Catholic faith and
piety. They maintained that in the statement of doctrine
and the interpretation of the Bible there was, excluding
definitions of faith, "here and there an element of human
philosophy or, again, of assumed fact, which is not of the
essence of the doctrine, and, which may, and sometimes ought
to be, rejected." Hedley noted that Ward had tried to make
it clear that hasty changes of current expressions of doctrine could do great harm among simple minds, and that it
was sometimes better to tolerate an error bound up with
truth than to attempt to eliminate it. At the same time,

174

he had tried to conciliate thinkers and critics, both Catholic and non-Catholic, by demonstrating that these errors were only accidentally bound up with doctrine and were not a part of the Church's faith. Hedley thought that on the whole Ward accomplished his objectives with ability as well as perfect respect to ecclesiastical authority.[14]

Replying to Hedley's intervention on Ward's behalf, Merry del Val said that he was not aware that Rome had received any delation of Ward. He added, however, that many competent persons considered the orthodoxy of some of Ward's writings in the Dublin and elsewhere to be "questionable." He described Ward's theology "as 'acrobatic'--he attempts the feat of sitting between two stools--and occasionally comes down with a bump--he quickly regains his balance and is able to assure everybody that he is all right again." The Papal Secretary of State remarked that he did not like to suppose for a moment that Ward was disloyal or lacked the best intentions.[15]

Although the modernist intellectuals lived in various parts of Europe and held diverse views, Hügel, more than anyone else, had acquainted them with each other's work and had established some contacts among them. For this reason as well as his views in the area of Biblical criticism, he was a leader among the modernists, even though he disagreed with immanentism and extreme subjectivism. In the first months of 1906, he had been alarmed by the placing of works of Fogazzaro and Laberthonnière on the Index, the Church-State conflict over abrogation of the century-old Napoleonic Concordat in France, a report that Pius IX might be beatified, and reports that the Roman officials had accepted a policy of repression. He became convinced that the time had arrived for him to take some steps to attempt to defend his cherished belief in freedom of inquiry for Catholic intellectuals. At the beginning of May, 1906, he

presided over a gathering in his home of some less influential English Catholic laymen to decide what could be done
to defend Loisy and others. Robert Dell and William Gibson--
who both had written some of the strongly worded articles
which had led to the joint pastoral in 1900--were among
those present. It was decided to get Edmund Bishop to
collaborate with Hügel in drafting an address to present to
Loisy should the long rumored syllabus of errors appear and
Loisy meet with excommunication in the event of being unable
to submit to it. Bishop was at first willing to participate
in drafting the address, for he thought that Loisy alone had
risked himself for the sake of the laity in attempting to
refute Harnack's Das Wesen des Christentums, which threatened
to trouble educated young laymen. But when he saw that the
signatories to this address would be few or insignificant,
he dismissed it as another futile gesture by liberal
Catholics. Another address was drawn up without his participation. It held that Loisy was a good Catholic driven
into perplexity by persecution even though he had submitted
to the decrees of the Holy See. It was never presented to
Loisy or published since Loisy believed that it had mis-
judged his position and that it would lead to a needless
condemnation of its signatories.[16]

     The next step Hügel took to defend freedom of
inquiry for Catholic intellectuals was a booklet entitled
The Papal Commission and the Pentateuch, published in col-
laboration with an American Protestant scholar, Professor
C. A. Briggs. It was a scholarly and respectful reply to
the Biblical Commission's decision upholding the Mosaic
authorship of the Pentateuch. Archbishop Mignot wrote to
Hügel about the booklet: "It would be impossible to warn
with greater competence and propriety the Biblical Commission of the dangers of the way it is going."[17] Although
becoming more antagonistic toward the actions and decisions

of the ecclesiastical authorities, Hügel was determined to keep his place within the Church. At the same time, he was becoming somewhat warier of excesses he encountered among other modernists. To Tyrrell, he said he had warned Loisy against radical liberals taking contemporary ultramontanism in the Church as final and rejecting it and the Church together. Moreover, he had told Loisy that religion was of greater depth and range than science, and should not be whittled down simply to the level of science.[18] While maintaining to Loisy that the individual soul needed an organized church, he simultaneously expressed his conviction that the Church could not remain a "prison for the critical and reasoning reason, indeed for the modern awakened conscience" and that it would have to undergo a transformation for the sake of spiritual life in the Church.[19] Hügel was determined to sacrifice none of his sometimes conflicting loyalties to Catholicism, to science, and to his modernist friends.

Cut loose from both the spiritual and temporal moorings to which he was accustomed, Tyrrell had a look of suffering and desolation about him in the first months after his dismissal from the Jesuit order. A post card from him led Hügel to tell Maude Petre that Tyrrell ever reminded him "of those beautifully delicate, and in their own way, wonderfully strong marine creatures," which used to delight him as a child during his summer Mediterranean bathings, for "in water and sunshine, how expansive, how delightful, how happy they were; and out of water and in the bleak winds, how shrunken, limp, mere husks and weeds they were!" He believed that if "ever a soul required trust, sympathy, affection, expansion, to be itself and to do its great, very great, work," it was Tyrrell's! He now felt that even their sympathy would not turn Tyrrell into a good fighter, by which he meant "not an 'effective' fighter, but a fighter

who does not damage his own self by the fighting." Tyrrell
was too utterly sensitive a human being "not to get dried-
up, embittered, unbalanced over such conflicts."[20] Also
concerned about Tyrrell, Wilfrid Ward had asked the Duke
of Norfolk, his wife's uncle, what could be done? Norfolk
answered that there was nothing he could do, as any representations of his would have no weight with ecclesiastical
authorities on such a matter.[21]

Without a permanent residence, Tyrrell constantly
moved about for over a year and stayed with friends. In
May, 1907, he finally settled at Storrington where a cottage
was made available by Maude Petre for his use. To forestall
scandalous rumors about his privately circulated "Letter to
a Professor of Anthropology," he felt obliged to publish it.
The work appeared in the autumn of 1906 under the title A
Much-Abused Letter.[22] Tyrrell was specially strained by his
preoccupation with the bearing of Biblical and historical
criticism on faith and the bearing of the centralization of
authority in the papacy on the individual conscience in both
spiritual and scientific questions.[23] In "Semper Eadem" and
the "Letter to a Professor of Anthropology," he had dealt
specifically with the former problem. In summer 1907, he
published under the title Through Scylla and Charybdis:
Or the Old Theology and the New a collection of his articles,
including a recent article entitled "From Heaven, or of Men?"
This article had been published in the April, 1907 issue of
Rinnovamento under the title, "Da Dio o dagli uomini." In
it, Tyrrell again specifically addressed himself to the
problem of authority in the Church, and elaborated on the
views he had first put forward in 1901 in his pseudonymous
writings on the joint pastoral.[24]

In "From Heaven, or of Men?" Tyrrell noted that the
abuse of authority often had its roots in an erroneous conception of the source of authority. Consequently, he raised

the question: where had ecclesiastical authority come from, heaven or men, God or people? If one pictured authority as having come from a transcendental God who ruled as a king over his subjects, as a shepherd over his flock, then the ecclesiastical official to whom this authority had been delegated was regarded as standing outside and above the flock and ruling over it. The official considered himself to be the superior of all collectively, not each singly, and to be in no way responsible to the flock or community but only to a transcendental God to whom an appeal was presently impossible. Contrariwise, Tyrrell suggested that the source of authority was from God immanent in the community. Thus, authority remained directly from God but it was also inherent in and inalienable from the community itself. All authority was from the Heavenly in man. Ecclesiastical authority stood above the laity solely as representative of the community's authority and was responsible to the community as to God. Perhaps no institutional tribunal could revise laws and formulas of either Pope or Council, but the Spirit of God immanent in the community effectively did so, for decrees which gave life to the flock survived and those of only relative and temporary value perished. In any case, democracy had come to stay, and the generations of the near future would accept no other conception of authority. If the authority of the papacy, councils, and bishops was not susceptible of a democratic interpretation, it was doomed. By democracy he did not mean, Tyrrell warned, subjection of clergy to laity or the few to the many, but all alike to the whole community.[25] In a note in Through Scylla and Charybdis on the article, he applied his views on ecclesiastical authority to the question of the infallibility of the pope. If papal infallibility was interpreted to mean that one individual, the pope, rather than the whole Church was the organ of truth, it was destructive of Catholicism. Popes, councils, and bishops had the responsibility of interpreting the Church's mind, not making their own formulations. Any theory of papal absolutism was to be rejected. The Vatican Council's decrees were ambiguous on this point, although an ultramontane party had attempted and was still trying to impose its absolutist interpretation on the Church.[26] Commenting on the article, Hügel said that he thought Tyrrell was right in his general conclusions but wrong regarding his preliminary point of an immanentist conception of God. "But I feel strongly, somehow, that your treatment of the old transcendent conception of God as requiring to be reformulated, en toutes pièces, by an immanental one, is somehow a bit of most tempting, yet nevertheless impoverishing, simplification."[27]

While Tyrrell had become a priest without a home and was drifting physically and theologically, Loisy had also lost permission to say Mass. After the controversy over L'Évangile et l'Église and Autour d'un petit livre, Loisy had been living in retirement and saying his Mass privately. In November, 1906, official authorization for him to say private Mass was due to expire; consequently, he applied to the French ecclesiastical authorities for renewal. Although he thought that his separation from the Church was inevitable and was not anxious to have his permission renewed, he decided to leave to the ecclesiastical authorities all initiative for his separation. His request for authorization to say Mass was refused.[28]

In spring 1907, there began a succession of Roman censures leading to the papal condemnation of modernism. These censures provoked from Loisy a bold reaction that was intensified by the even lower view of the Roman authorities that he had taken as a result of the Church-State conflict in France. He decided to let the authorities know what he thought of their measures. He was well aware that his action might lead to his excommunication. In an allocution in a consistory called to create new cardinals on April 17, 1907, Pius X denounced "those rebels who profess and repeat monstrous errors, under skilful disguises, . . . without definitely revolting, in order not to be expelled, but nevertheless without submission, in order not to be faithless to their own convictions." He referred to modernism as "that assault which does not constitute merely a heresy, but the summary and the poisonous essence of all the heresies which tend to undermine the foundations of the faith and to destroy Christianity." On April 29, Prefect of the Index Steinhuber wrote to the Archbishop of Milan censuring Rinnovamento, referring to "self-styled Catholics," who "in their self-pride pose as masters and doctors of the Church," and mentioning by name Hügel, Tyrrell, Fogazzaro, and Romulo Murri, an Italian modernist priest.[29] Hügel, hoping the incident would be dropped, decided to remain completely silent about the mention of his name. This hope was fulfilled.[30] In contrast, Loisy wrote to Merry del Val and denied that he had submitted in 1904 out of fear of being excommunicated; writing to Steinhuber also, he expressed his astonishment and distress that Hügel, whom he regarded as "the least wilfully proud of men," had been publicly accused of pride. At the end of May, the Pope ratified a decision of the Biblical Commission upholding the authenticity and historicity of the Gospel of John. Reacting to this latest event, Loisy wrote to Merry del Val, who was a member of the Biblical Commission, arguing against the decision. The final measure that preceded the papal condemnation of modernism came about one month later when the long expected syllabus of errors was promulgated.[31]

Two months previously, David Fleming, a Consultor of the Holy Office, had written to Wilfrid Ward a letter that he marked "Private." Saying that he knew nothing very definite about the syllabus, he added: "Anyhow, you need not be afraid, but von Hügel and the Subjectivists must be kept aloof." Fleming commented that the "whole philosophical question must be handled with great delicacy and accuracy in itself and in its relations to history, exegesis and dogma. Some writers have made a hash all round. Tyrrel [sic] wrote to the Pope that he had given up Catholicism. This he now denies with disconcerting effrontery. Some Italian Ecclesiastics are nearly as bad as Tyrrel [sic]. My information as to the latter comes from Merry del Val to whom he wrote the letter." Fleming observed that LeRoy in Paris had been "very injudicious" and others were moving in the same direction.[32]

Apparently misjudging the situation, Fleming was much too optimistic about the future in store for moderate liberal Catholics: "With Tyrrel [sic] out of the way and von Hügel hors de combat--not to speak of Dell and a few others--I think we shall get on well. . . . I don't think you have now to fear anything very formidable from the Holy See." Fleming believed that "the hour has come! The wheat is being separated from the chaff on both sides." He remarked that for many years he had a hard fight "to bring Theologians, Exegetes and Historians to understand each other. The greatest difficulty was the 'sheer ignorance,' . . . We are on the whole getting into smoother waters. . . . Loisy and company give [sic] us a tremendous 'set back', but we recovered and began to advance again." He concluded optimistically: "The future belongs to true pro-gress. The 'flowing tide' is with all honest and competent progressives."[33]

On July 3, 1907, the Holy Office enacted the decree Lamentabili Sane Exitu which listed and censured sixty-five propositions concerning, for the most part, Scripture and early Christian origins and their relationship to the Church,

dogma, and ecclesiastical teaching. The censured propositions were drawn mainly from works of Loisy, but also Tyrrell
and perhaps LeRoy.[34] The first propositions concerned the
authority of the Church and included: No. 3, From the
ecclesiastical judgments and censures rendered against "free
and more scientific (cultiorem) exegesis," it could be
gathered that the Church's faith contradicted history and that
Catholic dogmas could not really be reconciled with the true
origins of Christianity; No. 4, The Church's magisterium
could not "even through dogmatic definitions, determine the
genuine sense of the Sacred Scriptures"; No. 5, Since only
revealed truths were contained in the deposit of the faith,
under no respect did "it appertain to the Church to pass
judgment concerning the assertions of human sciences";
No. 6, In defining truths the Ecclesia discens (Church
learning) and the Ecclesia docens (Church teaching) collabo-
rated in such a way that it only remained "for the Church
docens to sanction the opinions of the Church discens"; and
No. 8, Persons who treated as of no weight the condemnations
passed by the Index or the other Roman Congregations were
free from all blame. The ensuing censured propositions
mostly concerned criticisms of Scripture, in particular,
opinions associated with Loisy, and included: No. 12, the
exegete must put aside all assumptions concerning Scripture's
supernatural origin and must interpret it as he would any
human document; Nos. 16, 17, and 18, denial of the historicity of the Gospel of John; No. 20, revelation was only
man's acquired consciousness of his relation with God;
No. 23, opposition could and did exist between the facts
narrated in the Bible and the Church's dogmas and, consequently, the critic might reject facts which the Church
held to be certain; No. 24, so long as the exegete did not
directly deny the dogmas, he might without blame construct
premises that led to the conclusion that dogmas were

historically doubtful or false; No. 27, Christ's Divinity
was not proved from the Gospels but was a dogma derived by
the Christian conscience from the idea of the Messias; and
No. 34, the critic could not admit that because Christ as
man had God's knowledge, His knowledge had no limits.
Propositions 39-51 concerned the sacraments. Proposition
54 apparently involved the apologetical theme developed in
Loisy's L'Évangile et l'Église: "Dogmas, sacraments, hierarchy, both as regards the notion of them and the reality,
are but interpretations and evolutions of the Christian
intelligence which by external increments have increased
and perfected the little germ latent in the Gospel." Proposition 57 stated that the Church had shown itself to be
"hostile to the progress of natural and theological
sciences." Propositions 59-62 concerned denials of the
Church's retention of dogma in the same sense. Proposition
65 was the final statement censured: "Modern Catholicism
cannot be reconciled with true science unless it be transformed into a non-dogmatic Christianity, that is into a
broad and liberal Protestantism."[35]

Loisy admitted that a large number of the propositions censured in Lamentabili were taken from his books,
especially L'Évangile et l'Église and Autour d'un petit
livre, but held that some of them had been altered from what
had actually appeared in his works. He also objected to the
Holy Office's requirement of complete obedience to its
decree while leaving open the possibility of a future
reversal of its position on this or that censured proposition.[36] Lamentabili also irked the other leading modernists.
Tyrrell thought the Pope intended to demand absolute assent
to the decree while it was avowedly fallible and might later
be reversed. He would hesitate to submit formally to its
censures, for he felt that many of them were certainly
false. Furthermore, he saw in the decree "a clearly

exercised claim to <u>direct</u> jurisdiction over the whole realm
of man's natural reason," and said that claim must be flatly
rejected.[37] Since <u>Lamentabili</u> was an official decree of the
Holy Office, Hügel thought it deserved respect, but felt
that neither he nor Tyrrell could sincerely accept some of
its censures. He found consolation in the idea he had
gotten from David Fleming that really important Holy Office
decrees were enacted on Thursdays; Wednesday decrees
(<u>Lamentabili</u> was such) "can go into the waste-paper basket."
In any case, he and Tyrrell decided for the time being to
keep silent about the decree.[38]

      William Barry wrote Wilfrid Ward: "What we foresaw
has come about in Rome. I have not seen the new document;
if the papers are correct it is a very light pronunciamento
from the doctrinal point of view, without definite notes of
censure or names of persons, and a mere utterance of the
Inquisition." It might embarrass writers, but "it decides
how much?" Barry thought that the English bishops might
have "saved the situation if they had realized its danger
in time and acted together." But now, he--like Hügel and
Tyrrell--judged silence to be prudent: "Time does
wonders."[39]

      <u>Lamentabili</u> appeared at a particularly bad time for
Tyrrell. Negotiations for regularizing his status as a
priest had recently been resumed. With the Prior of
Storrington and the Belgian Abbot of Leffe, his superior,
acting as intermediaries between Tyrrell and the Prefect of
the Congregation of Bishops and Regulars, the negotiations
seemed to be approaching a successful conclusion. On condition of his reinstatement as a priest, Tyrrell agreed to
publish no further theological teaching without due authorization nor to spread such teaching by epistolary correspondence that would be the equivalent of publication, these
duties being incumbent on all priests. At the end of

August, he received through the Prior of Storrington a
letter from Cardinal Ferrata, the Prefect, reproducing word
for word the terms that Tyrrell had suggested for reinstatement. Tyrrell immediately sent off a qualified statement of
acceptance. But Lamentabili had been promulgated that
summer, and he was under the pressure of conflicting advice
from all sides. When news of his reinstatement was leaked
to the press, he withdrew his submission. He feared that
press accounts would make it seem as if he had finally given
an unqualified submission and was allowing his scalp to be
brandished before fellow liberals.[40] A further development
would lead to his excommunication. A much heavier blow
than Lamentabili was about to be struck.

On September 8, 1907, Pope Pius X promulgated the
lengthy encyclical Pascendi Gregis[41] condemning modernism as
an extremely grave danger for the Church: the modernists
"lay the axe not to the branches and shoots, but to the
very root, that is, to the faith and its deepest fibres."
Moreover, the encyclical stated that the modernists presented their teachings cleverly in disordered and unsystem-
atic fashion so as to appear as if their minds were hesitant.
It sought to group together the modernist teachings and to
show their interconnection. It successively considered the
modernist as a philosopher, believer, theologian, historian,
critic, apologist, and reformer.[42] We will summarize the
papal encyclical on modernism in the following pages.

The encyclical considered modernist philosophy to
be agnostic. Modernist philosophy held that human reason
was confined entirely to phenomena. Consequently, it could
not attain knowledge of God and recognition of His existence,
even through visible things. Hence God was not to be considered a direct object of science nor a subject of history.
This meant the sweeping aside of natural theology and
external revelation. The Church had already condemned these

186

errors, which represented the negative side of modernist philosophy. The positive side was what the modernists called vital immanence. Like any other fact, religion must be explained. But since the modernists had rejected natural theology and all external revelation, they had to seek an explanation in man and his life, hence vital immanence. According to them, faith consisted in a certain interior religious sense, originating in a need for God. The modernists' neo-Kantian philosophy had important consequences for historical and Biblical criticism, for in accordance with it everything suggestive of the divine in the history and person of Christ had to be rejected. It affirmed that Catholic Christianity, in Christ as well as his successors, "emanated from nature spontaneously and of itself." Nothing could more completely destroy the whole supernatural order than this erroneous belief.[43]

The modernist philosopher recognized the phenomenon of the divine in the believer's heart as an object of the believer's feeling and affirmation, but whether a God existed outside his feeling and affirmation, the modernist as a philosopher did not inquire. The modernist as a believer did assert it to be established and certain that a God really exists independently of the believer. If one asked him on what ground his assertion rested, he would reply: in the individual's personal experience. In confronting the problem of the relations between faith and science, including, as he was accustomed to doing, history under the category of science, the modernist believer asserted that faith and science were concerned with completely separate spheres. Faith dealt entirely with the divine which science declared unknowable; science dealt entirely with phenomena. To the objection that some things appertaining to faith such as Christ's human life fall also within the realm of phenomena, the modernist believer

187

asserted that in so far as such things were lived by faith, which had both transfigured and disfigured them, they had been removed from the realm of phenomena. Did Christ work real miracles, make real prophecies, really rise from the dead and ascend into heaven? The modernist philosopher speaking as a philosopher and concerned only with the history of Christ answered no; the modernist believer speaking as a believer and concerned only with Christ's life as relived by and in the faith answered yes. While the modernist thought he had rendered faith independent of science, he had really subjected it to science. Excluding the divine reality and the believer's experience of it, he subjected to science every other religious fact, including religious formulas and the idea of God. He felt a need to reconcile faith with science so that faith never opposed science's general conception of the universe.[44]

While the modernists rebuked the Church for not accommodating her dogmas to modern philosophy, they tried to introduce a new theology supporting modern philosophy's aberrations. For the modernist theologian as for the modernist believer, the question was the reconciliation of faith with science by subjecting it to science. Applying the principles of immanence and symbolism to the believer, he concluded that "God is immanent in man" and "The representations of the divine reality are symbolical." These errors led to pernicious consequences. If dogma was merely symbol, then the dogmatic formulas were of account to the believer only as a means of uniting him to the absolute truth, which they symbolized but failed to express, and just so far as they proved helpful to him. The meaning of the modernists' principle of immanence that best fitted in with the rest of their teachings was pantheism. Moreover, immanence was connected with their teaching that Christ did not institute the Church and the sacraments, which they maintained were founded

only mediately by Christ. They argued that since all
Christians live Christ's life, just as the branches of a
plant live the seed's life, and since this life in time
produced the Church and sacraments, these can be said to
have their origin from Christ and to be divine.[45]

In addition to their teachings on the origin and
nature of faith, the modernists also propagated teachings
on such branches of faith as dogma, Scripture, and the
Church. They held that dogma was derived from a need of
the believer to elaborate his thought in order to make it
clearer to his conscience and the consciences of others.
This elaboration was carried out through investigation and
refinement of the primitive formula, not in itself and in
accordance with any logical explanation, but vitally, that
is, according to circumstances. Hence secondary formulas
were formed around the primitive formula and these when
grouped into a doctrinal construction and sanctioned by the
Church's public magisterium were called dogma. For the
modernists, this constituted the nature of dogma. Regarding
the Bible, inspiration was, according to them, the same as
the impulse which stimulated a believer to reveal his faith
orally or in writing, except perhaps that the inspiration
of Scripture was more vehement. It was something like
poetical inspiration: "There is a God in us, and when He
stirreth He sets us afire." Their assertion that Scripture
could be said in that sense to be inspired by an immanent
God was merely verbal conjuring on their part. For them,
the Bible was a human work, written by men for men; no room
was left for its Divine inspiration in the Catholic sense.[46]

The modernists taught that the authority of the
Church did not come to it from without, but came from the
Church itself, which derived from the collectivity of consciences. Thus, ecclesiastical authority originated in the
religious conscience and was subject to it. The present age

was an age of democracy and, therefore, ecclesiastical authority would have to adopt a democratic form or meet with disaster. The great anxiety of the modernists was to reconcile ecclesiastical authority with the freedom of the believers. They maintained that since the magisterium of the Church, its authority to teach doctrine and dogma, derived from individual consciences and had a mandate of public utility for their well-being, it must bow to popular ideals.[47]

Evolution was practically the modernists' chief doctrine: "To the laws of evolution everything is subject under penalty of death--dogma, Church, worship, the Books we revere as sacred, even faith itself." The modernists regarded it as their sacred duty to advance changes in the Church. If authority rebuked them, they had their own conscience and intimate experience to tell them they were certainly right. But their teaching on the evolution of revelation and dogma had been condemned. Pius IX's <u>Syllabus of Errors</u> had condemned the proposition that "Divine revelation is imperfect, and therefore subject to continual and indefinite progress, corresponding with the progress of human reason." And the Vatican Council had decreed: "that sense of the sacred dogmas is to be perpetually retained which our Holy Mother the Church has once declared, nor is this sense ever to be abandoned on plea or pretext of a more profound comprehension of the truth." This pronouncement, however, did not mean that knowledge concerning the faith could not develop. On the contrary, the same Vatican Council supported the legitimacy of accepting its development "but only in its own kind, that is, according to the same dogma, the same sense, the same acceptation."[48]

The modernists as historians professed to be objective and not to be biased in favor of any philosophical theories. Yet their history was agnostic, for they

maintained that history like science dealt entirely with
phenomena; therefore, it had to relegate God and every
divine intervention to the realm of faith alone. In treating Christ, the Church, the sacraments, and so on, history
dealt only with the human element. The modernist historians
proclaimed that Christ as a historical figure was not God
and did nothing divine and that his actions were those that
they, judging from his times, thought he ought to have done.
As apologists, a common axiom of theirs was "that in the
new apologetics controversies in religion must be determined
by psychological and historical research." The modernist
apologists proclaimed to the rationalists that they would
use real history based on modern principles and method.
They held that the dogmas of the Church were filled with
flagrant contradictions but that this was unimportant since
the dogmas were reconcilable with symbolical truth.[49]

The encyclical summarily defined the modernist
system as "the synthesis of all heresies," and attempted to
draw out the consequences of the modernists' teaching.
Acceptance of their teaching would be disastrous:

> What, then, remains but atheism and the absence of
> all religion. Certainly it is not the doctrine of
> symbolism that will save us from this. For if all
> the intellectual elements, as they call them, of
> religion are nothing more than mere symbols of God,
> will not the very name of God or of divine person-
> ality be also a symbol, and if this be admitted,
> the personality of God will become a matter of
> doubt and the gate will be opened to Pantheism?
> And to Pantheism pure and simple that other doc-
> trine of the divine immanence leads directly. For
> this is the question which We ask: Does or does not
> this immanence leave God distinct from man? If it
> does, in what does it differ from the Catholic doc-
> trine, and why does it reject the doctrine of
> external revelation? If it does not, it is Pan-
> theism. . . . And why this religion [of an unknow-
> able reality] might not be that soul of the
> universe, of which certain rationalists speak, is

191

something which certainly does not seem to Us apparent. These reasons suffice to show super-abundantly by how many roads Modernism leads to atheism and to the annihilation of all religion. The error of Protestantism made the first step on this path; that of Modernism makes the second; Atheism makes the next.[50]

The encyclical went on to say that although the proximate cause of modernism was an error of the mind, there were two remote causes, curiosity and, especially, pride: "It is owing to their pride that they seek to be the reformers of others while they forget to reform themselves, and that they are found to be utterly wanting in respect for authority, even for the supreme authority." The primary intellectual cause of modernism was ignorance, particularly of scholasticism; modernism "has been born of the union between faith and false philosophy." The modernists zealously and energetically propagated their system, but three chief obstacles stood in their way: the scholastic philosophical method, the Patristic authority and tradition, and the Church's magisterium. On these, they waged unrelenting war. Many young Catholics, although not modernists, already had been "so infected by breathing a poisoned atmosphere, as to think, speak, and write with a degree of laxity which ill becomes a Catholic."[51]

In the concluding section of the encyclical, the Pontiff ordered a number of stringent measures against modernism; regarding these measures, he adjured the bishops to be not "in the slightest degree wanting in vigilance, zeal, or firmness." The first remedy he prescribed was the study of scholastic philosophy. But he added that he considered worthy of praise those who, with full respect for tradition, the Fathers, and the magisterium of the Church, endeavored "with well-balanced judgment, and guided by Catholic principles (which is not always the case), to illustrate positive theology by throwing upon it the light of true history." Not one tainted with modernism, however, was to be chosen as a director or professor for a seminary or Catholic university; any director or professor so tainted was to be removed from his position. Equal care and severity were to be exercised in the examination and selection of candidates for the priesthood. Moreover, clergy enrolled in Catholic institutes or universities henceforth were not to take in secular universities courses for which their Catholic institutions had chairs.[52]

The bishops were to do everything in their power, including solemn interdict, to drive modernist writings, or writings savouring of or promoting modernism, out of their dioceses. Even if a book had been granted an _imprimatur_ elsewhere, a bishop, after taking "the advice of prudent persons," should condemn it if he saw fit. In certain cases it sufficed to prohibit a book only to the clergy. But Catholic booksellers were never to sell books condemned by the bishop. It was insufficient simply to hinder the reading and selling of bad books. Many publications required the permission of the bishop; he was to be most strict in granting it, and to make this control effective, official censors were to be appointed in each diocese. Furthermore, any priest already having permission to edit a paper or periodical was to be warned and then deprived of the permission if he misused it. Any priest who was a correspondent or collaborator of a periodical and who contributed matter contaminated with modernism was also to be warned and prevented from writing. And henceforth the bishop was to permit congresses of priests only on very rare occasions. All these remedies would be of little avail if not effectively carried out. Therefore, every diocese was to institute without delay a "Council of Vigilance," bound to secrecy in its deliberations and decisions. Its functions would include detecting and taking measures against all traces and signs of modernism in publications and teaching. Finally, all bishops were henceforth to submit to the Holy See periodically a careful report concerning the things decreed in _Pascendi_ and the doctrines current among their clergy, particularly in seminaries and other Catholic institutions.[53]

In concluding the encyclical, the Pope remarked that the Church's opponents "will doubtlessly abuse what We have said to refurbish the old calumny by which We are traduced as the enemy of science and of the progress of humanity." As a new answer to such charges, he announced his intention of establishing a special institute "in which, through the co-operation of those Catholics who are most eminent for their learning, the advance of science and every other department of knowledge may be promoted under the guidance and teaching of Catholic truth."[54]

Having summarized _Pascendi_, we must frankly recognize the following two things. On one hand, the encyclical had fabricated "modernism" in the Church--no Catholic intellectual held the system condemned as "modernism" in _Pascendi_. On the other hand (as Hügel once pointed out to Maude Petre in a letter of March 13, 1918), there were "strongly subjectivist" views really held which _Pascendi_ lumped together. Some views of some of the more extreme liberal Catholic intellectuals--most notably, Loisy--stood censured in and together with those of their views that the encyclical had distorted.

The moderate Wilfrid Ward had hoped that the Vatican would not think it necessary to combat excessive liberalism by striking a heavy blow. He had hoped for a minimum of censure by the church authorities and a maximum of intellectual freedom. At work on Newman's biography, he vividly recalled the 1860's and the reign of Pius IX.

Though he had concluded from his study of history that
there was a constant ebb and flow in the amount of activity
by Catholic intellectuals and its toleration by ecclesiastical authorities, he was sorry to see what he regarded as
the repression of the 1860's returning.[55]

The chapter on "The Encyclical _Pascendi_" in Maisie
Ward's biography of her father Wilfrid Ward depicts him
fairly accurately--<u>as far as it goes</u>.[56] But, while she
does tell us that his immediate reactions to _Pascendi_ were
often vehement and his private letters concerning the
encyclical were frequently "rash," the extent of his
vehemence and the details are not given. The inadvertent
result is a rather attenuated view of Wilfrid Ward among
some students of English Roman Catholic attitudes in the
late nineteenth and early twentieth centuries. In the
following pages, I shall attempt to add to the picture of
Wilfrid Ward and his distress in the months immediately
following the promulgation of _Pascendi_ in September, 1907.
In the final chapter of the present book, I shall discuss
the effects of the papal suppression of modernism on his
intellectual activities and, lastly, his retrospective
judgment of modernism.

Pascendi upset Ward intensely. He remarked that the
details of the encyclical were "the greatest triumph ever
obtained (perhaps) by the narrow school which Newman hated."
The people who were miserable over the encyclical were "the
moderate loyal party." Ward thought that Loisy and Tyrrell
rejoiced in the papal letter because its analysis of modernism, beside noting grave errors, included views that "nearly
all reasonable Catholics hold." And while Ward agreed that
an effective blow at the extreme modernists was needed, he
saw _Pascendi_ as "an appalling misfire both from its taking

up positions which cannot be held and for its impossible violence." It would have made Newman "miserable."[57]

The initial reaction of the Duke of Norfolk, Ward's confidant on ecclesiastical matters, was perhaps typical of many Catholics in England. He had expected that the encyclical would "deal with matters more concerning everyday life," and he was "rather relieved to find it only concerned philosophical problems" of which he knew nothing. He was surprised, therefore, to find that Ward thought so seriously of its probable results. He remarked that the tone in which modernists were spoken of seemed "unfortunate and undignified." He inferred that it was "a survival of ancient usage."[58]

In a letter to Norfolk marked "_Private_," Ward gave his view of _Pascendi_ in detail. He regarded it as the nemesis that Newman had foreseen "arising from Popes trying to give the Church _intellectual_ instructions by Encyclicals-- which was never done before Pius IX's time." Thus _Pascendi_ itself was "a piece of 'modernism.'" Its theology was drawn up not by a keen mind alive to contemporary religious controversies--or even to the established facts of history--but by "a scholastic theologian," who might be "an anti-Newmanist, as they often are," and who condemned modernists "on certain points in terms which beyond question equally condemn Newman's theories." The only simple way out of the situation--"preliminary to a more accurate statement for which they _must_ employ competent people and not exclusively mere scholastics"--was to say that the doctrines condemned in _Pascendi_ were condemned only in the sense in which they were found in the works "of the Modernist writers alluded to and based on their principles." In the long run, the new problems were so difficult and complicated that the pope would never be able to teach firmly on the matters in question until he had permitted the freest discussion--despite its

196

attendant dangers and the unsettlement it might hasten.
Yet the pope was now stopping free discussion. Ward thought
the writer of the encyclical had apparently said to himself:
"'there are dangerous men. What have they said? Let us
read it all carefully and condemn it all.'" Having thus
burnt the wheat with the tares, Pascendi then erected a
form of scholastic philosophy that even Ward's father,
William George Ward, "with all his love of scholastic
theology and desire to agree with Rome, said was a constant
trial to him from its hopeless inadequacy to convince any
thinking mind familiar with the problems now before us."
Ward noted that Pascendi nowhere said that the teachings
condemned were only condemned in the sense in which extreme
modernists held them, or so far as they involved certain
principles. He longed to find such a statement. Some condemnations struck him as justified: "A kind of subjectivism
which makes religion fundamentally emotion is condemned; the
view that dogmas are only the work of the intellect in
expressing religious experience is condemned. A form of
the doctrine of immanence which makes God almost undistin-
guishable from man is condemned." Alongside of such serious
errors, however, also condemned was the teaching that dogmatic propositions are the symbols of a reality surpassing
them—which, Ward remarked, "in propositions relating to
the infinite God is undoubtedly the doctrine of St. Thomas
Aquinas and of Newman and of every competent thinker."
Similarly censured was the idea that the laity could contribute to progress in the Church—as if a good thought
helpful to theology or philosophy was less valuable if it
came "from the brain of a layman, and a good work less good
from lay hands."[59] Norfolk wrote back to Ward in alarm,
and warned him not to publish anything at present on the
encyclical. He felt that if Ward now wrote and published a

criticism of _Pascendi_, no matter how respectfully worded, it would "prejudice you enormously with very many people."[60]

In a letter to _The Times_, the Newman scholar W. J. Williams maintained that _Pascendi_ had condemned Newman's most characteristic propositions. He remarked that many converts had been led into the Church by Newman's arguments which the encyclical treated "with a contempt not only injurious to the great writer who used them, but also grossly insulting to the majority of educated English Catholics." He added that he was only saying publicly what nearly every Catholic was saying privately.[61] Ward immediately wrote to Norfolk that Williams' statement was "precisely true. Not one or two but all the characteristic fundamental positions of Newman are included in close detail in what the Encyclical describes as modernism"--even though some other elements, condemned as modernism, would have "horrified Newman."[62] In reply to Williams' letter, John Norris, the superior of the Birmingham Oratory which Newman had founded, wrote _The Times_ that he had just received information "from the highest authority that the 'genuine doctrine and spirit of Newman's Catholic teaching are not hit by the Encyclical, but the theories of many who wrongly seek refuge under a great name are obviously censured.'" Writing to Norris immediately, Ward said: "'Deo gratias.' I simply can't express the relief I felt when I read your letter in the 'Times' and the words you quote."[63]

Before the appearance of Norris' letter on November 4, Ward had consulted some experienced theologians. He had remembered the mass of misunderstanding created in 1864 by Pius IX's encyclical _Quanta Cura_ and the _Syllabus of Errors_, "owing to a hasty interpretation of these documents, which ignored their technical character." The theologians Ward consulted about Pius X's _Pascendi_--"all, without exception"-- told him that the passages in question contained no censure

on Newman's opinions. Ward took Norris' disclaimer as con-
firming what they said.[64]

Gasquet, who had been asked a few months earlier to
preside over the Roman commission revising the text of the
Vulgate, replied in The Times to Williams' letter. Expressing amazement at Williams' tone toward the Pope, Gasquet
said that even if he had not comprehended the encyclical,
he would have felt obliged to submit to its directions. He
absolutely denied that Newman's thought had been censured
and pointed to Norris' disclaimer made on the "highest
authority."[65] Writing to a friend, Ward commented: "I do
not think Gasquet quite happy in today's 'Times.'" In a
postscript, Ward said: "Merry del Val is, I take it, the
high authority alluded to by Norris."[66]

Replying to Gasquet, Williams wrote The Times that
Newman's Oratorians themselves must have been concerned
whether their founder's teaching had been condemned, for
they had recourse to the "highest authority"; this indicated,
to say the least, that the encyclical was ambiguous on the
point. Williams cited a remark made by Newman in the notes
to his Letter to the Duke of Norfolk: "The Pope cannot help
having sycophants." Although saying he was far from suggesting that Gasquet was a sycophant, Williams maintained
that this quotation exemplified what Newman thought not
about liberal Catholics but about extreme ultramontanes.
He denied that he had spoken disrespectfully of the Pope.[67]

Williams' second letter again drew replies from
Norris and Gasquet. Norris denied that the Oratorians had
thought Newman's teaching was censured, and said that it
had been Williams' first letter to The Times which led them
to apply for an authoritative disclaimer.[68] Gasquet
repeated that the disclaimer received by Norris ought to
settle the matter. He cited as additional proof The Times
Roman correspondent's report of an article in the

Osservatore Romano. The article denied absolutely that Pascendi had identified Newman with the modernists, and maintained that scholars could easily show the deep difference between Newman's teachings and those condemned in Pascendi.[69] Gasquet added that he had received no order or word from Rome to write his previous letter to The Times. He concluded that if one should appeal to Newman at all, his life and work taught a sincere submission to authority.[70] In an ensuing letter to The Times Robert Dell, identifying himself as a "modernist," maintained that despite what had already been said the encyclical had condemned Newman's essential idea of the development of dogma and had denied that dogma could undergo any modification. This was, he wrote, the natural and plain meaning of the encyclical.[71]

The Pope himself was apparently pleased with Gasquet's replies to Williams denying that Newman had been hit. By the end of the month Gasquet had what he described as a delightful interview with the Pope who had on his table translations of Gasquet's two letters to The Times.[72] But Ward was suspect in some quarters in Rome. He heard from John S. Vaughan, a friend in Rome, that Williams "has done you harm. They, in some way, seem to connect you two together."[73] Vaughan had already asked Ward whether, as editor of the Dublin Review, he was going to write anything on the encyclical: "They are all on the look out for some pronouncement [of yours]; and will read what you write with a judicial not to say critical spirit."[74]

Ward had thought of entering the public controversy over Newman. In a draft of a letter to The Times, he said the authoritative disclaimer from Rome should have disposed of the suggestion raised by Williams and Dell that Pascendi struck Newman's teaching. Nevertheless, he understood that "so far as the real meaning and intention of a technical Roman document are concerned the way in which the ordinary

reader may approach it at first sight is a misleading one."
Pascendi had been to him a matter of some difficulty, but
the theological experts whom he consulted had informed him
that Newman's views were not censured.[75]

In an ensuing private correspondence with Williams,
Ward explained further. He told Williams that the very
narrowness of Pascendi justified the view of theologians
that, technically speaking, the only condemnation was "on
the whole system--which includes sheer subjectivism and a
God immanent and not transcendent." Now preparing an article
on Pascendi for the Dublin Review, Ward felt justified in
his article in making the most of the authoritative disclaimer from Rome--Newman's God was transcendent, and he
was no mere subjectivist. On the other hand, Ward had
informed the Dublin's censor that he would resign as editor
unless he could intimate that, though he accepted the
encyclical as a pontifical act, he did not like it. Moreover, as editor, Ward had formed certain criteria for a
candid and truthful article on Pascendi, and he had already
declined an article by Bishop O'Dwyer of Limerick because
it had not met them. At present, O'Dwyer was threatening
to denounce Ward publicly, but Ward hoped it would not lead
to his resignation as editor. He went on to tell Williams
that he thought "theological minimism a necessity." Yet it
was now getting close to "sheer equivocation, owing to the
high hand of Roman authorities"--"'our present system is
papal absolutism tempered by theological equivocation.'"
Ward believed even excessive minimism to be justifiable
under the present system, "as the only way out of greater
evils."[76]

In another letter, he told Williams that he had
deplored Pascendi deeply "to everyone, in England and Rome
as well." The Vatican knew his views fully. He had consistently held that the true course was to make it understand

201

that much of what it included in modernism was true and indispensable, and could only be censured as found in a censured system. All the theologians whom Ward had consulted took this view--including those "in constant communication with the Vatican." The Vatican confirmed the view in regard to the Newman passages. Ward held that the only way out of the situation--aside from revolution--was this theological interpretation, which enabled "the authorities to retreat from an untenable position without explicitly admitting a mistake." While it involved a non-natural interpretation of parts of Pascendi taken alone, it was "the most natural and only possible interpretation of all relevant authorities taken together." It was, therefore, the most straightforward course available--despite any quibbling involved. Ward informed Williams that Archbishop Bourne told him that even the Revue du Clergé Francais, which was much more liberal than the Dublin, had accepted Pascendi, and Ward must do likewise. Nevertheless, Ward's article would clearly intimate that he sacrificed none of his convictions and that, intellectually, he accepted Pascendi only in the most minimistic sense. He agreed with Williams that things were "terribly bad in Rome from an intellectual point of view."[77]

Williams, on the other hand, started from a different standpoint and with a different object than Ward. He had always hoped that Catholics would take the first opportunity to show that papal power was not absolute against a majority of educated Catholics. He was looking out for a chance to establish a precedent "for what you call rebellion, but what I call lawful and constitutional resistance." Such an occasion had now arisen, and Williams hoped that Catholics would make it impossible for popes to be tyrannical again.[78] He regarded Ward "as the only representative of sane Catholicism left to us in the Catholic Press who is at

the same time a recognized spokesman of English Catholics."[79]
But he thought that, within a short time, it would appear
completely absurd to have acquiesced in a document "which
is openly ridiculed as coming from a Pope who is half off
his head."[80] Williams said he felt keenly with Ward in his
terribly difficult situation and apparent isolation. The
ecclesiastical authorities stamp on every hand held out in
an attitude of reverence. Williams did not think that Ward
should resign his editorship yet. Even if Williams had
been imprudent, he was sure "it is historically useful that
an apparent condemnation of Newman should not be allowed to
pass without strong and even immoderate opposition." But
he did not think he was imprudent.[81]

Ward published his article on Pascendi in the
January issue of the Dublin Review.[82] He began by saying
that he was bound to accept and obey the encyclical. He
identified the root principle censured in the encyclical
as subjectivism in religion: "the identification of religion
with sentiment or emotion rather than with belief in objective truth, issuing in the conception of a deity immanent
in man and not transcendent, and of dogmatic formulæ as no
longer the expression of facts--of the dogmatic truths of
revelation--but as the mind's reflection on its subjective
religious experience." He thought it very strange that
persons had associated Newman with modernism, for Newman
had been a life-long opponent of that form of liberalism
represented by subjectivism in religion. Ward observed
that Pascendi had been severely criticized and attacked in
several English periodicals. Many questions, including the
expediency of the encyclical, its direct bearing on Catholic
thought, and its consequences, had been raised. He had been
asked to discuss these questions fully, particularly in
relation to the activity of Catholic thinkers in the Dublin
and elsewhere. But now was not the time for such a public

discussion since it would be incompatible with Catholic obedience and loyalty when the highest authority had just rendered a decision. Nevertheless, he could attempt to correct certain misrepresentations of the encyclical. In this, he had already consulted with expert theologians and received their sanction for what he had to say. Ward stated his arguments that the encyclical was a technical document, that it had to be considered in relation to traditional Catholic theological positions, and that each part of it had to be read in context and not taken as an isolated statement. "But in our modern world a document of this kind, technical and almost medieval in its construction, is read by large numbers as a newspaper article. Or more probably scraps or isolated passages are read, and their prima facie meaning, if each be taken alone, is flourished before the world as the real one, and as containing a position which opposes what all great Catholic theological thinkers have taught."[83]

In concluding his article, Ward referred to the historical example of Aristotelianism in the thirteenth century. In the early part of that century, rationalistic and pantheistic excesses accompanied the introduction of Aristotelianism, yet even those who advanced unorthodox excesses had not labored in vain. What was good in their writings was subsequently used by Thomas Aquinas and other theologians, who by the middle of the century had successfully purged Aristotelianism of rationalist and pantheistic excesses and had made it serviceable to Catholic theology. Ward suggested that perhaps in a similar manner what was true in the early work of some of the modernists would not be lost. In any case, Pascendi was a solemn warning against modernist excesses in future Catholic writings. In conclusion, Ward assessed the immediate future for the Catholic intellectual:

Toleration and sympathy for the attempt to accomplish what may be a pressing necessity in the interests of Catholic thought, can only be won now by scrupulously preserving the attitude of loyalty without which such work is disintegrating and cannot be assimilated by Catholic theology. Even if this may sometimes involve for a time abstaining from the public discussion of some problems raised by the new sciences, which must ultimately be dealt with, such self-restraint avoids also what is even intellectually a great evil from the point of view of Christian thought, namely, that rationalistic "Liberalism" which follows, in Cardinal Newman's phrase, from "the exercise of thought upon matters in which, from the constitution of the human mind, thought cannot be brought to any successful issue."[84]

Congratulating Ward on his treatment of _Pascendi_, William Barry commented that it was certainly no time for plunging into details. Ward would be "scanned with great and not always benevolent curiosity in Rome."[85] The influential Bishop Hedley regarded Ward's article as satisfactory; his only criticism was that he wished Ward would have welcomed the encyclical more warmly. On the other hand, liberal Catholics to the left of Ward were not so satisfied. Hügel told Ward that he could hardly have said less in favor of _Pascendi_ and remained editor of the _Dublin Review_. Hügel suggested that Ward's resignation might have been "more satisfactory to your own conscience and more useful to the cause, as not only I, but as I think you yourself understand it."[86] In reality, Hügel's suggestion was at odds with Ward's understanding of the cause of the reconciliation of modern science and faith. Ward was determined to prove that a Catholic intellectual could remain absolutely orthodox while modernists hoped to show the opposite. He refused to resign the _Dublin_ when his resignation might be taken to mean that a Catholic position could not be at once both intellectual and orthodox.[87]

In contrast to these agitated reactions to Pascendi, Edmund Bishop regarded the encyclical as a relief. He took it as a final confirmation of his pessimistic predictions. He had regarded the reign of Leo XIII only as an interlude; in his view, Lamentabili and Pius X's Pascendi completed Pius IX's crushing of lay intellectual activity within the Church. But if Pascendi had denied the laity an ecclesiastical function, it had also thereby relieved the laity of responsibility and freed it to serve God by serving truth as conscience might dictate. Bishop was not despairing of the Church, but he believed that at the time laymen had no chance of changing the policy of the Roman authorities.[88] He had attempted neither to influence the policy of ecclesiastical officials nor to deal with the burning contemporary intellectual issues facing Christianity; he had confined himself to scholarly research in the history of Western liturgy and related areas.

Alec R. Vidler, in his Variety of Catholic Modernists, Ch. vi, "An Unrecognized Modernist," argues that Bishop was in private a modernist, although he has not been recognized as such. He was not known to the public as a modernist, nor were his public actions such. In that chapter, Dr. Vidler presents a very good case for his point about Bishop--which I accept. There is a letter from Bishop to James Hope, dated January 5, 1908, among the Wilfrid Ward Papers that somewhat qualifies Bishop's modernism, however. The relevant part of the letter is not in the draft of the letter among the Bishop Papers at Downside Abbey. Apparently, Bishop added it in writing the letter: "With all the will in the world to be brief, this is terribly long already. I dare not therefore aborder your letter to the Rota. Needless to say how entirely I agree with you as to 'resistance,' a surcease of the 'Newman boom'; also doubtless as to the need of a warning, a danger signal, from Rome as to excesses already committed; or indeed of a condemnation of a certain limited number of definite exorbitations. But the gravamen against the Encyclical is that it has taken advantage of this occasion to promulgate a whole positive system in both the intellectual and spiritual domains. I do not see how this objection is to be got over."[89]

Bishop told his friend Everard Green that he was determined not to reflect upon either Loisy or Tyrrell. He would join in no shouting at them since, though neither had helped him, both had tried "their best to help others whom the priests and levites passing by on the other side of the way just neglected and left helpless."[90] About the same time, he wrote that what he objected to was this: conjectures were made the basis of school doctrines that were used in turn "to override the mere plain evidence of documents. This has been going on for now nearly 250 years."[91]

Hügel read Pascendi as a climactic blow dealt by the Roman authorities for the purpose of suppressing completely freedom of thought and attempts to reconcile Catholicism to the modern world. He told Loisy that the encyclical demonstrated the incompatibility of scholastic epistemology with the results of criticism and that it showed a total lack of Christian charity by attacking the persons of modernists. Using his favorite argument, he added that it had not condemned his modernist friends since the modernism condemned was the inverse of scholasticism and, therefore, just as opposed to their views as was scholasticism. To Tyrrell, he said he could sympathize with the position of the Pope, "a peasant of simple seminary training and speaking to some 200 million souls, of whom doubtless a good nine-tenths, at least, are even less cultured than himself, and whom he is sincerely trying

to defend against what he conceives to be deadly error.
We can afford to be magnanimous; and is it not a duty to
be so?"[92] Although feeling a deep aversion toward
Pascendi, Hügel was still determined to maintain as best
he could his different loyalties to the Church, to historical and Biblical criticism, and to his modernist friends.

In November, Pius X issued the motu proprio
Praestantia excommunicating all who defended any of the
doctrines or views condemned by Lamentabili or Pascendi.
Although seemingly falling under this category, Hügel was
informed by Bishop Bonomelli and others that no individual
need apply to himself such a general excommunication; it
was up to ecclesiastical authority to apply it individually.
That same November, all writers, buyers, sellers, and
readers of the Italian radical liberal periodical Rinnovamento were threatened with ecclesiastical penalties.
Responding to this development, Hügel advised the Rinnovamento group not to cease publication. He thought that it
was necessary to continue within the Church the fight for
the cause of "sincere Science linked hand in hand with
the sincerest Faith," and that if Italian Catholics stood
firm, Rome would treat Catholics in other countries more
discreetly. He told Tyrrell that in order to advance the
cause the Rinnovamento group would have to face excommunication. Following St. Augustine, he thought that sometimes
God allowed good men to be excommunicated; if excommunicated, they should try to remain close to the Church and
not advance heresies or schisms. In his view, the modernist crisis was such a case.[93]

Hügel himself continued to submit some articles to
Rinnovamento, but preferred not to sign them. He did not
want to provoke the authorities just when he was about to
publish The Mystical Element of Religion as Studied in
Saint Catherine of Genoa and her Friends, a book that he

had been writing for ten years.[94] Some radical liberals
thought that Hügel might unwittingly be guilty of cowardice
in seeking to decrease the risk of excommunication for himself while advising the Rinnovamento group to face excommunication.[95] But the Rinnovamento group had to choose
between the alternatives of risking excommunication or
ceasing publication; Hügel did not. By avoiding condemnation he avoided discrediting the work he had already done
within the Church. Moreover, his views were quite different from those of some of his more radical friends.[96]

Loisy reacted more vehemently to Pascendi than did
Hügel. He was annoyed by what he regarded as the personal
defamation of modernists and the caricaturing of their
ideas. Furthermore, he thought the encyclical had wrong-
fully constructed a modernist system and imputed it to
each individual modernist, although he admitted the Pope
was within his rights in indicating the logical connections
among the various elements of modernism and in drawing out
the ultimate consequences of its ideas. Writing to Merry
del Val to tell the Pope of his attitude toward Pascendi,
Loisy said he was deeply depressed by the encyclical, its
denunciation of opinions not really held by those to whom
they were imputed, and, even more, its defamation of the
persons of modernists. He added that he recognized neither
his teaching nor himself in the modernist system depicted
by the encyclical. Loisy had already concluded that his
excommunication was inevitable. He realized that his
actual views stood censured in and together with those of
his views that he thought Lamentabili and Pascendi had
altered. While awaiting further developments, he prepared
for publication his Les Évangiles Synoptiques and also a
new little book, Simples réflexions, which dealt with
Lamentabili and Pascendi.[97] The decision to publish the
latter was made against the advice of his friend Hügel,

who thought that a new polemical work would hurt many people.[98]

In January, 1908, the Bishop of Langres, the diocese in which Loisy resided, received an order from Merry del Val demanding in the Pope's name that "Abbé Loisy must declare without restriction that he condemns all and every one of the propositions condemned by the decree Lamentabili as confirmed by the motu proprio Praestantia, as Holy Church condemns them, and that he condemns Modernism as the Holy Father has condemned it in the encyclical Pascendi." Otherwise the Pope would be obliged "to terminate the scandal which his continuance in the Church creates." Loisy refused to submit and announced the imminent publication of his work on the synoptic gospels. At the end of the month, Les Évangiles Synoptiques and Simples réflexions were published. On February 14, the Archbishop of Paris forbade in his diocese the reading of Loisy's latest two books "under penalty not only of mortal sin but also of excommunication expressly reserved to the Supreme Pontiff," the same penalty applying to those who possessed or published the two books or sought to defend them. A few days later Merry del Val ordered the Bishop of Langres to give Loisy a final warning to submit, failing which he would be excommunicated. The decree of the Holy Office excommunicating Loisy was pronounced on March 7, 1908. It stated that Loisy had failed to recant his errors and had even stubbornly maintained them in further writings and in correspondence with his superiors.[99]

Shortly before Loisy's excommunication, Hügel had told Maude Petre that Loisy was "so Catholic still, thank God and not thanks to the official world."[100] On the same day that the Holy Office published its decree excommunicating Loisy, there appeared in the Tablet, by an odd coincidence, a letter by Hügel saying that Loisy did not intend to leave the Church or to deny its definitions of the faith. Nevertheless, Hügel had already become warier of some of Loisy's views. Immediately after Loisy's excommunication, Archbishop Mignot, who more than anyone else among the hierarchy had been his friend and defender, wrote to Hügel. He remarked that Loisy's confining himself only to the role of a historian and neglecting the Church's tradition meant that "either he has lost the Faith as understood by the Church--and then he will find all our observations importunate, or he is still a believer; if so, he should reassure those who believed in him and were glad to take him as a guide." Not long thereafter, Hügel, while still admiring Loisy's critical work, complained to him that in his philosophy "God is conceived as being at bottom no more than the sum of individual consciences . . . that this anima mundi hardly seems to differ essentially from matter."[101] For his part, Loisy ceased to be concerned with the affairs of the Roman Church. He was elected in 1908 to the chair that Renan had once held at the Collège de France. Subsequently, he professed a religion of humanity.

The most vehement reaction to Pascendi came from Tyrrell, who had already been distressed by the promulgation of Lamentabili and by the frustration of negotiations to regularize his status as a priest. In a memorial of his friend, Hügel analyzed in retrospect the root causes of Tyrrell's anger over the Roman pronouncements:

> These were, as to Lamentabili, its continuous assumption, indeed insistence, that official theologians have, as such, a direct magisterium over historical science, and the manner in which absolute interior assent was being expected of scholars concerning condemnations to which the condemning authorities did not bind themselves for good and all. And, as to Pascendi,

> his anger arose from its apparent contempt for
> mysticism and all the dim, inchoate gropings
> after God; its wholesale imputation of bad
> motives to respectable, hard-working scholars
> and thinkers; and its disciplinary enactments.
> It was these last two characteristics and sec-
> tions that he felt unable not to attribute to
> the Pope personally; hence his tone towards the
> Pontiff.[102]

Although Hügel agreed completely with Tyrrell on these
points,[103] his circumspect nature and Tyrrell's impetuosity
were poles apart. Responding to invitations by The Times
and by the Giornale d'Italia, Tyrrell agreed to write
articles on Pascendi while expecting to be excommunicated
for his action.[104] Commenting on notes apparently sent to
him beforehand in preparation for The Times articles,
Hügel told Tyrrell that he was impressed by his calling
attention to the most important point about Pascendi: its
rejection of the claim for the autonomy of historical
criticism from the Church's direct, not merely disciplinary,
jurisdiction.[105]

In his first Times article, Tyrrell maintained that
the encyclical had identified Catholicism with scholasticism. It asserted that the root principle of modernism
was agnosticism, meaning not that the modernist "denies
that the divine and the real are knowable; but merely that
they can be known by the scientific faculty, the Verstand
of Kant, the ratio and intellectus of the Schoolmen. . . ."
It took the object of faith as a revealed theological
statement, and denied the modernist contention that it was
on a completely different plane from science and history
with which it consequently could not conflict. Pascendi
maintained that in conflicts science must give way to
revelation, and said modernists erroneously held the opposite: that revealed statements should be subjected to
science. "If faith is revealed formula," Tyrrell admitted,

212

"no heresy could be more deadly. . . ." The encyclical also censured the conception of the source of ecclesiastical authority that he had advanced in "From Heaven, or of Men?" Moreover, according to him, it held that the "individual mind of the Pope, not the collective mind of the Church, is, of course, the sole immediate subject of Divine guidance and the ultimate source of dogmatic authority." "Is this Pius X. who speaks, or some purple 'dignitary'?" Tyrrell asked. In conclusion, he maintained that since Pascendi was based on scholastic philosophy, when this was hit the whole argument of the encyclical was in ruins.[106]

As the encyclical had distorted many of the positions of modernists, Tyrrell in his second Times article grossly caricatured its teaching:

> Religion is derived by deductive reasoning from
> natural and miraculous phenomena. God is not
> reached through inward religious experience, but
> by argument. The divinity of Christ and
> Christianity can be thus argued so as to coerce
> the understanding. The Roman Catholic Church,
> with the Papacy, the sacraments, and all its
> institutions and dogmas, was, in its entirety,
> the immediate creation of Christ when upon earth.
> There has been no vital development, but only
> mechanical unpacking of what was given from the
> first. The Scriptures were dictated by God, and
> are final in questions of science and history.
> All doctrinal guidance and ecclesiastical
> authority is mediated through the infallible
> Pope from God to the Church. The Church is the
> purely passive recipient of the guidance so
> received. The Bishops are mere delegates of the
> Pope; the priests of the Bishops. The laity have
> no active share of any kind in ecclesiastical con-
> cerns; still less in the so-called growth of the
> Church's mind. Obedience and pecuniary succour
> are their sole duties. Science is subject to the
> control of scholastic theology; secular govern-
> ment is subject to the control of ecclesiastical
> government in mixed matters. Their jurisdiction
> is in the same order; only in different depart-
> ments. There has been no true enlightenment and

213

                    progress in modern times outside the Church.
                    There is no element of truth in any other
                    religious system.

The encyclical was a "clear exposition of the tenets of
scholastic theology and of its claim to control and dictate
to history and science," had adopted "frankly inquisitorial
methods by which this claim is to be enforced," and provided "a clear and final demonstration of the futility of
pouring new wine into old bottles." But history had now
worked out to their impossible results both sixteenth-
century solutions to the problem of liberty and authority
in the Church: the Reformation solution of unfettered
liberty and the Counter-Reformation solution of unfettered
authority. Perhaps the problem of liberty and authority
could now admit of a better solution. A modernist should
not leave the Roman Church since by so doing he would
admit "that Catholicism was bound hand and foot to its
scholastic interpretation and to its medieval Church polity;
that the Pope had no duties and the people no rights."
Nevertheless, many people would be lost to the Church
because Pius X came forward in Pascendi "with a stone in
one hand and a scorpion in the other." In conclusion,
Tyrrell remarked that the encyclical had not gotten to the
root cause of modernism; until this had been grasped, the
remedies might be much worse than useless.[107]

        After seeing Tyrrell's Times articles in print and
his Giornale d'Italia article, Hügel commended him on his
philosophical and theological expositions but regretted
his hot tone toward the Pope. Tyrrell replied: "With more
time and quiet the shots could have been better aimed.
Now they are delivered for better or for worse, and I leave
the rest to God and Law."[108] On October 22, 1907, he
received notice from the Bishop of Southwark, in whose
diocese he was residing, that his articles had raised a

                            214

question about his right to receive the sacraments; having referred the matter to Rome, the bishop had been informed that Tyrrell was forbidden the sacraments and his case reserved to the Apostolic See.[109] Tyrrell's response to what was tantamount to excommunication contrasted with Loisy's reaction. Whereas Loisy said, in effect, that he would go when he was put out, Tyrrell maintained that he would stay and the ecclesiastical authorities could not cast him out.[110]

Wilfrid Ward privately commented to Norfolk that the Pope utterly misconceived Tyrrell's motives and work, but Tyrrell lost his temper and placed himself in the wrong. Ward thought that when the ecclesiastical authorities began to snub Tyrrell years ago, he "became too modern and fell too much into the arms of non-Catholic thinkers." Ward believed that he had now said some really unorthodox things, though he could modify and correct them "without a _very_ deep change." Nevertheless, he started "with a wonderfully keen perception of present difficulties and the lines of reasoning necessary for keeping Catholicism in such a position as to appeal to educated men." Ward had just returned from St. Edmund's: "Nearly every able divinity student there has all Tyrrell's earlier works. He helped them as no one else did." Though he had now gone too far, he had written "much more that is good than bad; I refer to his earlier writings." But _Pascendi_ took pretty well all that he had said and condemned it all--"good and bad alike."[111] In addition, W. J. Williams told Ward he heard that many Roman ecclesiastics, who were authorities on the subject, thought "the excommunication of Tyrrell, without any process, extremely doubtful."[112]

Pascendi and his excommunication embittered Tyrrell against Rome. Writing to friends, he was inclined to make remarks such as: Rome has always shifted the cry for reform "by the same methods, for the same ends, money and power." "Rome cares nothing for religion--only for power; and for religion as a source of power."[113] Moreover, he began to move further in an immanentist direction. To a French friend, he wrote: "My imagination is quite cured of the outside God; for I feel that the inward spirit pervades and transcends the whole universe and reveals to me but an infinitesimal fraction of its Will and End and Truth and Nature. I find most help in reading the Psalms and interpreting them into this immanent view of God, e.g. . . . Tu est Deus fortitudo mea--all fortitude and strength is the strength of Conscience. . . . That is our Refuge, our Rock, our consolation in trouble."[114] Concerned about Tyrrell, Hügel--who had seen him almost daily for about seven weeks--wrote to Maude Petre that he had noticed again Tyrrell's unappeased craving for the kind of activity he had when giving conferences, retreats, "and trusted by and helping souls as a Catholic Priest and religious." Tyrrell had told Hügel: "all this controversial, church-political, newspaper writing makes one empty and bitter. I long to get back to mystical ways and mystical subjects, and yet I cannot, I am out of tune for them."[115] Writing to Tyrrell, Hügel acknowledged that his friend was in "fog and darkness" but was confident that it would pass and hoped that his mystical bent toward the spiritual life would soon be reawakened.[116]

In a Lenten pastoral in spring 1908, Archbishop Mercier of Malines addressed himself to modernism and pointed to Tyrrell as its chief exponent. This provoked from Tyrrell a book in reply. In discussing the forthcoming publication, Hügel told Tyrrell that he felt apprehensive, for Tyrrell's true vocation lay in his mystical bent toward the spiritual life and not in controversy, even though he was admittedly a brilliant controversialist.[117]

216

Nevertheless, Tyrrell's Medievalism, written hastily and under pressure, was printed in July. If more eloquent and impassioned than some of his other work, it was not, in his own opinion, so thoughtful and constructive.[118] In it, he maintained that the modernist and the scholastic, whom he referred to as the medievalist, were both Catholics in that both believed in the Church as a living organism. While caricaturing the position of the "medievalist," Tyrrell expressed a significant quality of modernism: "The difference is that, whereas the Medievalist regards the expression of Catholicism, formed by the synthesis between faith and the general culture of the thirteenth century, as primitive and practically final and exhaustive, the Modernist denies the possibility of such finality and holds that the task is unending just because the process of culture is unending."[119]

For a time, especially after the publication of Medievalism, Tyrrell thought of returning to the Anglican Church of his youth. But he eventually decided to continue his attempts to advance the modernist cause within the Roman Church.[120] Hügel stood opposed to conversion to any other church, and his opposition provoked some passing irritation from Tyrrell: "In your just revolt against the fallacy of simplification, I sometimes wonder whether you are not driven to value complexity for its own sake."[121] Nevertheless, Hügel persisted in his hopes that Tyrrell would again take up his bent toward mysticism and the spiritual life. He told him that he was a mystic who could find God, Christ, and the Church only "in deep recollection, purification, quietness, intuition, love." Hügel warned, "not all the wit, vehemence, subtlety, criticisms, learning that you can muster (and how great they are!) will ever, without those, be other than ruinous to others as well as to yourself."[122]

217

Unaware that he had Bright's disease, Tyrrell in the last few months of his life was moving away from ideas of immanence toward a reemphasis on transcendence. Three months before his death, he wrote to Hügel: "I feel that my past work has been dominated by the Liberal-Protestant Christ, and doubt whether I am not bankrupt. . . . If we cannot secure huge chunks of transcendentalism, Christianity must go. Civilisation can do (and has done) all that the purely immanental Christ of Matthew Arnold is credited with. The other world emphasis, the doctrine of immortality, was what gave Christianity its original impulse and sent martyrs to the lions."[123] And about a month before his death, he wrote to Alfred Fawkes, a minor modernist figure who had recently returned to the Anglican Church:

> As to "development," we all want to claim Jesus. But I fear He belongs to the obscurantists. . . . Eternal life, which was the substance of His Gospel, was not the moral life, but the super-moral. . . . Liberal Protestantism is the development of the ethic He adopted and exemplified in common with the prophets and saints of all times; but not of His Gospel, His Message. Of that, Catholicism is the development. . . . I hope I am wrong; but I feel I have been reading the Gospel all my life through nineteenth-century glasses, and that now scales, as it were, have fallen from my eyes.[124]

Tyrrell was now at work on what proved to be his last book, Christianity at the Cross-roads. Reemphasizing the transcendency of God, he depicted a Christ not of Catholic orthodoxy but still contained within the Church's faith and worship although disfigured by Catholic theology. He believed Catholicism still taught the true Christ more adequately than other religions, even if in his view official Catholicism needed a modernist transformation.[125] In his memorial of his friend, Hügel said that the book contained "some passages which may easily give more pain

than help," but was suffused "by a keen sense of the close-
ness and continuity between our Lord's preaching, precisely
where it is now liable to sound strange and difficult to us
all, and the Catholic Church's practice, temper, and teaching down to our times." Hügel concluded: "Never was there
a less 'liberal' book, if by 'liberal' be meant any weaken-
ing of the sense of the transcendency of God, and of
religion as essentially neither science nor even ethics,
but the hunger for and certainty of God, a super-earthly,
future life, and Christ, God with us."[126]

In July 1909 while Tyrrell was residing at Storrington the final stages of his disease suddenly began. He
became violently ill and was bed-ridden for the last days
of his life. In an apoplectic condition, he received conditional absolution and the last rites, and died on July
15. Fearing that reports of a death-bed retractation by
Tyrrell might arise, his friend Maude Petre, with Hügel's
advice and consent, published a letter in The Times saying
that he had received the last rites but had made no last
minute retractation. Although his friends tried to secure
a Catholic burial for him, ecclesiastical officials refused
to permit it.[127]

Tyrrell's Christianity at the Cross-roads was published posthumously. It contains his last assessment of
the status and prospects of Christianity vis-a-vis modern
thought. He succinctly expressed his view in the Preface
to the work: "With all its accretions and perversions
Catholicism is, for the Modernist, the only authentic
Christianity. Whatever Jesus was, He was in no sense a
Liberal Protestant. All that makes Catholicism most repugnant to present modes of thought derives from Him. The
difficulty is, not Catholicism, but Christ and Christianity.
. . . We may be sure that religion, the deepest and most
universal exigency of man's nature, will survive. We cannot

be so sure that any particular expression of the religious idea will survive."[128]

Contemporary historical criticism had raised the question: could ecclesiasticism of any sort be found in Jesus? Could even the earliest Christianity be reconciled with Christ? Taking up the problem, Tyrrell rejected the liberal Protestant interpretation of Jesus once and for all; instead, he adopted the consistent eschatological interpretation of Weiss, Schweitzer, and Loisy: "Jesus did not come to reveal a new ethics of this life, but the speedy advent of a new world in which ethics would be superseded." Tyrrell clearly distinguished his view of the Gospel of Christ from that of liberal Protestantism: "The whole tendency of Liberal Protestantism is to minimise the transcendence by establishing a sort of identity of form between this life and the other. . . . Without this concession to transcendentalism [other-worldliness], Liberal Protestantism would not be a religion at all." Against Liberal Protestantism he sought to justify Catholicism, but a Catholicism which stood in need of a modernist transformation: "As 'dogma' usually stands for some defined point of theology, imposed by ecclesiastical authority, it is affirmed confidently [by liberal Protestantism] that Jesus was not dogmatic. But it is vain to deny that Jesus imposed, with the authority of Divine revelation, and as a matter of life and death, that vision of the transcendental world which the Church has clothed in a theological form. If He did not impose philosophical formulas He imposed the revelation, the imaginative vision, which they formulate." But Catholicism's underlying fidelity to the Christianity of Christ was just the problem for Tyrrell: what value could Jesus' apocalyptic visions now have for modern religious thought?[129]

Tyrrell's radical distinction between Catholicism's dogmas and what he considered to be Jesus' apocalyptic revelation constituted the basis of his attempt to reconcile Catholicism with contemporary thought. He argued that whereas Jesus had regarded His own apocalyptic imagery as literal fact, the modern mind might be able to accept it as imagery, but not as fact. Although some of the other modernists eventually abandoned belief in a transcendent God when they had adopted such symbolism, Tyrrell's Christian mysticism helped to preserve his belief in the transcendent. He suggested that the sense of the supernatural had much to do with Jesus' mysterious power over people. He doubted that even Christian morality would be able to hold its own if Christianity were purged of all transcendent meaning and value. He saw Jesus satisfying the mystical and moral needs of millions of people for centuries, and considered His moral influence to have depended largely on His mystical influence. Tyrrell's mysticism was not one-sided. He maintained that Jesus' mysticism "in embracing God, embraced the whole world and all its spiritual interests--truth of feeling, truth of conduct, truth of knowledge. . . ." Like Hügel in The Mystical Element of Religion, Tyrrell believed that the health of a religion consisted "in the balancing and holding together of principles that tend to fly asunder and become independent and exclusive."[130]

Tyrrell was critical of traditional Catholic orthodoxy, but he was also critical of modern thought. If he shared the confidence of many of his contemporaries in the conclusions of the Biblical and historical criticism of his times, he rejected the faith that some of them had in progress: that man by his own efforts would inevitably realize something like a heaven on this earth. He stated that the optimism of "Modern Christianity" was begotten not of faith in the other world but in this world; its courage and hope depended on the belief that the Kingdom of God was the natural term of a process of social and moral development. Tyrrell commented: "Nothing is more evident than that Jesus had no such faith or hope." Liberal Protestantism had a "bland faith and hope in the present order"; it refused "to face the incurable tragedy of human life."[131] If Tyrrell here vehemently over-reacted against liberal Protestantism, his previous leanings toward immanentism as well as his desire to distinguish clearly his modernism from liberal Protestantism were reasons for his reaction.

He at least had not lost the capacity to be critical of his contemporary culture. In prophetic tones, he warned: "To-day we are so enamoured of our scientific and material progress that we have no eyes for our many decadences, even though we are face to face with social and moral chaos. We believe, with childish simplicity, that we are making straight for the millennium." He regarded the times as unfavorable to any form of Christianity that remained true to the Gospel of Christ: "At present the world that is heard and seen in public, elated with the success of science and the triumphs of invention, confident that what has done so much will do everything, is blind to the appalling residue of human misery and to the insoluble problems that are coming up slowly like storm-clouds on the horizon. Once more we are told that life will work out the cure of its own evils and change the world into Paradise." He thought that the Gospel of a transcendent life would not meet with enthusiastic faith in such a period; religion was liable to come to terms with the temper of the times. While insisting on the necessity of the transcendent element in Christianity, Tyrrell held that Christianity must also be concerned with this world: "Yet this emphasis on the other world, however necessary as a corrective, needed to be

checked and balanced by a just estimate of the meaning and
value of time in relation to eternity. He who said
'Blessed are the poor, the hungry, the suffering,' spent
His life in relieving their needs; He who said 'The night
cometh,' gave it as a motive for working while it was yet
day; He who said 'The Kingdom is at hand,' was urging men
to repentance and righteousness."[132]

In the second part of <u>Christianity at the Cross-roads</u>,
Tyrrell took up a problem suggested by the comparative study
of religions: the relation of Christianity to other religions. He said that the religious idea revealed itself
"more fully in some religions than in others; but in all,
more than in any one." Nevertheless, his view of the
Christian ecumenism of his day was unfavorable: "The tendency towards reunion among the Christian sects of to-day
is the result of weariness and decay; of scepticism as to
the value of their several systems." Was there ever to be
a universal religion? he asked. If so, he answered, it
would not come about by sinking differences; instead, it
would occur through the growth and triumph of one religion,
either new or old. Here Tyrrell expected far too much from
applications of science to religion: "May we not then con-
jecture that a relatively universal and permanent religion
would be one that rested on a knowledge of the laws and
uniformities revealed by a comparative study of religions
and a study of religious psychology? that it would be, in
some reserved sense, a scientific religion?" He had, however, another reason for his belief in the possibility of a
future unification of religion: "Yet what brings it within
the field of the possible is the growing recognition of the
universality and perpetuity of man's religious need and of
his effort to satisfy it. . . . The notion that religion is
a disease of man's intellectual childhood, something that
he throws off with his bibs and tuckers, is being rapidly

223

discredited." Might Christianity in any form ever become a universal religion? In Tyrrell's view, Protestantism could not: "Lutheranism is a development, not of Catholicism from which it is a departure, but of certain elements of Catholicism; Liberal Protestantism is a development of certain elements of Lutheranism." By their very formation and history, many religions thus excluded the possibility of Catholicity: "They have cut off too much and cannot take it on again." Tyrrell thought that Catholicism transformed by modernism might still grow into a universal religion. In his view, it was "more nearly a microcosm of the world of religions than any other known form; where we find nearly every form of religious expression, from the lowest to the highest, pressed together and straining towards unification and coherence; where the ideal of universal and perpetual validity has ever been an explicit aim; where, moreover, this ideal is clothed in a form that cannot possibly endure the test of history and science and must undergo some transformation."[133]

Whatever Tyrrell's hopes for a future Catholicism, they included no hopes for the Vatican: he was thinking "not of Catholicism in the grip of the exploiter [the Curia], but of Catholicism as a living and lived religion, as a school of souls." He observed that, in contrast, the moderate liberal Catholics entertained the hope--"which no sane Modernist entertains for a moment"--that one day some spiritual-minded Pope might, "in spite of the bureaucracy that exploits his primacy as a political asset, approve and give force to their ideas. Any sort of revolution seemed to them incompatible with substantial continuity."[134] Thus, Tyrrell did not foresee the appearance of a Pope John XXIII.

There was much of substance in Tyrrell's thought, in spite of inadequacies also present in it. His insistence that faith is more than doctrinal belief and

224

that theology is more than the intellectual elaboration of propositions was echoed in Catholic theology later in the twentieth century.[135] Tyrrell's insights also included: the higher estimation of religious experience and spiritual anthropology, the deeper examination of the relation of psychology to religion, the reemphasis on the sense of mystery, the renewed awareness of the pastoral function of theology, the less mechanical appraisal of the role of authority, greater insight into the development of dogma, the emphasis on the organic nature of the Church and the significance of the laity, a higher regard for Biblical scholarship and natural science, an appeal to leave a cultural ghetto.[136]

Tyrrell's death marked the end of open modernist resistance to the decisions of the ecclesiastical authorities.[137] Loisy had been excommunicated and ceased to be concerned with the affairs of the Roman Church; Hügel was determined to remain within the Church; Tyrrell was gone. Lesser figures involved in the modernist controversy also either parted ways with the Church, submitted to its decisions, or kept silent. In 1910, Pius X dealt the coup de grâce to modernism. He issued a motu proprio requiring all clerics before advancing to major orders and all clergy exercising ministerial functions to take an anti-modernist oath that included submission to Lamentabili and Pascendi. With this oath, modernism practically disappeared within the Roman Church.[138]

CHAPTER VI

THE AFTERMATH

The suppression of modernism was accompanied by a
virulent anti-modernist reaction which affected not only
modernists but orthodox scholars and thinkers as well.
Indeed, the immediate outcome of the modernist movement was
directly opposite to what modernists had intended. From
the beginning, Wilfrid Ward had feared that extremes would
compromise Catholic scholarship and thought. His fears
were now justified. Modernists had hoped to reconcile the
Roman Church to modern culture and, in particular, to
modern scientific criticism. Instead, attempts to effect
this reconciliation were now looked upon with greater suspicion than before, and liberals making such attempts ran
a far greater risk of ecclesiastical censure. The anti-
modernist reaction that followed the condemnation of modernism hit some orthodox scholars who had acquired reputations
for moderate steps in the direction of reconciliation.
Although the Dominican Lagrange, the foremost moderate
Catholic Biblical critic, and Mgr. Batiffol, a leading
historian of the early Church, had been among the first to
dissociate themselves from Loisy and to attack modernism,
they were struck. Lagrange had to curtail his work in
Biblical criticism and was forced for a time to leave the
École Biblique in Jerusalem. Batiffol's L'Eucharistie was
placed on the Index in 1907, and he himself was replaced as
rector of the Institut Catholique of Toulouse, a position
he had held for a decade. Duchesne was also hit. Even

226

though his L'Histoire ancienne de l'Église had received an
imprimatur, it was consigned to the Index. In fact, the
number of titles added to the Index from 1907 to 1914 was
twice the number from 1900 to 1907, and averaged fourteen
a year.[1]

Denunciation of modernists and modernist sympathizers was encouraged. This encouragement unfortunately
resulted in the formation of a private, unofficial secret
society, the Sodalitium Pianum, known also as the Sapinière,
by a certain Mgr. Umberto Benigni(1862-1934). Scattered
about Continental Europe, Sapinière agents and informers
denounced and delated persons of whom the society disapproved. The Sapinière denounced even Cardinal Amette of
Paris, Cardinal Mercier of Malines, Cardinal Piffl of
Vienna, and many diocesan Committees of Vigilance. Rome's
toleration of Benigni's activities was an indication of
the virulence of the anti-modernist reaction.[2]

Yet Gasquet was able to tell Pius X personally that,
in the present age, clergy educated without knowledge of
current literature would be useless in England at least.
But the Pope had Italy always in his thought and said that
the inroads of modernism among the clergy was very terrible.
Gasquet regarded the situation in Rome as a very difficult
one. Though Pius X was "always very good in allowing one
to speak fully and frankly" to him, many persons were
"pushing him" and the Italian seminaries gave him "great
anxiety."[3]

Two events in 1914 checked the anti-modernist
reaction. World War I began and questions of life and
death, peace and war, soon absorbed the attention that had
been focused on modernism; moreover, a new pontificate was
inaugurated upon the death of Pius X in 1914. On becoming
pope, Benedict XV issued an encyclical demanding that dis-
sension and discord among Catholics cease, stating that

where Rome had not decided views could be freely expressed without fear of denunciation, and discountenancing the use of certain appellations to distinguish Catholic from Catholic.[4] Cardinal Bourne told Mrs. Josephine Ward that this declaration of the new Pope "brought solace to many minds."[5] In a memoir to Cardinal Ferrata, the new Papal Secretary of State, Archbishop Mignot summarized some of the effects of the anti-modernist reaction on Catholic scholarship and thought; while accepting the absolute necessity of the papal condemnation of modernism in Pascendi, Mignot observed:

> Within the bosom of the Church, discouragement has
> seized upon intellectual and social workers.
> Denounced, spied upon, abused by the papers of the
> occult power [Benigni's Sapinière]; held in sus-
> picion by those who, deceived by false reports,
> suspected the honesty of their intentions--they
> found their work grown very difficult. Many a
> man withdrew once and for all from the lists who
> might have won many a victory for the Christian
> cause.
>
> This sense of unrest has made itself most
> unfortunately evident in many major seminaries,
> in religious houses of study and in university
> centres. Upon this, testimony is unanimous:
> our young men have lost the sacred passion for
> intellectual labour, and it is very difficult
> for their professors to stimulate it. After the
> enthusiasm--the often feverish enthusiasm
> admittedly--for the study of apologetics,
> exegesis, positive theology, philosophy and
> sociology, the students are now satisfied with
> a dull flat study, and theology of the hand-
> book sort.[6]

Although the anti-modernist reaction may be said to have ended in 1914, serious after-effects lingered on. In the crucial area of Biblical scholarship, fears had not yet calmed after the war and were aggravated by several ecclesiastical decisions. The Holy Office, with Cardinal Merry del

Val as its secretary from October 1914 to February 1930, decreed in May 1920 that the view advanced by Abbé Touzard in two articles on Moses and Joshua and on Moses and the Pentateuch was unsound. And in December 1923, a new edition of the Manuel biblique of Saint Sulpice, which had been widely used in seminaries in France for forty years, was placed on the Index and a severe explanatory letter was sent by Merry del Val to the Superior General of Saint Sulpice.[7] The Biblical scholar Jean Levie, a moderate French Jesuit, summarized the situation in an article in 1929: "Lastly, many exegetes, often those most competent and penetrating, fully aware of the grave historical or theological problems raised by the Old Testament, consider that any attempt at a synthesis should be put off for a while. They specialize in one of the auxiliary subjects of the Bible--Assyriology, Hebrew Grammar, problems of style, textual criticism, the history of exegesis, or the study of a limited period or a particular book--all matters less likely to be controversial." Catholic exegesis was not liberated until 1943 when Pope Pius XII promulgated the encyclical Divino afflante Spiritu, which sanctioned and ratified the work of moderate Catholic exegesis just as Leo XIII's Rerum Novarum (1891) had earlier sanctioned and ratified the social work of Manning, Ketteler, and others.[8]

The avoidance of controversial areas or taking up only specialized topics within such areas was not confined to Biblical scholarship alone. In 1922, Abbot Cuthbert Butler of Downside, the historian of the First Vatican Council and a pupil of Edmund Bishop, told Hügel: "In regard to what you say about your regret that I am not giving myself up to early Christian things,--years ago I recognized that these things--Xtian origins, New Testament, History of Dogma, etc.--have been made impossible for a priest, except on the most narrow apologetic lines. A

229

priest can publish nothing without 'imprimatur'. . . .
When the Biblical Commission got under way, and the Lamentabili and Pascendi were issued, I deliberately turned away
from all this work."[9] Butler's attitude appears to have
been typical of the attitude of many other Catholic
scholars. Some creative yet orthodox efforts in theology,
philosophy, and apologetics must have been forestalled by
the lingering after-effects of the anti-modernist reaction.
The modernist movement and its repression engendered fears
and counter-fears which produced in England, as elsewhere,
"a somewhat arid piece of intellectual history in the
twenty years subsequent to Pascendi and it was only as the
1930s wore on that, at last, a certain relaxation of institutional tension became apparent coupled with a very considerable infusion of new blood."[10]

Except for Tyrrell and Hügel, modernism had hardly
emerged in the Roman Church in England. The only other
persons who were at all conspicuous modernists were Alfred
Fawkes and Maude Petre. As we have noted, Fawkes cannot be
considered an actual adherent of Catholic modernism but
only a figure who was in touch with it and reported on it.
He left the Roman Church quietly to return to Anglicanism
in 1909.[11] Maude Petre remained faithful to Tyrrell's
general position and adopted his attitude of refusal to
leave the Church. In 1910, her bishop harassed her and
demanded that she subscribe to the condemnations of modernism. She protested and countered by asking--if an unqualified submission was required of her--would the bishop
assure her that each condemnation or proposition in
Lamentabili and Pascendi was de fide? Of course he could
not do this, since theologians generally acknowledged the
encyclical and the Holy Office decree to be non-infallible
decisions. The ·bishop responded by privately ordering the
clergy of his diocese to refuse to administer the sacraments

to her. She was able, however, to receive the sacraments elsewhere.[12] The only other significant English Catholic figure who appears to have had a close connection with the modernist movement was Robert Dell. He left the Roman Church,[13] and fell away from positive Christian belief. In a book published in 1920, he advocated a completely rationalistic position modelled on Voltaire.[14]

   The following developments in Roman Catholic intellectual life in England seem at least in part to have been a consequence of the papal suppression of modernism and the anti-modernist reaction. Even though Hügel's major published works after 1907 were generally of an orthodox nature, his influence in theology and philosophy was largely outside the Roman Communion in spite of the fact that he was one of the most influential religious thinkers of his time in England.[15] Furthermore, after the suppression of modernism, Roman Catholic scholarship in England generally avoided those areas which were most involved in the modernist controversy.[16] The phenomenon of liberal-minded English Catholics turning away from ecclesiastically controversial areas after the papal censures of the 1860's (Newman, Acton, and Simpson) had recurred after the condemnations of 1907. After _Pascendi_, Wilfrid Ward felt obliged to give up his attempts to serve as a liaison officer between orthodox Catholic positions and modern thought in England; he now turned to literary subjects, in part as an indirect means of apologetics. "Literature is the simplest way now to spread the light," William Barry remarked.[17] No other English Catholic in the succeeding years was able to fill the role of liaison officer that Ward had abandoned; his intellectual ability, literary talent, moderation, tact, wide acquaintances, and family connections had made him ideally suited for that role. After the years when Ward, Hügel, and Tyrrell were active,

one tends to think of men of letters such as G. K. Chesterton,
Hilaire Belloc, and Ronald Knox when one thinks of Catholics in intellectual life in England. In particular,
Belloc and Chesterton seem to become the most conspicuous
figures in Catholic apologetics in England after World War
I. Although they engaged in some effective apologetics,
their apologetics differed from that of Ward, Hügel, and
Tyrrell. It was not an attempt to state and develop the
grounds for Christian and Catholic belief in as precise and
clear a manner as possible,[18] and did not try to take
account of the discoveries of modern science, particularly
Biblical and historical criticism. Chesterton's apologetics, for instance, tended to attack modern civilization
which he regarded as having become ill because it had
abandoned Christianity; he sought to show how Christianity
was needed if modern man was to be restored to good health.
Indeed, Christian apologetics itself perhaps also needed a
tonic like Chesterton's brand of apologetics. It was
invigorating now to launch an offensive after having been
on the defense so long.

There were other reasons besides the anti-modernist
reaction for turning away from the problems involved in the
apparent conflict between modern scientific criticism and
religion, problems with which Ward, Hügel, and Tyrrell,
each in his own way, had dealt. For one thing, Catholic
intellectuals became preoccupied with other questions in
the twentieth century. Moreover, some problems involved in
the conflict of science and religion were resolved or demonstrated to be only apparent; for instance, some radical
criticisms of nineteenth-century Biblical critics were
rejected or altered by later scholars. Yet the feeling
that scientific criticism had irretrievably discredited
orthodox positions often remained and continued to exert an
influence on the popular mind. Thirdly, faith in science

as a substitute for religion declined among scientists
themselves in the twentieth century. In sum, the conflict
between science and religion, which had been hot in the
nineteenth century, abated. Jacques Maritain described the
new situation as follows: "the cast of mind of scientists
regarding religion and philosophy, as it appeared in the
majority of them a century ago, has now profoundly changed.
There are, no doubt, atheists among scientists, as there
are in any other category of people; but atheism is not
regarded by them as required by science. The old notion of
a basic opposition between science and religion is progres-
sively passing away. No conflict between them is possible,
Robert Millikan declared. In many scientists there is an
urge either toward more or less vague religiosity or toward
definite religious faith."[19]

In addition to its aforementioned general consequences, the papal suppression of modernism had a number of
important specific effects on the work of the leading
English liberal Catholics. After Pascendi, Wilfrid Ward
had to halt much of his intellectual work. He told a convert that it was a trial of patience, not of faith. In
January 1908, Archbishop Bourne wrote to Ward regarding his
conduct of the Dublin Review:

> In theological and philosophical matters the
> Dublin now hardly represents the ordinary views
> of Catholics in this country: it is representa-
> tive rather of that particular school of thought
> which has your sympathy. As Ordinary I am not
> called upon to intervene, as long as you remain
> within the bounds of Catholic orthodoxy, what-
> ever my private opinions may be. Were I, how-
> ever, to exercise rights of proprietorship, my
> intervention might be more insistent and more
> frequent. And the existing state of things can
> evidently continue only on the understanding
> that the peculiar nature of your Editorship is
> made quite manifest and that the views in the
> Review are accepted as the views which you

personally hold, and not the opinions of the
Proprietors, still less of the Archbishopric.

In reply to Bourne's letter, Ward wrote: "I quite understand Your Grace's view and am grateful for your letter."
Ward was grateful for the continued liberty that Bourne was
willing to allow him and for the recognition that he
remained within the bounds of orthodoxy. But he concluded
that for the time being it was best to set aside in the
pages of the Dublin Review theological and philosophical
subjects in their relation to modern thought and, instead,
to emphasize the literary side of the periodical.[20] From
his article on Pascendi in January 1908 down to his death
in 1916, only two of the more than thirty articles appearing over his name in the Dublin were directly concerned
with the reconciliation of traditional Christian beliefs
with modern thought, and both articles were published in
the form of a commentary on recently published books.[21]
Nevertheless, the Dublin was a success during his editorship. "The D. R. under your editing has achieved success,
equalled or surpassed other Quarterlies, and thereby done
Catholics credit where they need it most," William Barry
told him.[22]

     Ward experienced a number of trials during the anti-
modernist reaction. Because of his earlier association with
Tyrrell, he was accidentally listed as a modernist in some
of the Continental books that treated the subject of modernism. He had to request friends such as Bishop Hedley to
get the authors of these works to withdraw his name from
their lists of modernists. Moreover, when Cardinal Mercier,
another of his friends in the hierarchy, proposed his name
in 1908 for membership on an international committee on
Catholic learning that Mercier planned to form, Cardinal
Rampolla, then Secretary of the Holy Office, vetoed the

selection of Ward. In 1910, Rampolla requested Bourne to ask Ward to withdraw the epilogue to his book on Cardinal Wiseman, due to be re-printed again. To the contrary, Father Basil Maturin remarked to Ward that his books had been an immense help to Maturin personally and in dealing with educated and intelligent people who had felt drawn to the Church, but had been held back by difficulties. Maturin thought Ward's line of thought in such of his writings as the epilogue to Wiseman had been "the means of removing these difficulties more than any other I know."[23] Ward wrote to Hedley and received a testimony from him defending and praising the epilogue. He then saw Mercier who agreed to write to Rampolla on his behalf. Meanwhile, Bourne, who was in Rome, spoke to Rampolla and understood from him that the matter was to go no further. In 1911, however, Rampolla repeated his request that Ward withdraw the epilogue. Mercier this time advised Ward to be silent and do so, and Bourne concurred in this advice. Ward consented, and with-drew the epilogue from his next edition of Wiseman.[24]

In a memorandum drawn up for presentation to Rampolla but never sent, Ward remarked that Pascendi had necessitated the suspension of his work toward "the reconciliation of Christian faith with what is sound in modern thought and science and research."[25] Nevertheless, he retained the basic moderate liberal Catholic position he had always held. In the Preface to his Men and Matters (1914), a collection of his old articles, Ward carefully reaffirmed his position:

> This endeavour [to bring Catholic thought to a position equally advanced with the times] has led some writers into disastrous errors and excesses. But there are also signs in certain quarters of reaction to an opposite extreme--to suspicion of those who have continued to attempt the same difficult task with greater caution and submission to authority. It seems to be assumed in some quarters

235

that submission to ecclesiastical authority must suffice for guidance on the most intricate problems, and that active thought savours of a wanton and dangerous love of innovation. This view I venture strongly to deprecate, on lines laid down in Cardinal Newman's writings, as opposed to the traditions of the Church. For it is the great theological thinkers who have been our intellectual guides in times past--ecclesiastical authority approving.[26]

Ward went on to employ again his favorite example of Aquinas in the thirteenth century and to reaffirm that the history of the Church taught that it was unjustifiable to presume positions to be false simply because they apparently resembled erroneous positions. Moreover, he pointed out that even men who were the authors of heretical writings might, like Tertullian and Origen, have something of value to contribute to Christian thought.[27] Of Ward's Preface, Hügel commented: "as a piece of writing that has passed the Censors in these our times, it possesses a certain remarkable breadth of its own. Yet, of course (as you must no doubt feel yourself) it cannot but leave the practical troubles of Catholicism . . . pretty well where it found them."[28]

Since 1905 Ward had been working on what he regarded as his magnum opus, a biography of Newman based on Newman's papers. But after Pascendi and the debate over whether Newman could be considered a modernist, the biography itself threatened to become an item of controversy. Gasquet told Ward to hold back nothing in the work but to be careful in his philosophical statements, for heresy-hunters were after him.[29] Indeed, in the aftermath of Pascendi, Ward was being pulled at from all sides in writing the biography. Newman's literary executors were worried lest Newman's reputation should suffer from too frank disclosures; heresy-hunters were looking for traces of modernism; modernists were ready to pounce on any traces of lack of candor concerning Newman's views. At one point while writing the study, Ward had aged, his family doctor said, ten years in a few months. When it was finally published in 1912, the work was received very well by critics, and confirmed Ward's reputation as a biographer. Moreover, Rome seemed satisfied with it. From Rome, Gasquet commented that the Vatican was as unlikely to condemn Ward's study of Newman as it was to condemn an encyclopedia, for the work was a truthful record of facts.[30]

Although Ward continued to disagree with "the present Roman extreme policy of suppression," he did not regard Pius X's policy as simply a failure in the sense that a total lack of suppression would have been more successful or that entire freedom of discussion was without dangers: "The repression policy has done a good deal in keeping alive faith and esprit de corps among the less educated, and guarding faith for them . . . increasing the influence of the Church in some spheres, and strengthening the quality of Catholic zeal and keeping out secularism in others."[31] Ward came to believe that he had been mistaken in thinking that Leo XIII's reign had ended what he considered to be a state of siege in the history of the Church; nevertheless, he remained optimistic about the future. Writing to Lord Hugh Cecil in 1911, he summarized his view of the situation:

> You assume that the Catholic Church is essentially what the party opposed to Newman made it out to be. Newman's position was that though in practice it has become in our day something like what you describe, that is a passing phase quite separable from its essential constitution and due to circumstances. I think my own analogy of the martial law in a city under a siege, which I drew long before I read the Newman correspondence, illustrates my meaning. The position of Pope and

Hierarchy becomes autocratic when the Church is
being persecuted on the very principles involved
in the establishment of martial law. The important
thing is that some man of influence like Newman
himself should point out that this is only a
practical necessity in an emergency and not a part
of the necessary Constitution of the Church. The
ablest men of science may be called out as con-
scripts, and their individuality and genius made
useless in the press of an exceptional war. . . .[32]

Like Wilfrid Ward, Edmund Bishop regarded the anti-
modernist reaction as a trial of patience, not of faith.[33]
His scholarly work in the history of liturgy was largely
in areas not involved in the modernist controversy; thus
it was not touched by the reaction. In the decade before
his death in 1917, Bishop produced "work as full of originality and seminal power as the productions of any comparable
period of his youth or middle age."[34] Yet he developed a
personal antipathy toward the anti-modernist reaction. In
1908, he asked to be released from a commitment to write a
handbook of Western liturgies. The reaction played an
important part in this decision, for Bishop felt that he
could not write the handbook unless he had "entire freedom
to do or not do, to speak or keep silence completely."
Moreover, after Pascendi he felt obliged to be reserved in
intellectual questions before Catholic clergymen: "As
things are, I should never address any priest, at once
intelligent and informed, on any matter of intellectual
difficulty and interest; one has no right I think to expose
them [sic] to the alternative of exposing himself or utter-
ing insincerities."[35] Bishop told his friend Everard Green
that nothing would make him say the "dark" things were
clear, and the "hard" things were plain. He insisted that
"they are what they are, 'dark,' 'hard,' and we must bear
with them as such, as best we can."[36]

Bishop had always looked upon the conflicts between liberal Catholics and the Roman ecclesiastical authorities as essentially a struggle between the laity and the clergy, and had drawn the conclusion that the cause of the laity was hopeless under conditions then pertaining within the Roman Church. To Maude Petre, he wrote in 1913: "Of course one did not cease to work or to be interested, because to live at all meant to labour, to be interested in things around--but for the layman I think now as I have continuously felt--the layman 'of sorts';--he is not wanted in our Church, in our day. I neither resist nor rebel. . . ."[37] Several years after Bishop's death, Hügel wrote of him and his views: "I knew Mr. Bishop well, a great scholar, one of Lord Acton's disciples, whose only faults, in my mind, were those of his master. He had a persistent irritation against Philosophy, or what he took to be such; and again, his suspicion and antipathy towards the Vatican were, as I know well, from far greater personal experience than ever had Bishop, distinctly excessive."[38] Indeed, in his personal copy of the Autobiography and Life of George Tyrrell (1912), Bishop underlined Tyrrell's remark on p. 407, "The misery is that she [Rome] is both Christ and anti-Christ." Bishop commented: "that is the bother!"[39]

One of the harshest criticisms of Hügel that I have seen was pencilled by Bishop in the margins on two pages of his personal copy of Tyrrell's Autobiography and Life. There he remarked: "F. v. H. has been at 'tactics'--wire-pulling and making his puppets work--Loisy, Tyrrell and Co.--for years." "The Pharisaism of the man [Hügel]!" "But when has v. H. ever cared for 'the sheep'--except for one, himself."[40] Nigel Abercrombie's Life and Work of Edmund Bishop notes that, in November 1912, the shock of reading Tyrrell's Autobiography and Life, together with other mental and physical factors of disturbance at the time, had plunged Bishop into a short, bitter crisis. In February 1913, he began to reread the book--he had received a personal copy from Maude Petre--and to make marginal notes. Abercrombie states that some of Bishop's notes were poignantly precise in their indication of the effect of the first reading on him.[41] This may explain the harshness of the marginal notes on Hügel.

The scholarly work of Bishop's friend Gasquet had been in areas not involved in the modernist controversy. At the turn of the century, Gasquet's scholarly reputation had stood high. Although he had made many inaccuracies earlier, only after about 1900 did the pages of his works begin to "crawl with errors and slips."[42] After he had been elected Abbot President of the Anglo-Benedictine Congregation in 1900, Gasquet became involved in administrative work and lost touch with scholarship. Yet this was only one reason among many for the decline of his scholarship.[43] His ecclesiastical career, at any rate, was not adversely affected by the waning of his reputation among scholars. Nor was it significantly affected by the anti-modernist reaction. In defending Newman against charges of modernism and professing his own submission to Pascendi in his letters to The Times in 1907, Gasquet had demonstrated his loyalty to the Holy See. Some months earlier he had already received a vote of complete confidence when Pius X appointed him to supervise the revision of the Vulgate, a task which he pursued until his death in 1929. In 1914, he was made a cardinal in curia by Pius X and became a resident in the Vatican. During the war years, he was the leading ecclesiastical spokesman in Rome for the Allied cause.[44] Under Benedict XV, he received further ecclesiastical appointments. In 1917 he was made prefect of the Vatican archives and in 1919 librarian of the Holy Roman Church. His services in these positions had their own significance, but he had become far less engaged in the liberal Catholic attempt to reconcile Catholicism with modern scientific thought and scholarship.

Although he remained on terms of personal friendship with some of the modernists, Hügel was led by the development of an immanentist theology among them to dissociate himself from the remnants of that movement. By the end of 1909, the modernist controversy was over for him. Only "absolutist ultramontanism" and "sceptical modernism" were still in the field as he saw it.[45] To the end of his life, he remained faithful to the principle of complete autonomy for science and scholarship and appears to have neither abandoned nor revised point by point his opinions in Biblical criticism. But he was convinced that belief in a transcendent God was essential to religion and that belief in the divinity of Christ was vital to Christianity, beliefs that a number of modernists had challenged. The modernist trend toward immanentism led Hügel to become more highly conscious of and to emphasize these two beliefs and other positions he held in common with orthodoxy.[46]

His rejection of immanentism became an anxiety. In a letter to Maude Petre in February 1910, he criticized the immanentism of Buonaiuti and Minocchi.[47] Several months later, he wrote to Professor Clement Webb of Oxford that another of the stricken modernists was "declaring himself a pure Immanentist. After Bonajuti [sic] and Minocchi, now Murri [all Italian modernist priests], cleric as they, is defining God as a purely abstract term for the totality of humanity's quite immanental aspirations. . . ."[48] In March 1910, he wrote to Loisy: "As for the divinity of Christ, I have well noted the brusque and absolute way in which you put it to one side, as foreign to the subject of a scientific teaching on the history of Jesus. But here

241

again I believe that this can or cannot have an acceptable meaning for modern man according as one holds by or abandons faith in a transcendental, ontological God; and that one does not look for in the doctrine of Christ's divinity all that theology finds in it."[49] And years later in answer to a query by a Swiss professor, Hügel felt obliged to write: "I simply had to put this introduction here--it has cost me much--because otherwise you might think that my love for Loisy and Tyrrell, and my persistent admiration for some of their older books, mean that I am with them in their Immanentisms etc., which is not at all the case."[50]

In his book, Baron Friedrich von Hügel and the Modernist Crisis in England (1972), Lawrence F. Barmann showed that Hügel had been very much involved in the modernist movement. A reader unfamiliar with the subject, however, will probably not get a balanced view of Hügel from Dr. Barmann's book. The modernist Hügel is writ large there; in contrast, the Baron's thought after the modernist controversy is writ very small.[51] Since the latter is crucial to a balanced appraisal of Hügel's relationship to modernism, we will explore some of the developments in his thought after the modernist controversy. In some ways Hügel was "Consistent to the End"--the title of the last chapter of Dr. Barmann's book. In other ways, however, he was not.

While remaining critical of the ecclesiastical officials of his day, Hügel began to take a somewhat higher view of their actions than he had previously held. To Maude Petre in 1911, he wrote of a Vice-Rector of Propaganda who had become an immanentist, been removed from his position, and left the priesthood: "I am very sorry for him, for generations of arrears of study, candour, etc., in the ecclesiastical world, are doubtless chiefly responsible for such states of soul." But Hügel added: "Would you or I have kept him, as Vice-Rector of Propaganda, to form the

consciences of young missionary Priests?"[52] In an address
delivered in July 1914 and later published, Hügel balanced
criticism of the Roman acts condemning modernism with a
criticism of a number of modernists: "Under the rapid
succession of almost numberless condemnations and restrictions [during the pontificate of Pius X] . . . , it is no
wonder if (especially in cases where the critical, or even
hypercritical, acumen and activity of men is greater than
their philosophical training, self-discipline and insight,
or, especially, than the depth, delicacy and urgency of the
spiritual life within their souls) certain extreme effects
are now traceable, within the Roman Catholic Church, as
truly in the direction towards the left as in that towards
the right."[53] In a paper published in 1918, Hügel expressed
his gratitude not only to scientific workers, even if they
sometimes opposed Christianity, but also to those men "who
indeed failed to understand the worth, and who opposed the
growth, of such other activities, yet who preserved the
sense of the specific character of Religion,--that it deals
primarily, not with ideas, but with realities, and that a
certain superhumanness is of the very essence of all full
Religion."[54] To Maude Petre in 1918, he suggested that he
would prefer even Mgr. Umberto Benigni to scepticism:
"Certainly, in so far as one has moved any soul away, even
from the Civiltà Cattolica or Benigni, to scepticism, one
deeply regrets it, one most humbly begs God's pardon for
it."[55]

Hügel made perhaps the clearest statement of his
views of the Church's authority itself--not merely of the
ecclesiastical officials of his time--in a letter of June
1912. In the course of advising a mother in regard to the
moral guidance of a son at Downside, he wrote:

Certainly it will be well for your own peace and fruitfulness of mind and heart, if you can get yourself habitually to see, feel, and practise a catholicism which recognizes itself bound to two things, but to two things only:

(a) the acceptance, ex animo, of all the solemn definitions and condemnations of the Church; and

(b) the avoidance of ignoring or contravening even lesser ecclesiastical decisions (e.g. Pius Xth's Encyclicals and the Decisions of the Biblical Commission) without serious reasons and real careful study and knowledge of the subject matters, or without restraint, and, wherever possible, silence. . . . Certain it is that any attempt to force our minds to a final, unhesitating, interior assent to professions, to which the authorities themselves do not so bind themselves, can only end in unreality and scepticism. Yet if you would have it out with the now dominant authorities that is what they would exact. Let us be satisfied with the attitude and dispositions of a Sir Thomas More and many another great saint of God.[56]

On papal infallibility, he told Maude Petre he wanted something to the effect that the dogma "will have to be so restated, and so included in a wide and deep declaration of the Church at large being, in the long run and in her deepest and final apprehensions or decisions not forsaken by, indeed guided by God's Spirit, as to be completed, checked etc. by the other parts of a much larger whole." He added that, "of course, this is all too long, complex, etc.; but I am very clear that inclusion, softening, reinterpretation, and not a simple, direct repeal would be the right course." And he cautioned: "Let us not have sheer 'reactions' [against the dogma of papal infallibility]."[57]

Hügel's major published works--The Mystical Element of Religion (1908), Eternal Life (1912), and Essays and Addresses on the Philosophy of Religion (two series, 1921 and 1926)--established his reputation as one of the most respected writers on religion in England. He was perhaps

244

a more profound philosopher of religious experience than the influential William James. Although the Germanic Hügel never became a master of English literary style, the quality of his works earned him academic recognition. He was named one of the seven electors to the Wilde Lectureship in Natural and Comparative Religion at Oxford in March 1914, awarded an honorary LL.D. Degree by St. Andrews University in July 1914, awarded an honorary Doctorate of Divinity by Oxford in June 1920--the first Roman Catholic so honored since the Reformation--and elected Gifford Lecturer by Edinburgh University in June 1922, a position he eventually had to decline due to the very poor health that preceded his death in January 1925.[58]

His published works after the Roman acts against modernism did not involve him in ecclesiastical controversy; they were not directly concerned with the modernist controversy or its hottest specific issues. Yet they did give expression to some of the views he had been developing on problems involved in the modernist controversy. In particular, he discussed the epistemological problem, general problems raised by historical criticism, and the problem of authority in the Church. He sought to correct the immanentist tendency found in the modernists' attempts to deal with these problems by instead advocating a realist epistemology and by insisting on the necessity of the historical and institutional elements in Christianity.[59]

In a letter to the editor of The Times Literary Supplement in 1922, Hügel stated that his acceptance of suffering as an aid to sanctity and his mind's need of a philosophical realism helped him to keep his faith and his reason during the period 1906-1914.[60] In Eternal Life (1912), he criticized the idealist epistemology:

For if Knowledge, even of the least thing, is ever,
for us men, not knowledge of that thing's Reality,
but only of its appearance to our senses and of the
elaboration of this appearance by our minds; if of
Reality we only know, somehow, that it exists distinct from our senses and minds, and, somehow, that
it is radically different from these our apprehensions and elaborations; if hence everywhere our
strongest impressions that we know Reality are but
illusions: then the Existence of an Infinite,
Necessary Reality will, in a supreme degree and in
a normative manner, be absolutely unreachable from
any amount or kind of impressions or implications
to that effect. For here we have the supreme
application of, and trust in, that minimum of a
realistic conviction, the denial of which indeed
lands Kant, elsewhere, in continuous difficulties
of various kinds, and, at this point, tears up the
elementary experience and affirmation of religion
by the roots.[61]

To a correspondent in 1921, he wrote criticizing pragmatism:
"I entirely doubt the full pragmatising of the Dogmas,
because the Religious Sense itself is, to itself, Eviden-
tial, Realist, Metaphysical--essentially so. All that is
alive with a coming quality amongst my philosopher friends
is getting definitely away from Pragmatism; and I think
they are profoundly right."[62] As his mind shifted toward a
position of critical realism in epistemology, it moved away
from the philosophies of action of Blondel and
Laberthonnière. To Professor René Guisan he wrote in 1921
that he found himself "driven, in simple loyalty, to go,
and to remain, still more to the right of the Modernists."
He still greatly admired "certain pages of my (always well-
loved) friends Maurice Blondel and Louis [sic]
Laberthonnière; but I must confess that my fully living
interest is now given to thinkers--almost all German,
English, and Italian--who are now constituting for us a
critico-realist epistemology. This and the problem of
nature and supernature binds me very closely with Prof.

[Ernst] <u>Troeltsch</u> in Berlin and <u>Prof. Norman Kemp Smith</u> in Edinburgh."[63]

Hügel warned against subjectivist philosophies, which had been fashioned in response to Kantian criticisms, leading sometimes to pantheism. In notes prepared for a discussion of a paper at the London Society for the Study of Religion meeting in December 1916, he remarked that Kantian epistemology and agnosticism had had their day. In various degrees and ways, thinkers were, in his judgment, "articulating the rebirth of Realism, a sobered, critically purified, psychologically and historically delicately sensitive Realism, but a Realism indeed. Agnosticism is going, going, gone. Not it, but Pantheism is now, and will long be, the danger of Religion."[64] In an address delivered in 1918 and later published in his <u>Essays and Addresses on the Philosophy of Religion</u> (1926), he again commented on the challenges of agnosticism and pantheism to theism. Had he been speaking on the idea of God from 1850 to 1900, he would have had "specially to consider Materialism and Agnosticism. . . . But the twentieth century has seen, amongst leading thinkers, a marked retrocession--for a while--of Materialism and Agnosticism, and as real a return of Pluralism and especially of Pantheism." He was convinced that theism would never fully escape "all ultimate Dualism, or final Pluralism, or essential Agnosticism, without some . . . insistence upon Wholeness, Unity, and Knowableness of the World."[65]

His acceptance of a realist epistemology led Hügel to a new appreciation of scholasticism, although hardly detailed agreement with it. He commended scholasticism at its best: "But its central search and insight remains deathless--its sense of the necessity to find room for, and the place and the function of Nature and Grace, Reason and Faith, Discursive and Intuitive Reason, Reason and Will,

etc."[66]   In _Eternal Life_, he noted that an intelligent Neo-
Scholasticism might be "more adequate to the abiding necessities of the human mind and of the religious and Christian
experience" and "more appropriately penetrative of the
Christian theology throughout the centuries" than the
systems of Kant, Hegel, Descartes, or Leibniz. His appreciation of Neo-Scholasticism was, however, far from unquali-
fied--the liberty of philosophy was, he remarked, incompatible with the obligatory acceptance "of a philosophical
proposition or system as true, simply and directly because
of its imposition by Church Authority."[67]

      Hügel also began to emphasize and insist upon the
necessity of the historical element in Christianity in
response to modernism's challenging of it. His views again
found expression in his major published works. In _Eternal
Life_, he stated: "Nor will any systematic or radical distinction between Historical Happenings and Dogmatic 'Facts'
or Doctrines really suffice here." All genuine religion,
not only Rome, absolutely required "Ontology, a really
extant God, and really happened Historical Facts and
Persons." Regarding New Testament and primitive Christian
matters, he agreed with the ecclesiastical authorities'
insistence upon the need for reasonable certainty "as to
the factual character of a nucleus in the Christian complex
of doctrines . . . ; upon all the great Christian doctrines
as finally true, as interconnected, and as all either
directly descriptive of actual spiritual Realities and
Persons and factual Events, or as closely interpretative
and protective of those Realities, Persons, or Events; and,
finally, upon the possession by the Church, and by the
Church alone, of the grace and the right fully to penetrate,
and finally to decide, the spiritual truth and ultimate
meaning of Scripture." Hügel's emphasis on the necessity
of the historical element was, however, also far from

unqualified: "Yet Theologians, both as Catholics and as
reasonable men, will have not to insist upon historians
finding more, or different, historical Happenings in documents put forward as historical proofs, than these documents will yield to careful and candid critical analysis."[68]

Hügel elaborated on these views in his later major
published works. In an address delivered in 1913 and
printed in his Essays and Addresses on the Philosophy of
Religion (1921), he remarked that "an abiding nucleus of
factual happenings is essential to Catholicism, as
Christian, as incarnational." As to what this nucleus of
factual happenings might consist of, he continued: "And
though the great central figure--Our Lord, and the main
outlines of His life and teaching, death and apparitions--
require, for the integrity of Catholicism, to be not only
spiritual truths but factual happenings, it does not follow
that the same is necessarily the case with every truth and
doctrine concerning Him."[69] In an address delivered in 1914
and printed in the second series of his Essays and Addresses,
Hügel referred again to a nucleus of historical facts and
said that the Creeds would remain true, even if some of
their articles "would have slowly, cautiously, to be reinterpreted as true in not a factual sense or in a factual
sense somewhat different from the old one."[70]

Although he ultimately rejected theological immanentism and philosophical subjectivism, he retained here a
modernist view of the relationship between dogma and
Biblical history, a view similar to that of Tyrrell. When
Maude Petre was about to publish her volume of George
Tyrrell's Letters (1920), Hügel commented on Tyrrell's
letter of February 10, 1907, to him: "A great letter, this,
surely." Thus the Virgin Birth, to take the example used
by Tyrrell in his letter, apparently would not be among the
nucleus of historical happenings which Hügel thought

249

the Creed must retain. Here his views, like Tyrrell's, bear some similarity to the later movement of "demythologizing."[71] But even when Hügel put forward bold suggestions regarding dogma, he agreed that the decision on matters of dogma was the prerogative of the Church and its legitimate heads.[72] His relationship to orthodoxy was heavily influenced by personal factors which he had poignantly expressed during the Loisy affair:

> I long tried to reach truth, directly through
> orthodoxy, and feel very sure that, for many, this
> is the only way. But I found, for my own case,
> that I was thus losing both truth and orthodoxy,
> and with them, all fruitfulness as well. Since I
> have been taught, by saintly spiritual leaders,
> to try and find orthodoxy through ever increasing,
> ever toilful, self-renouncing sincerity of mind,
> and to gladly will that the majority, largely
> without doubt much better than myself and with
> idiosyncrasies other than my own, should, at
> best, just simply bear with me: I have found
> interior strength and a joyous love of the
> Catholic Church.[73]

A major area of historical controversy during the modernist crisis had been the question of the Church's origins and later development. As with the historical element in general, Hügel began here to emphasize the necessity of the element of the divine upheld by orthodoxy against modernism. In an address on "Institutional Christianity," delivered in 1918 and printed in the first series of his Essays and Addresses, he said that "developments may well be in substantial accord with the deepest implications and acts of Jesus, Paul and the early centuries, and with the immanental necessities of a Church called upon to endure and to spread throughout our earth's time and space, and may yet show, in the details of their evolution, unhistorical imagination, pseudonymous documents, even now and then some dishonesty. It is really time that such

250

discriminations became the common property of all serious scholars whatever their religious allegiance."[74] In another address, Hügel spoke still more explicitly of his view of the Church's origins and development: "With regard to God and Christ in the Church, religion will have somehow not to conceive and practise the Kingdom of God and the Church as something simply built up by their human constituents, as something growing up, coral-reef like, from below, but as something also, indeed primarily, given by the Divine generosity, as something descending from above. 'You have not chosen Me, but I have chosen you,' says Christ to His Apostles." He added that it was not only he, the Roman Catholic, who, amidst these problems, still saw this--saw this, in fact, "with a (for me) quite fresh keenness and poignancy."[75]

Hügel gave a sincere intellectual assent to the authority of the Church within what he regarded as its proper limits.[76] For him the problem of the authority of the Church was largely not the intellectual problem that it became for Tyrrell. It was a problem of the practical order concerning the specific actions of the ecclesiastical authorities and the extent to which they were obliging Catholics to respect decisions that were admittedly fallible. He thought papal authority had in practice so overextended itself as to have deleterious effects. In Eternal Life, he expressed his hope that zealous Catholics would come to agree "with Newman the far-sighted, and with many a great Saint down to our own acutely saddening times, that revolution and despotism are ever the fruitful parents of each other," and that even the pope could never "come to be beyond learning and receiving from men and through men-- those very men to whom he has so much to teach, and so much to give." In characteristically hopeful fashion, he made a

statement that in retrospect seems prophetic of the
pontificate of John XXIII:

> Providence . . . may utilize this very power [of
> the papacy], which now appears as though finally
> omnipotent, to give all the larger scope to some
> Papa Angelico who will know how to conjoin with
> the simple, traditional piety and goodness, still
> genuinely amongst us, a sensitive sympathy, as
> yet lacking or angrily suspected, with all that
> is true and generous in the very troubles and dim
> aspirations of our greatly altered world. Such
> a figure would in some way severely check, and
> perhaps for ever repress all directly political
> ambitions, through a great increase, in the
> Servant-Mistress of all the Churches, of the
> sense and practice of Eternal Life.[77]

Hügel has been viewed as a forerunner of Vatican
II.[78] He hoped that the Church would adapt itself, as far
as it legitimately could, to the modern world. He stood
for ecumenism in his insistence that Catholics should
attempt to see positive value besides defects in other
religions and in his contacts and friendships with religious
thinkers of many different denominations and nationalities.
He hoped Catholic theology would bring itself abreast of
modern knowledge and looked forward to the development of
Catholic Biblical studies, an area in which he specialized.
For Catholic scholars, he urged much more freedom than was
allowed in his day. He thought that the tendency toward
centralization of authority in the Church had gone too far
and needed to be checked. Moreover, he always desired to
see the reform of the Curia. He stood for greater participation by the laity in Catholic life. Of The Mystical
Element of Religion (1908), his magnum opus, he stated:
"And lastly a lay lover of religion speaks throughout, a
man to whom the very suspicion that such subjects should
or could, on that account, be foreign to him has ever been
impossible. A deep interest in religion is evidently part

252

of our very manhood, a thing previous to the Church, and
which the Church now comes to develop and to save. Yet
such an interest is, in the long run, impossible, if the
heart and will alone are allowed to be active in a matter
so supremely great and which claims the entire man. 'Where
my heart lies, let my brains lie also.'" Yet he believed
that the layman's views on Church matters are unofficial.
Emphasizing the interrelationship and complementary nature
of different elements in religion, he was opposed to undue
exaltation of either authority or personal independence and
opposed to the denigration of the institutional side of
religion.[79]

Still another way in which Hügel anticipated
Vatican II was in his understanding of the term "Church."
This was evident in a letter to Wilfrid Ward. Hügel felt
sure that "we ought never to use the term 'Church' pure and
simple, for 'official Church,' 'teaching Church.' It is
simply un-Catholic to restrict 'Church' in such a manner.
Though the 'Ecclesia Discens' is not, and should not aspire
to be, the official tester, formularizer, and proclaimer of
the collective Church's experience, tradition, analysis
etc., that 'Ecclesia Discens' is an integral part of the
material and means on which and by means of which the
Ecclesia Docens thus acts."[80] On this point, Hügel was
indebted to Tyrrell, who had suggested it first in his pre-
modernist days.[81]

In "The Essentials of Catholicism," Hügel expressed
yet another of his hopes for the future of the Church. He
tried to strike a just balance between transcendence and
this world:

> There must at no time be any question of eliminating
> or weakening the transcendental, other-world, God-
> ward, recollective movement; it, on the contrary,
> will have, as keenly and penetratingly as ever, to

253

be the great sheet-anchor of our souls and the
great root of the self-identity of the Catholic
religion and of its world-conquering peace. We
shall only, in our other movement--in the out-
going, the world-ward, the incarnational movement,
have, far more keenly than men were able to realise
in the past, to be attentive, active, observant,
hospitable, there also--not merely with the sense
of doing good, or with the wish directly to find
or to introduce religious facts and categories,
but especially with the conviction that these
various stages and ranges, each and all, come
from God, possess their own immanent laws and
conditions of existence and growth, and deserve
our love and service in this their nature and
development. We shall feel sure that they will,
in the long run, benefit (often in the most
unexpected but most real ways) regions of life
apparently far apart from them, and especially
will aid religion, the deepest life of all.[82]

To an Anglican bishop, he expressed the balance he had
struck: "Very certainly, the Church has also to help in
the amelioration of this life; but, I submit, always after,
and in subordination to, and penetrated by, that metaphysical, ontological, other-worldly sense and life which
alone completes and satisfies fully awakened man."[83]

Hügel's revised judgment of the papal condemnation
of modernism was less critical than his earlier judgments.
In a letter in 1918 to Maude Petre, who was then preparing
a book on modernism, he distinguished between two different
meanings of the term "modernism." He defined one as "a
permanent, never quite finished, always sooner or later,
more or less, rebeginning set of attempts to express the
old Faith and its permanent truths and helps--to interpret
it according to what appears the best and the most abiding
elements in the philosophy and the scholarship and science
of the later and latest times." He said that such work
never ceased for long, and to it he still tried to contribute
his "little share," with such improvements as the experiences of Pius X's pontificate had taught him--in part only

slowly--to be desirable or necessary. He described the other modernism as "a strictly circumscribed affair, one that is really over and done--the series or groups of specific attempts, good, bad, indifferent, or variously mixed, that were made towards similar expressions or inter- pretations, during the Pontificate of Pius X." This modernism ended with Tyrrell's death "and with Loisy's alienation from the positive content that had been fought for"; its end could also be dated from the suppression of Rinnovamento onward, "and the resolution of so much of the very substance of the movement, not only, or even chiefly, under the stress of the official Church condemnations, but from within the ranks--scepticism dominating what remained of organs claiming to be 'Modernist.'" Then he raised an objection against a list of his writings since 1914 appear- ing in Petre's book on modernism, and expressed in personal terms his revised judgment of the papal condemnation of modernism:

> It [the objection] arises forcibly in my mind--as far as I know myself--from a strong desire not to appear (it would be contrary to the facts, and indeed contrary to my ideals and convictions) as though all that action of the Church authorities had, in no way or degree, been interiorly accepted by me. Certainly that action was, very largely, violent and unjust; equally certainly, if one had been required definitely to subscribe to this or that document [Lamentabili, Pascendi, anti- modernist oath] without express reservations, one could not, with any self-respect left, have done so. Yet it is not cowardice or policy, it is in simplest sincerity, that I have come to see, more clearly than I used to do, how much of serious unsatisfactoriness and of danger there was especially in many of the philosophical (strongly subjectivist) theories really held which Pascendi lumped together. And [Ernst] Troeltsch has taught me vividly how profoundly important is Church appurtenance, yet how such appurtenance never, even at best, can be had without some sacrifices--even of (otherwise) fine or desirable

liberties or unhamperednesses. These two things--
the actual fact of a very real, though certainly
not unlimited submission, and the duty of such
submission--I care much should not be left
uncertain, on occasion, in my own case.[84]

There was perhaps no more precise a statement by Hügel of
his retrospective judgment of the modernist controversy
than this letter.[85]

Like Hügel's revised judgment of the papal condemnation of modernism, that of Wilfrid Ward, who best represented moderate English liberal Catholicism, was less
critical than his earlier judgments. Upon the death of
Pius X in 1914, Ward wrote in the Dublin that the Pope had
probably judged the danger presented by the modernist movement to be so grave that "its power had to be broken before
that calm and dispassionate discussion which may be needed
for the sifting process I have indicated could be wisely
undertaken." Ward came to think that he himself had under-
rated the strength of modernism and overrated the strength
of theological thought to counter it at the time, for
Catholic theology was hardly as vigorous in the late nineteenth and early twentieth centuries as at some other times
in the Church's history. These considerations did not alter
his view of the normal relationship of Catholic intellectuals and ecclesiastical authorities in the constitution of
the Church, but he did come to look upon the modernist
crisis as an abnormal period calling for unusual action on
the part of the authorities.[86]

Looking back on modernism, Ward described what he
regarded as the typical reaction of "the abler Catholic
readers" to it--a reaction that was indubitably his own
response also. They were proud of the modernist writer's
open-mindedness when he tried to reconcile the recognized
achievements of modern scientific criticism with Catholicism,

256

so long as he accepted the dogmas and respected the authority of the Church. They regarded the modernist as pioneer-
ing in enlightened theology. But when he went beyond the
bounds of orthodoxy, there was a reaction and the esteem
in which he was held vanished. The modernist's former
admirers took him at first to depict a wise and comprehensive Christianity, ready to assimilate truth wherever found,
only later to discover he had been depicting what he
regarded as a discredited Christianity which could be saved
from destruction only by adopting his personal views.[87]

In his posthumously published Last Lectures (1918),
Ward's views on modernism from the overall point of view of
the history of civilization are given. He reaffirmed
Christianity's irreconcilable opposition to naturalistic
world views and to conclusions based not on scientific
knowledge but on naturalistic assumptions: "Christianity
included from the first a challenge to the secularism and
naturalism which reappear in different forms in successive
civilisations and bear fruit in the culture and philosophy
of each. . . . If consideration for modern necessities means
that Christianity must be evacuated of antagonism to the more
important historical and philosophical speculations of the
day [Ward's day], it will mean the denial of much that
revelation has stood for from the first." Ward thought
that many theories of the higher criticism were speculations
based on naturalistic assumptions in addition to wide critical knowledge. These assumptions were "the rival assumptions to those of Christianity." Though a naturalistic
habit of mind undoubtedly came easily in an age of science,
it was unchristian. Then recalling the views of the intellectual who had been regarded by a number of English liberal
Catholics as their forerunner, Ward commented:

Newman repeatedly urged, from his Oxford days to
his very last publication on the 'Development of
Religious Error,' that the human reason, in a
highly developed civilisation, always tends to
negation in matters of religious belief. In its
abnormal activity it outstrips its legitimate
competence, and it unconsciously adopts in a
greater or less degree current intellectual and
ethical assumptions which in a fallen world are
apt to be secularistic. The heretic has again
and again been the 'modern man' of his age. How
striking is the prima facie appearance of intelligent common sense in some of the arguments of
Nestorius! The orthodox on their side have
vindicated the traditional revelation against a
reason that was overstepping its legitimate
province. If this is true it is necessary, when
conclusions are claimed as demanded by modern
conditions of thought and knowledge, closely to
cross-examine this claim. We must ascertain
whether it is not in reality reinforced and the
issue determined not by new . . . knowledge, but
by fragments of the inveterate rationalism which
recurs in all epochs of active speculation.88

Ultimately, Friedrich von Hügel and Wilfrid Ward
possessed a remarkable centrality--as I hope the present
book has shown.

Efforts to reconcile Catholicism with contemporary
culture recur in Church history. They may remain within
the bounds of orthodoxy or exceed these limits. They may
be concerned with intellectual questions, political developments, or social conditions. Such efforts reached a
critical point in the 1860's with Pope Pius IX's censures.
Nevertheless, by the 1890's the attempts to reconcile
Catholicism with nineteenth-century political developments
and social conditions had achieved a fair measure of success. They received some sanction from Pope Leo XIII in
his ralliement policy and his encyclical Rerum Novarum. The
apparent conflict of science and religion, however,

challenged belief directly and remained a burning issue. The 1890's saw the emergence of a new group of liberal Catholics and a new set of attempts to reconcile Catholicism with scientific criticism and contemporary thought. Although they seemed promising at first, these new efforts became endangered when a number of controversies arose between liberal Catholic writers and ecclesiastical officials. The danger became graver as a modernist wing emerged among the liberal Catholics after the turn of the century. Unlike the moderate liberals, modernists sought to reconcile Catholicism with scientific criticism and contemporary thought by radically altering the meaning of dogma and of the Church's authority. With Pope Pius X's condemnation of modernism, the liberal Catholic attempts at reconciliation reached a turning point. Not only was modernism almost totally suppressed but also moderate efforts suffered from the virulent anti-modernist reaction, which spilled over even into areas unrelated to the modernist controversy. Thus liberal Catholicism again disappeared beneath the surface of ecclesiastical affairs.

Even though sharply curtailed after 1907, moderate liberal efforts at reconciliation continued. They received some later sanction when Pius XII's encyclical on Biblical studies, _Divino afflante Spiritu_, quietly appeared in the midst of World War II. The pontificate of John XXIII and the Second Vatican Council appear to have given a final approval to such efforts so long as they remain within orthodox limits. Just as the pontificate of Leo XIII gave rise to a set of liberal Catholic attempts at reconciliation, John XXIII's brief pontificate appears to have sparked a new and far more extensive endeavor at reconciliation of Catholicism and the modern world. What degree of success these new attempts will achieve remains highly problematical.

Nor do we know how many efforts, like modernism, may go beyond orthodox limits.

But modernism, strictly speaking, is over and done--as Hügel pointed out to Maude Petre in his letter of March 13, 1918. In conclusion, there were both valuable insights and serious inadequacies in the thought of the modernists. The ecclesiastical authorities both preserved older valuable insights and were unjust in certain judgments and actions. The modernist crisis was a tragic drama, and I see no gain for historical understanding should--to put it hyperbolically--the old view that the modernists were all wrong be replaced in Roman Catholic circles by a new view that the church authorities were completely wrong, the modernists quite right. Nor does intolerance today--whether from the left, right, or center, and whether secular or "religious"--seem to me any better in principle than nineteenth-century neo-ultramontane intolerance.*

---

*A curious phenomenon today is that some educated men and women, including some academics, who decry the intolerance of past ages, sometimes act very intolerantly themselves and, on occasion, thereby cause much suffering and very serious harm to other human beings. Neither the past nor any one ideological orientation has a monopoly on intolerance. It, and its accompanying self-righteousness, exist today, in perhaps less evident forms. Genuine tolerance--which should not be identified with indifference nor with wishy-washiness in moral or intellectual matters--is a precious commodity.

NOTES TO THE INTRODUCTION

[1]As used here, the term "science" includes any branch of study based on research and the inductive method. It should not be taken to mean the natural sciences only. While the latter is the more common meaning of "science" today, nineteenth-century writers were inclined to employ "science" in its broader sense when referring collectively to those disciplines which challenged religion. They applied the term to Biblical criticism and historical scholarship, as well as other contemporary disciplines.

[2]Attempts to reconcile Catholicism with contemporary culture occur repeatedly in the history of the Church. They may be concerned with questions of belief, political issues, social concerns, or other problems of life within the culture. They may remain within the bounds of orthodoxy or stray beyond. Thus, "liberal Catholicism," used to refer to such attempts, is a term with a very broad meaning. Objections can be raised against this use of the term. For one thing, "liberal Catholic" was often used by Church officials in the nineteenth century to signify a disloyal or unorthodox Catholic. For another, on a number of issues, some "liberals" agreed with "conservatives" against other "liberals"--and "conservatives" likewise divided at times. Nevertheless, in writing on the efforts to reconcile Catholicism with contemporary culture in the nineteenth century, the historian must use some term to refer to these attempts. "Liberal Catholicism" presents at least no more problems than alternative terms, such as "progressive Catholicism," or "aggiornamento," an anachronism when applied to the nineteenth century. Moreover, many of the protagonists in the nineteenth-century attempts at reconciliation referred to themselves as "liberal Catholics"--and their opponents often applied the same term to them. This is true both of leading figures in mid-century and, to a lesser degree because of the unfavorable connotations the term had taken on within the Church, of protagonists in similar efforts in the late nineteenth and early twentieth centuries. As used in this study, the term implies no greater or lesser degree of orthodoxy between "liberals" and "conservatives." It must be recognized that they had much in common as Catholics; they shared basic religious beliefs and practices: most of them accepted the Church's dogmas and authority, worshipped

at Mass, received the sacraments, etc. Their different per-
spectives on the relations of Catholicism with contemporary
culture were secondary to their Catholicism itself.

[3]Josef L. Altholz, The Liberal Catholic Movement in
England: The "Rambler" and Its Contributors, 1848-1864
(London, 1962), p. 221.

[4]The earlier ultramontanes had looked to the papacy
to support the Church against the new secular state that had
arisen out of the French Revolution. The neo-ultramontanes
believed, in addition, that authority within the Roman Church
should be fully centralized in the hands of the papacy.

[5]See Edmund Sheridan Purcell, Life of Cardinal
Manning, 2nd ed. (London, 1896), Vol. II, Ch. vii, "The
Temporal Power of the Pope."

[6]See Altholz, The Liberal Catholic Movement in
England . . . 1848-1864, Ch. viii, "Catholic Politics and
Catholic Intellect, 1860-1861," and Ch. ix, "Friends and
Enemies, 1861."

[7]Ibid., pp. 131-32.

[8]Purcell, Life of Cardinal Manning, II, 322-23,
quoting a letter by Manning to Talbot, February 25, 1866.

[9]J. G. Snead-Cox, The Life of Cardinal Vaughan
(London, 1910), II, 297, quoting from a letter by Acton to
The Times, November 24, 1874.

[10]See E. E. Y. Hales, Pio Nono (Garden City, N.Y.,
1962), Ch. vii, Sec. 1, "The Syllabus of Errors (1864)."

[11]Altholz, The Liberal Catholic Movement in England
. . . 1848-1864, p. 229, quoting from a letter by Newman to
Acton, March 18, 1864.

[12]His refusals may occasionally have resulted from
an over-scrupulous conscience and a shy nature, but his
intellectual honesty and discrimination seem to have been
the more common reason.

[13]See A. O. J. Cockshut, Anglican Attitudes (London, 1959), Ch. iv, "The Doctrinal Crisis."

[14]Henry E. Manning, "On the Subjects Proper to the Academia," Essays on Religion and Literature, ed. Manning, 1st ser. (London, 1865), pp. 43-44, 46; [Manning], "The Work and the Wants of the Catholic Church in England," Dublin Review, n.s., I (July, 1863), 165.

[15]Manning, "On the Subjects Proper to the Academia," pp. 50-51.

[16]Ibid., p. 64. For Manning's views on the conflict of science and religion, see his "On the Inspiration of Scripture," Essays on Religion and Literature, ed. Manning, 2nd ser. (London, 1867), pp. 380-85, and his "On the Subjects Proper to the Academia," pp. 50-66.

[17]Vincent Ferrer Blehl, ed., The Essential Newman (New York, 1963), p. 212.

[18]Meriol Trevor, "Manning's University and Newman's Aloofness," Tablet, January 5, 1963, p. 8.

[19]Newman, "Christianity and Scientific Investigation," in his The Idea of a University, new edition, ed. Charles Frederick Harrold (New York, London, and Toronto, 1947), p. 339. For his views on the conflict of science and religion, see his "Christianity and Physical Science" and "Christianity and Scientific Investigation" in The Idea of a University, and Blehl, ed., The Essential Newman, pp. 211-13, 228-38. See also Wilfrid Ward, The Life of John Henry Cardinal Newman, new impression (London, 1921), Vol. I, Ch. xiii, "University Lectures (1854-1858)."

[20]Ward, Life of Newman, I, 5.

[21]Newman, "A Form of Infidelity of the Day, 1854," in his Idea of a University.

[22]Ward, Life of Newman, I, 8.

[23]See Lewis Freeman Mott, _Ernest Renan_ (New York and London, 1921), pp. 16-17, 26-28; H. W. Wardman, _Ernest Renan: A Critical Biography_ (London, 1964), pp. 11-12.

[24]Ward, _Life of Newman_, II, 246-48.

[25]Manning, "The Work and the Wants of the Catholic Church in England," pp. 153-55, 157, 165-66.

[26]Trevor, "Manning's University and Newman's Aloofness," p. 8.

[27]See Vincent Alan McClelland, _Cardinal Manning_ (London, 1962), Ch. iv, "Higher Education"; McClelland, "Manning and the Universities: A Reappraisal of the Background to the Kensington Venture," _Tablet_, March 30, 1963, p. 336.

[28]The repeated frustrations that his work encountered during the 1850's and 1860's are well-known. Besides two attempts to found an oratory at Oxford, his efforts to establish a Catholic University in Ireland, his editorship of the _Rambler_, and his plans to prepare a translation of Scripture to replace the old Douay version all failed in the face of outright opposition or lack of support from ecclesiastical authorities.

[29]Ward, _Life of Newman_, II, 204.

[30]See Altholz, _The Liberal Catholic Movement in England . . . 1848-1864_, pp. 233-34, 240-41.

[31]Hales, _Pio Nono_, p. 284.

[32]His father, Carl von Hügel, a baron of the Holy Roman Empire, had served in the diplomatic service of the Hapsburg Emperor. Carl, a Roman Catholic, married Elizabeth Farquharson, a Scotswoman who subsequently converted to Roman Catholicism from Presbyterianism. Two years after the marriage, Friedrich was born. In 1867 the family moved to England. In 1873 Friedrich married Lady Mary Herbert, a convert from Anglicanism; thereafter, he made his home in England.

[33]Alec R. Vidler, _A Variety of Catholic Modernists_ (Cambridge, Eng., 1970), Ch. vi, "An Unrecognized Modernist," argues that Bishop was in private a modernist, although he has not been recognized as such. He was not known to the public as a modernist, nor were his public actions such. In that chapter, Dr. Vidler presents a very good case for his point about Bishop--which I accept. But see my qualification on Bishop's modernism (and Vidler's point) in Ch. v of the present book and in my article, "Von Hügel after the Modernist Controversy," _Clergy Review_, LXIII (June, 1978), 214.

NOTES TO CHAPTER I

[1]I have examined Lord Acton's papers at the Cambridge University Library. My research in his papers did
not uncover expressions by him on the new liberal Catholicism that emerged in England during the 1890's. Wilfrid
Ward and Acton did exchange letters, but their correspondence mainly concerned historical matters, not the contemporary ecclesiastical scene. Acton remained aloof from
liberal Catholic efforts in England in the 1890's and he
was most reticent about them.

[2]The Jesuit priest George Tyrrell was not yet a
leading figure among the liberal Catholics.

[3]Shane Leslie, Cardinal Gasquet (London, 1953),
pp. 9, 13.

[4]Henry VIII and the English Monasteries: An
Attempt to Illustrate the History of their Suppression,
2nd ed. (London, 1888), Vol. I, "To the Reader," p. xi.

[5]Ibid., 3rd ed. (London, 1889), Vol. II, "To the
Reader," p. viii.

[6]"Edmund Bishop's account of his state of mind at
17," two pages of typescript, in the Bishop Papers at
Downside Abbey.

[7]See Nigel Abercrombie, The Life and Work of
Edmund Bishop (London, 1959), pp. 20-21, 26, 30-32, 45,
68-69.

[8]Francis Aidan Gasquet and Edmund Bishop, Edward
VI and the Book of Common Prayer: An Examination into Its
Origin and Early History with an Appendix of Unpublished
Documents (London, 1890), "To the Reader," page unnumbered.

NOTES TO CHAPTER I

[9]Friedrich von Hügel, "The Case of the Abbe Loisy,"
Pilot, January 9, 1904, p. 31.

[10]This analysis of Hügel's position on the conflict
of science and religion is partially based on an analysis of
his philosophy of life in Michael de la Bedoyere, The Life
of Baron von Hügel (London, 1951), pp. 112-19.

[11]Maisie Ward, The Wilfrid Wards and the Transition
(London, 1934), Vol. I: The Nineteenth Century, pp. 335,
337-38, quoting from "The Conservative Genius of the Church,"
an address by Wilfrid Ward to the English Catholic Conference of 1900. The address was later published in Wilfrid
Ward's Men and Matters (London, 1914).

[12]Maisie Ward, The Wilfrid Wards, I, 341-42,
quoting from Father Cuthbert, O.S.F.C., "Wilfrid Ward,"
Dublin Review, CLIX (July, 1916), 9-10.

[13]Wilfrid Ward, William George Ward and the
Catholic Revival (London, 1912 reissue), Pref., p. xii.
His two volume biography of his father was his first major
published work and was received well. The first volume,
William George Ward and the Oxford Movement, appeared in
1889. The second volume, William George Ward and the
Catholic Revival, was published in 1893.

[14]See Wilfrid Ward, W. G. Ward and the Catholic
Revival, Ch. xvi, "An Epilogue"; also Wilfrid Ward's comments on his book in his reminiscences as quoted in Maisie
Ward, The Wilfrid Wards, I, 183-84. Edmund Bishop's views
were not in agreement with this assessment of the situation
of the new liberal Catholics. Although he admired Leo XIII
for opening the Vatican archives to historians and inaugu-
rating the ralliement policy, Pope Leo's reign had not
essentially changed his pessimistic assessment of the
prospects of success for the liberal Catholics. See
Abercrombie, Life of Edmund Bishop, pp. 195-99.

[15]Charles Gore, ed., Lux Mundi, from the 5th
English ed. (New York, n.d.), Pref., pp. viii-ix.

[16]Wilfred L. Knox and Alec R. Vidler, The Development of Modern Catholicism (Milwaukee, 1933), pp. 107-10.

[17]For a summary of the various theological essays in Lux Mundi see Knox and Vidler, Development of Modern Catholicism, Part I, Ch. viii, "Lux Mundi," pp. 94-102. The brief analysis given in the above paragraph is based upon this summary.

[18]James Tunstead Burtchaell, "The Biblical Question and the English Liberal Catholics," Review of Politics, XXXI (January, 1969), 112.

[19]Review (unsigned) of John William Colenso, The Pentateuch and Book of Joshua Critically Examined, Part III, in Home and Foreign Review, III (1863), 222-23, cited in ibid., pp. 112-13. The versatile Simpson wrote on a very wide range of subjects for the Rambler and the Home and Foreign Review. For a study of Simpson, see Damian McElrath, Richard Simpson, 1820-1876 (Louvain, 1972).

[20]Altholz, The Liberal Catholic Movement in England . . . 1848-1864, p. 204. Some Biblical critics, Renan among them, were criticized by the Home and Foreign Review for being insufficiently scientific, lacking objectivity, and depending on unproven hypotheses. Ibid., p. 205.

[21]Burtchaell, "The Biblical Question and the English Liberal Catholics," pp. 114-15.

[22]N. N. [Acton], "The Danger of Physical Science," Rambler, N.S., VI (1861-62), 528, cited in ibid., p. 115.

[23]James Tunstead Burtchaell, Catholic Theories of Biblical Inspiration since 1810 (Cambridge, Eng., 1969), pp. 176-77.

[24]Burtchaell, "The Biblical Question and the English Liberal Catholics," pp. 118-20.

[25]Ronald Roy Nelson, "The Life and Thought of William Robertson Smith, 1846-1894," Diss. University of Michigan 1969, pp. 82-92.

[26]John Kenneth Mozley, Some Tendencies in British Theology: From the Publication of Lux Mundi to the Present Day (London, 1951), pp. 19, 21.

[27]H. G. Wood, Belief and Unbelief since 1850 (Cambridge, Eng., 1955), pp. 70-71, 122-23.

[28]Knox and Vidler, Development of Modern Catholicism, p. 58.

[29]Arthur Michael Ramsey, An Era in Anglican Theology: From Gore to Temple (New York, 1960), p. 2. See also G. L. Prestige, The Life of Charles Gore (London and Toronto, 1935), p. 9.

[30]Knox and Vidler, Development of Modern Catholicism, pp. 191, 214.

[31]Ramsey, An Era in Anglican Theology, p. 96.

[32]C. H. Dodd, The Founder of Christianity (New York and London, 2nd printing, 1970), pp. 26-27.

[33]C. H. Dodd, History and the Gospel (New York, 1938), pp. 11, 14.

[34]James Carpenter, Gore: A Study in Liberal Catholic Thought (London, 1960), pp. 100-104, 108-109.

[35]Charles Gore, "The Holy Spirit and Inspiration," Lux Mundi, pp. 272-73, 277, 281-83.

[36]Ibid., pp. 276, 293-98, 300-302.

[37]Wilfrid Ward's reminiscences, Maisie Ward, The Wilfrid Wards, I, 182.

[38]Nineteenth Century, XXVII (June, 1890), 942-56. See also Wilfrid Ward's comments on his article in his reminiscences, Maisie Ward, The Wilfrid Wards, I, 183.

[39]Nineteenth Century, XXII (July, 1887), 31-51. Mivart had lived through the liberal Catholic-neo-ultramontane controversies of the 1860's. He belonged to an older generation, that of Acton (1834-1902), than did the younger liberal Catholics of the 1890's.

[40]John Cuthbert Hedley, "Dr. Mivart on Faith and Science," Dublin Review, CI (October, 1887), 401-19.

[41]See Jacob W. Gruber, A Conscience in Conflict: The Life of St. George Jackson Mivart (New York, 1960), p. 174.

[42]"The Catholic Church and Biblical Criticism," p. 50.

[43]Hedley, "Dr. Mivart on Faith and Science," pp. 402-405.

[44]See J[ames] F[itzjames] Stephen, "Mr. Mivart's Modern Catholicism," Nineteenth Century, XXII (October, 1887), 581-600, and an unsigned commentary on the Mivart-Stephen controversy, "A Triangular Duel," Saturday Review of Politics, Literature, Science, and Art, LXIV (December 3, 1887), 760-61.

[45]"A Triangular Duel," p. 761.

[46]Gruber, A Conscience in Conflict, p. 175.

[47]John Ratté, Three Modernists (New York, 1967), pp. 52-59, 61.

[48]Alec R. Vidler, The Modernist Movement in the Roman Church (Cambridge, Eng., 1934), pp. 78-86.

[49]See ibid., pp. 75-80.

[50]Bedoyere, Baron von Hügel, p. 74, quoting from a letter by Gasquet to Hügel, November 1, 1892.

[51]Wilfrid Ward's reminiscences, Maisie Ward, The Wilfrid Wards, I, 310.

[52]See "Providentissimus Deus," The Great Encyclical Letters of Pope Leo XIII, ed. John J. Wynne (New York, 1903), pp. 271-302.

[53]"The Encyclical Letter Recently Issued by Pope Leo XIII on the Study of Holy Scripture," Guardian, XLIX (April 11, 1894), 530-31. See also "Mr. Gore on the Pope's Encyclical," Spectator, LXXII (April 28, 1894), 578-79.

[54]"The Papal Encyclical on the Bible," Contemporary Review, LXV (April, 1894), 576-608; "Intellectual Liberty and Contemporary Catholicism," LXVI (August, 1894), 280-304; "Theological Book-Keeping by Double Entry," LXVI (September, 1894), 351-73. Bedoyere, Baron von Hügel, p. 76, states that the author was an ex-seminarian journalist, E. J. Dillon, but that some people even suspected Hügel of writing the articles. The Wellesley Index to Victorian Periodicals, 1824-1900, ed. Walter E. Houghton, Vol. I (Toronto and London, 1966), pp. 299-300, 875, gives Dillon as the author.

[55]"The Church and the Bible: The Two Stages of Their Interrelation," Dublin Review, CXV (October, 1894), 313-41; CXVI (April, 1895), 306-37; CXVII (October, 1895), 275-304.

[56]Ibid., CXV (October, 1894), 314.

[57]Ibid., p. 313.

[58]Ibid., CXVII (October, 1895), 278-83.

[59]Ibid., CXV (October, 1894), 323-24.

[60]Bedoyere, Baron von Hügel, p. 77, quoting from a letter by Mignot to Hügel, January 4, 1894.

[61]Ibid., p. 76.

[62]Ibid., p. 77, quoting from a letter by Duchesne to Hügel, March 2, 1894.

[63]Abercrombie, Life of Edmund Bishop, p. 198.

[64]Bishop to Ward, February 7, 1893, Wilfrid Ward Family Papers. Hereafter cited as Ward Papers.

[65]Hügel to Maude Petre, April 20, 1902, British Museum Additional Manuscript 45361. Hereafter cited as Add. Ms. 45361.

[66]J[oseph] Anselm Wilson, The Life of Bishop Hedley (New York, 1930), pp. 214-15, quoting from a letter by Hügel to Hedley, May 27, 1894.

[67]Maisie Ward, The Wilfrid Wards, I, 311, quoting a letter by Hügel to Wilfrid Ward, June 14, 1894.

[68]Wilfrid Ward's reminiscences, ibid., pp. 309-10. See also Bedoyere, Baron von Hügel, pp. 79-80.

[69]Wilfrid Ward's reminiscences, Maisie Ward, The Wilfrid Wards, I, 309.

[70]See Bedoyere, Baron von Hügel, p. 76; Friedrich von Hügel, letter to the Spectator, LXXII (May 19, 1894), 684-85.

[71]Bedoyere, Baron von Hügel, pp. 78-79, quoting from a letter by Hügel to Ward, May 21, 1894.

[72]Nineteenth Century, XXXII (December, 1892), 899-919.

[73]Ibid., pp. 918-19.

[74]"Happiness in Hell" was followed by two other articles by Mivart on the subject: "The Happiness in Hell: A Rejoinder" and "Last Words on the Happiness in Hell: A Rejoinder" in the Nineteenth Century (February and April, 1893).

[75]Gruber, A Conscience in Conflict, p. 185.

[76]Maisie Ward, The Wilfrid Wards, Vol. I, Ch. xvi, "The University Question."

[77]Ibid.; and J. G. Snead-Cox, The Life of Cardinal Vaughan (London, 1910), II, 80-85.

NOTES TO CHAPTER II

[1]Snead-Cox, Life of Cardinal Vaughan, II, 141-45;
Abercrombie, Life of Edmund Bishop, pp. 224-29; Viscount
Halifax, Leo XIII and Anglican Orders (London and New York,
1912), pp. 362-67, quoting from the pamphlet Risposta all'
Opuscolo De Re Anglicana (1896) by Gasquet and J. C. Moyes.

[2]Abercrombie, Life of Edmund Bishop, p. 214.

[3]See Arthur C. Benson, The Life of Edward White
Benson: Sometime Archbishop of Canterbury (London, 1899),
II, 610, quoting a memorandum by Archbishop Benson attached
to a letter from Halifax to Benson, December 12, 1894, and
p. 616, quoting an entry in Benson's diary, April 26, 1895.

[4]Halifax, Leo XIII, pp. 200-201.

[5]Maisie Ward, The Wilfrid Wards, I, 287-90, 293-94;
Halifax, Leo XIII, Appendix 3, pp. 443-45, quoting a
memorandum by Wilfrid Ward on his views concerning the
Anglican orders question; Bedoyere, Baron von Hügel, pp.
82-84.

[6]Halifax, Leo XIII, pp. 110-11, quoting a letter
by Ward to Halifax, September, 1894.

[7]"The Rigidity of Rome," Nineteenth Century,
XXXVIII (November, 1895), 786-804.

[8]Ibid., pp. 787-91, 800-804.

[9]See Halifax, Leo XIII, pp. 105-12, 145-53; Benson,
Life of E. W. Benson, p. 604.

[10]Abercrombie, Life of Edmund Bishop, p. 215;
Leslie, Cardinal Gasquet, p. 79.

[11]Snead-Cox, Life of Cardinal Vaughan, II, 186.

[12]Fleming, born at Killarney in 1851, was an Irish friar attached to the English province. Ordained at Ghent in 1875, he was Lector of Philosophy for nine years. He became first Provincial-Minister, English Province, Order of Friars Minor, 1891; Definitor-General of the United Franciscan Order, 1897; and Vicar-General of the Order of Friars Minor, 1901-1903. F. C. Burnand, ed., The Catholic Who's Who and Year-Book (London, 1910), p. 122.

[13]Snead-Cox, Life of Cardinal Vaughan, II, 194-201. See also Leslie, Cardinal Gasquet, pp. 55-57.

[14]Bedoyere, Baron von Hügel, p. 83; Halifax, Leo XIII, pp. 218, 240 (quoting a letter by Ward to Halifax, January 1, 1896), 292.

[15]Snead-Cox, Life of Cardinal Vaughan, II, 190-91, 223.

[16]Maisie Ward, The Wilfrid Wards, I, 295, quoting a letter by Wilfrid Ward to Halifax, September or October, 1896.

[17]Ibid., Ch. xx, "From the Metaphysical to the Synthetic," and Appendix B, pp. 417-20, giving the Synthetic Society's rules and membership (1896-1908) as well as the premises that it granted and the questions that it sought to answer concerning theism.

[18]Tyrrell was a convert from the Church of Ireland. In 1879 he had left Ireland for England where he converted to Roman Catholicism and entered the Jesuit novitiate the following year. Toward the end of the century he began to emerge as one of the leading figures among the English liberal Catholics.

[19]Barry to Ward, March 9, 1896, Ward Papers. William Francis Barry (1849-1930) studied at Oscott and at the English College and the Gregorian in Rome. He was ordained in 1873, and subsequently taught philosophy at the Birmingham diocesan seminary and theology at Oscott. He was made pastor in Dorchester in 1883. Embarking on a career as an author, he wrote many books, including several novels and some literary and historical studies. See

John J. Delaney and James Edward Tobin, <u>Dictionary of Catholic Biography</u> (Garden City, N.Y., 1961), p. 104.

[20]Gasquet to Ward, March 11, 1896, Ward Papers.

[21]Bedoyere, <u>Baron von Hügel</u>, pp. 87, 89, 95.

[22]1 Jn. 5:7, "Thus we have a threefold warrant in heaven, the Father, the Word, and the Holy Ghost, three who are yet one."

[23]Bedoyere, <u>Baron von Hügel</u>, pp. 96-97, quoting from a letter by Hügel to Ward, May 25, 1898.

[24]Ibid., p. 97; Snead-Cox, <u>Life of Cardinal Vaughan</u>, II, 400-401.

[25]Bedoyere, <u>Baron von Hügel</u>, p. 105.

[26]Ibid., pp. 112-13, quoting from a letter by Hügel to Ward, June 6, 1899.

[27]"Physical Science and Faith," <u>Dublin Review</u>, CXXIII (October, 1898), 241-61.

[28]Ibid., pp. 243-47.

[29]Ibid., pp. 248-50, 258, 260.

[30]Bedoyere, <u>Baron von Hügel</u>, p. 120; Alfred Loisy, <u>Mémoires pour servir à l'histoire religieuse de notre temps</u> (Paris, 1930), I, 500.

[31]Letter by Bishop J[ohn] C. Hedley to the <u>Tablet</u>, January 14, 1899, p. 59, quoting from Leroy's letter.

[32]In 1902 Hedley stated that since this incident of January 1899 he had been informed that no Roman congregation had condemned the thesis of Mivart and Leroy; if there was a real condemnation it emanated from the Dominican Superior of Leroy and not from the Holy See. In April 1902, however, the <u>Civiltà Cattolica</u> quoted Hedley's statement and commented that he had been badly informed. Hedley's biographer says that the Bishop left no papers that would throw further light on the controversy. In any case, there was no public censure of the thesis of Mivart and Leroy by the Holy See. Wilson, <u>Life of Bishop Hedley</u>, pp. 171-72.

[33]Letter by Hedley to the Tablet, January 14, 1899, p. 59.

[34]This letter had appeared in an Italian newspaper, Gazetta di Malta, on May 31, 1899, and was reprinted by the Tablet, June 24, 1899, p. 970.

[35]Tablet, June 24, 1899, p. 970.

[36]See Thomas T. McAvoy, The Americanist Heresy in Roman Catholicism, 1895-1900 (Notre Dame, Indiana, 1963).

[37]"An American Religious Crusade," National Review, XXXIII (March, 1899), 115-28; "'Americanism,' True and False," North American Review, CLXIX (July, 1899), 33-49; "The Troubles of a Catholic Democracy," Contemporary Review, LXXVI (July, 1899), 70-86.

[38]"'Americanism,' True and False," p. 36.

[39]Ibid., pp. 41, 44.

[40]"The Troubles of a Catholic Democracy," p. 70.

[41]"An American Religious Crusade," p. 126.

[42]"The Troubles of a Catholic Democracy," p. 84.

[43]"'Americanism,' True and False," pp. 47-48.

[44]Ibid., pp. 48-49.

[45]"The Troubles of a Catholic Democracy," pp. 78-79.

[46]Bedoyere, Baron von Hügel, p. 123.

[47]William Gibson, "An Outburst of Activity in the Roman Congregations," Nineteenth Century, XLV (May, 1899), 785-94; Wilfrid Ward, "Catholic Apologetics: A Reply," Nineteenth Century, XLV (June, 1899), 955-61. William

Gibson (1868-1942) was the first son of Edward Gibson, who in June 1885 was made Lord Chancellor, Kingdom of Ireland, and in July was created Baron Ashbourne. William Gibson was educated at Dublin and Oxford, where he received a M.A. and converted to Rome. See Vicary Gibbs, ed., The Complete Peerage of England, Scotland, Ireland, Great Britain, and the United Kingdom, new edition, Vol. I (London, 1910), p. 268; F. C. Burnand, ed., The Catholic Who's Who and Year-Book (1910), p. 136. Upon the death of his father in 1913, William Gibson became the second Lord Ashbourne.

[48]Gibson, "An Outburst of Activity in the Roman Congregations," pp. 785, 788-89, 792-94.

[49]Wilfrid Ward, "Catholic Apologetics: A Reply," pp. 955-58.

[50]Ibid., pp. 959-61.

[51]Gibson to Ward, June 1, [1899], Ward Papers.

[52]Tyrrell to Hügel, November 20, 1899, British Museum Additional Manuscript 44927. Hereafter cited as Add. Ms. 44927.

[53]Bedoyere, Baron von Hügel, p. 122.

[54]Letter by Vaughan to The Times, September 18, 1899, p. 9.

[55]"The Roman Catholic Church and the Dreyfus Case," The Times, September 18, 1899, p. 7.

[56]Letter by Ward to The Times, September 21, 1899, p. 10.

[57]"The Roman Catholic Church and the Dreyfus Case," The Times, October 17, 1899, p. 9.

[58]Letter by Mivart to The Times, October 17, 1899, pp. 13-14.

[59]Ibid., p. 14.

[60]Maisie Ward, The Wilfrid Wards, I, 332, quoting a letter by Wilfrid Ward to Hügel, June 28, 1900.

[61]Leslie, Cardinal Gasquet, pp. 156-57, quoting from two letters by Gasquet to Bishop, July 1, 1899 and October 19, 1899.

[62]The New Era was a short-lived periodical edited by Robert Dell, a liberal Catholic.

[63]Abercrombie, Life of Edmund Bishop, pp. 248-50.

NOTES TO CHAPTER III

[1] "The Continuity of Catholicism," Nineteenth Century, XLVII (January, 1900), 51-72; "Some Recent Catholic Apologists," Fortnightly Review, N.S., LXVII (January, 1900), 24-44. These two articles together with Mivart's ensuing correspondence with Cardinal Vaughan, published in The Times, January 25, January 28, and February 1, 1900, were conveniently reprinted in Mivart, Under the Ban (New York, 1900).

[2] "The Continuity of Catholicism," in Under the Ban, pp. 100-101. See also Gruber, A Conscience in Conflict, pp. 191-92.

[3] "The Continuity of Catholicism," in Under the Ban, pp. 68-69, 71-76, 80, 82-83.

[4] Ibid., pp. 87-88, 93-99.

[5] The Wellesley Index to Victorian Periodicals, ed. Houghton, I, 780, 1129, identifies Wilfrid Ward as the author.

[6] "Some Recent Catholic Apologists," in Under the Ban, pp. 34-40, 44, 48-49, 57, 64-65.

[7] Gruber, A Conscience in Conflict, pp. 203-205. Gruber quotes the relevant passage from "Dr. Mivart's Heresy," Tablet, January 6, 1900, p. 7.

[8] See Mivart's letter to Vaughan, January 6, and Vaughan's letter to Mivart, January 9, 1900, with the accompanying profession of faith, in Under the Ban, pp. 3-9.

[9] See letters from Mivart to Vaughan, January 11, Vaughan to Mivart, January 12, and Mivart to Vaughan, January 14, 1900, in ibid., pp. 9-14.

[10]Vaughan to Mivart, January 16, Mivart to Vaughan, January 19, Vaughan to Mivart, January 21, and Mivart to Vaughan, January 23, 1900, in ibid., pp. 14-19.

[11]Mivart to Vaughan, January 27, 1900, in ibid., pp. 29-30.

[12]N[igel] J. Abercrombie, "Edmund Bishop and St. George Mivart," Month, Vol. CXCIII (March, 1952), pp. 176-78 (quoting a letter by Vaughan to Bishop, January 2, 1900, and a letter by Mivart to Bishop, January 7, 1900, with Bishop's underlinings and comments written on the letters), and p. 180 (quoting a draft of a letter by Bishop addressed to Vaughan, a letter Bishop seems never to have sent).

[13]Abercrombie, Life of Edmund Bishop, p. 241.

[14]Leslie, Cardinal Gasquet, p. 198, quoting from a letter by Gasquet to Fleming, January 16, 1900. Apart from Mivart, Gasquet was, in Edmund Bishop's opinion, the only English Catholic who had "taken a place on common ground" and commanded "attention from the ordinary public" in England (Bishop to Everard Green, January 30, 1900, Bishop Papers). Hügel also regarded Gasquet highly at this time (as evident from a compliment by him in a letter to Gasquet, February 17, 1901, Gasquet Papers at Downside Abbey).

[15]Maisie Ward, The Wilfrid Wards, I, 323, 326 quoting from a letter by Tyrrell to Ward and quoting a letter by Ward to Hügel, February 27, 1900.

[16]Ibid., pp. 323-24, quoting a letter by Hügel to Ward, February, 1900.

[17]Hügel to Tyrrell, March 4, 1900, Add. Ms. 44927.

[18]See George Tyrrell, "A Perverted Devotion," in his Essays on Faith and Immortality, arranged by M[aude] D. Petre (London, 1914), pp. 158-71. This article is reprinted from the Weekly Register, December 16, 1899.

[19]Ibid., pp. 161, 170-71. There was perhaps much truth in Tyrrell's complaint that many neo-scholastics at that time were aggravating rather than lessening difficulties by emphasizing their reasoning and by their supposed elucidations of mysteries of faith. John Macquarrie, Twentieth-Century Religious Thought: The Frontiers of Philosophy and Theology, 1900-1960 (New York, 1963), pp. 278-79, notes that the revival of scholasticism was still in an early stage; not until after World War I did Neo-Thomism establish itself as a major strand in contemporary thought and have a number of first-rate thinkers among its representatives.

[20]M[aude] D. Petre, Autobiography and Life of George Tyrrell, 2nd impression (London, 1912), II, 118-20.

[21]Tyrrell to Hügel, February 14, 1900, Add. Ms. 44927.

[22]Maisie Ward, The Wilfrid Wards, I, 326-27, quoting a letter by Ward to Hügel, February 27, 1900.

[23]Maude D. Petre, Von Hügel and Tyrrell (London, 1937), pp. 124-25, 128, quoting a letter by Hügel to Tyrrell, March 4, 1900.

[24]Tyrrell to Hügel, March 10, 1900, Add. Ms. 44927.

[25]Petre, Life of George Tyrrell, II, pp. 120-21, 123-24, quoting passages from Tyrrell's reply, and Appendices 1 and 2, pp. 451-58, which give the entire Latin texts of the two censors' criticisms.

[26]He had already done much the same thing in an article entitled "The Relation of Theology to Devotion" in the Month, November, 1899. This article, however, did not become controversial at the time of its publication.

[27]Petre to Ward, April 30, 1900, Ward Papers.

[28]Petre, Life of George Tyrrell, II, pp. 126-29, quoting from Dell's article, a letter by Tyrrell to Père Henri Bremond, S.J., a letter of instructions by the

General's assistant, Rudolf Meyer, S.J., to the English
Jesuit Provincial, May 16, 1900, and a letter by Tyrrell
to Hügel, June 6, 1900.

[29]Copy (made by Wilfrid Ward in 1910 and sent to
Lord Halifax) of a letter by Tyrrell to Ward, June 18, 1900,
Hickleton Papers, Archives of the Wood Family of Hickleton
and Garrowby. The letter is cited in Petre, Life of George
Tyrrell, II, 109-10. Another letter by Tyrrell gives a
similar assessment: "At present the tension between the
old and young, between those who would yield nothing to
modernism and can see no good in it, and those who would
yield everything and can see no evil in it, is very acute
and dangerous; but such crises are nothing new in the
Church's story . . . growth means sameness and variety, and
the guardians of both interests should tolerate one another
seeing the truth is divided between them" (Tyrrell to Mrs.
Storer, March 9, 1900, Ward Papers).

[30]See Petre, Life of George Tyrrell, II, 70, 130,
137-42.

[31]See ibid., pp. 137-45.

[32]Maude D. Petre's Diary, October 23, 1900,
January 11, 1901, and February 25, 1901, British Museum
Unbound Additional Manuscript 52372. Hereafter cited as
Add. Ms. 52372. Maude Petre (1863-1942), daughter of the
Hon. Arthur Petre, of Coptfold Hall, Essex, and Lady
Catherine Howard, daughter of the 4th Earl of Wicklow,
shared in common with Tyrrell a keen interest in writing on
the life of religion.

[33]Tyrrell to Petre, November 16, and December 18,
1900, British Museum Unbound Additional Manuscript 52367.
Hereafter Add. Ms. 52367.

[34]"A Liberal Catholic View of the Case of Dr.
Mivart," Nineteenth Century, XLVII (April, 1900), 669-84.
Robert Edward Dell (1865-1940), who had been educated at
Oxford, converted to Roman Catholicism in 1897. He edited
the Catholic Weekly Register in 1899-1900. Burnand, ed.,
The Catholic Who's Who and Year-Book (1910), p. 89. From
October 30, 1899 to January 19, 1900, he also edited the

New Era. Dell, letter to the editor, Tablet, March 3, 1900, p. 336.

[35]Dell, "A Liberal Catholic View of the Case of Dr. Mivart," pp. 669-71, 674-80.

[36]Ibid., pp. 681-84.

[37]Nineteenth Century, XLVII (June, 1900), 960-73.

[38]Ibid., pp. 960-63.

[39]Ibid., pp. 963-65, 968-71. See Maisie Ward, The Wilfrid Wards, I, 333-34, for a personal note by Wilfrid Ward concerning the main points he made in this article.

[40]Nineteenth Century, XLVIII (July, 1900), 127-36.

[41]Ibid., pp. 127-31.

[42]Ibid., pp. 132-36.

[43]Maisie Ward, The Wilfrid Wards, I, 327-30, quoting two letters by Hügel to Wilfrid Ward. In the second letter, Dell is referred to as "A. B."

[44]Ibid., pp. 331-32, quoting two letters by Ward to Hügel, June 24 and June 28, 1900. In these two letters, Dell is again referred to as "A. B."

[45]Hügel to Tyrrell, July 7, 1900, Add. Ms. 44927.

[46]Hügel to Tyrrell, September 30, 1900, Add. Ms. 44927.

[47]Maisie Ward, The Wilfrid Wards, I, 318-21, quoting Wilfrid Ward's reminiscences.

[48]"A Convert's Experiences of the Catholic Church," Contemporary Review, LXXVII (June, 1900), 817-34; "The Movement for Reform within the Catholic Church," Contemporary Review, LXXVIII (November, 1900), 693-709.

[49]"A Convert's Experiences of the Catholic Church," pp. 828-32.

[50]"The Movement for Reform within the Catholic Church," pp. 696-702, 707-709.

[51]Petre, Life of George Tyrrell, II, 147.

[52]Robert Dell, letter to the editor, Tablet, March 3, 1900, p. 336.

[53]Maisie Ward, Insurrection versus Resurrection (New York, 1937), The Wilfrid Wards and the Transition: Vol. II, p. 143, quoting a letter by James Britten to Wilfrid Ward, 1901. Britten was the founder of the Catholic Truth Society and on close relations with several English ecclesiastical officials.

[54]"The Church and Liberal Catholicism: Joint Pastoral Letter by the Cardinal Archbishop and the Bishops of the Province of Westminster," [printed in full in the] Tablet, January 5, 1901, pp. 8-12, and January 12, 1901, pp. 50-52 [concluded].

[55]Ibid., pp. 8-9.

[56]Ibid., pp. 9-10.

[57]Ibid., pp. 10-12.

[58]Ibid., pp. 50-52.

[59]Mary Jo Weaver, "George Tyrrell and the Joint Pastoral Letter," Downside Review, XCIX (January, 1981), 19. Weaver's article contains some incorrect statements. In trying to use Wilfrid Ward as a backdrop against which to silhouette Tyrrell, Weaver asserts: "To Ward's way of

thinking, the Church (by which he meant ecclesiastical officials) could not make a mistake" (p. 18). On the contrary, Ward did not identify the Church with ecclesiastical officials, and he recognized that ecclesiastical officials sometimes made mistakes. Moreover, Weaver incorrectly says that the article, "An Outburst of Activity in the Roman Congregations," by William Gibson (later Lord Ashbourne), appeared in the May issue of the Nineteenth Century after Robert Dell's article, "A Liberal Catholic View of the Case of Dr. Mivart," had appeared in the April issue (p. 38, n. 6). In fact, as we have seen in the present book, Gibson's article appeared eleven months before Dell's article: the Nineteenth Century published Gibson's article in May, 1899, and Dell's article in April, 1900. Later in her article, Weaver asserts that Tyrrell "essentially demolished the value of Ward's works in 1904" (p. 27). Tyrrell tried to do that in 1904. Though I believe his attempt was quite unsuccessful, I wish to point out here that it is a matter of opinion and point of view (not fact) whether Tyrrell "essentially demolished the value of Ward's works in 1904" or failed to do that.

[60]"The Pope and Liberal Catholicism: Letter to the English Bishops," [from Leo XIII, Pope, printed in full in the] Tablet, March 23, 1901, p. 441.

[61]"The Joint Pastoral," news commentary in the Tablet, January 5, 1901, pp. 5-6.

[62]Leslie, Cardinal Gasquet, p. 198, quoting from a letter by Gasquet to Fleming, March 25, 1901; Abercrombie, Life of Edmund Bishop, p. 300.

[63]Bedoyere, Baron von Hügel, p. 129.

[64]Maisie Ward, Insurrection versus Resurrection, p. 142.

[65]See E. F. G. [Tyrrell], letter to the editor, Pilot, July 6, 1901, pp. 23-24. See also Maisie Ward, Insurrection versus Resurrection, p. 143, quoting a letter by James Britten to Wilfrid Ward in which Britten said that he knew at least one bishop did not ex animo accept the pastoral.

[66]Abercrombie, Life of Edmund Bishop, pp. 301-303.

[67]Williams to Ward, n.d., Ward Papers. William
John Williams, B.A., Oxford, converted to Rome in 1890.
Hügel once described him as "so shy and sensitive, thoughtful and original" (Bedoyere, Baron von Hügel, p. 90, quoting
a letter by Hügel to Tyrrell, October 19, 1897). Williams
later published a book, Newman, Pascal, Loisy and the
Catholic Church (1906).

[68]Abercrombie, Life of Edmund Bishop, pp. 302-303,
quoting from a letter by Barry to Bishop, August 31, 1901.

[69]Maisie Ward, Insurrection versus Resurrection,
pp. 136-37, quoting a letter by Barry to Wilfrid Ward,
September 3, 1901.

[70]Bishop to Green, October 23, 1901, Bishop Papers.

[71]Petre, Life of George Tyrrell, II, 152, quoting a
letter by Tyrrell to F. Rooke Ley, January 5, 1901.

[72]Copy (made by Wilfrid Ward in 1910) of a letter
by Tyrrell to Ward, January 22, 1901, Hickleton Papers.

[73]Tyrrell to Hügel, February 20, 1901, Add. Ms.
44927.

[74]A Conservative Catholic, letter to the editor,
Pilot, March 2, 1901, p. 282. Petre, Life of George
Tyrrell, II, 154, states that this letter was written by
Tyrrell under the aforementioned pseudonym.

[75]Petre, Life of George Tyrrell, II, 155-57, quoting
a private letter by Tyrrell to F. Rooke Ley in explanation
of his article.

[76]Ibid., pp. 158-60, quoting a letter by S.T.L.
[Tyrrell] to the Weekly Register, May 24, 1901, and from a
letter by Tyrrell to F. Rooke Ley, April 27, 1901. Cf.
Lord Halifax, "The Recent Anglo-Roman Pastoral," Nineteenth
Century and After, XLIX (May, 1901), 736-54. Thomas
Michael Loome, "A Bibliography of the Published Writings of

George Tyrrell (1861-1909)," Heythrop Journal, X (July, 1969), 305, attributes the article to Tyrrell and gives evidence that only a few pages of it were by Halifax. Also, Loome lists the Weekly Register writings by Tyrrell, Ryder, and Ward.

[77]Joseph Rickaby, "The Church and Liberal Catholicism," in the Month, XCVII (April, 1901), 337-46.

[78]Tyrrell to Hügel, June 17, 1901, Add. Ms. 44927. Additional remarks by Tyrrell in a temper indicate his growing dissatisfaction with his order. Commenting on congregations drawn by a popular Jesuit preacher at Farm Street, London, Tyrrell said there was not even the ghost of the Jesuit pretence to address itself to the educated classes. He impetuously remarked that the Society maintained its ascendency through its power over the wealthy bourgeoisie and over the silliest kind of women.

[79]Wilfrid Ward, "Doctores Ecclesiæ," Pilot, June 22, 1901, pp. 774-76.

[80]Hügel to Tyrrell, August 6, 1901, Add. Ms. 44927.

[81]Tyrrell to Hügel, September 22, 1901, Add. Ms. 44927.

[82]M[aude] D. Petre, ed., George Tyrrell's Letters (London, 1920), pp. 72-74, letter by Tyrrell to Ward, August 1, 1901.

[83]Tyrrell to Petre, August 2, 1901, Add. Ms. 52367. In August 1901, Tyrrell was still able to say to Cardinal Vaughan that he did not think they differed more than they had a few years before. Vaughan had then told Tyrrell he was moving too rapidly and should await more propitious times; Tyrrell, in turn, had suggested that Vaughan was moving too slowly. Tyrrell to Vaughan, August 26, 1901, archives of the Archbishop of Westminster. In the following years, further important differences developed between Tyrrell and ecclesiastical authorities.

[84]Maisie Ward, Insurrection versus Resurrection, p. 143, quoting Britten's letter to Wilfrid Ward.

NOTES TO CHAPTER IV

[1]Maisie Ward, Insurrection versus Resurrection,
pp. 493-95, quoting a letter by Hügel to Wilfrid Ward,
January, 1902; Bedoyere, Baron von Hügel, pp. 137-38,
quoting an undated letter by Hügel to Ward and from a letter
by Hügel to the same, February 12, 1902.

[2]Maisie Ward, Insurrection versus Resurrection,
p. 494, quoting Hügel's letter to Ward, January, 1902. See
also Maisie Ward, The Wilfrid Wards, I, 317, quoting Wilfrid
Ward's reminiscences.

[3]Leslie, Cardinal Gasquet, pp. 161-62, quoting
letters by Gasquet to Bishop, January 3 and January 9, 1902.

[4]See Vidler, The Modernist Movement, pp. 106-108,
113-22; Macquarrie, Twentieth-Century Religious Thought,
pp. 88-89, 93-94.

[5]Maisie Ward, Insurrection versus Resurrection,
p. 161.

[6]Bedoyere, Baron von Hügel, pp. 144-45, quoting a
letter by Hügel to Loisy, November 15, 1902, cited in Alfred
Loisy, Mémoires, I, 377.

[7]Maisie Ward, Insurrection versus Resurrection,
p. 162, quoting from Loisy, Mémoires, II, 226.

[8]Maisie Ward, Insurrection versus Resurrection,
p. 162.

[9]Bedoyere, Baron von Hügel, p. 147.

[10]See Alfred Loisy, My Duel with the Vatican, trans.
Richard Wilson Boynton (New York, 1924), Appendix 9,
"Ordinance of Cardinal Richard, dated January 17th, 1903, in
condemnation of The Gospel and the Church," p. 341.

NOTES TO CHAPTER IV

[11]Bedoyere, Baron von Hügel, p. 143, quoting from Loisy, Mémoires, II, 168.

[12]Loisy, My Duel with the Vatican, pp. 227-28.

[13]Leslie, Cardinal Gasquet, p. 202, quoting from a letter by Barry to Gasquet, February 16, 1903.

[14]Bedoyere, Baron von Hügel, p. 149.

[15]Ibid.

[16]Loisy, My Duel with the Vatican, p. 240.

[17]Ibid., p. 186.

[18]Maisie Ward, Insurrection versus Resurrection, pp. 164-65.

[19]Leslie, Cardinal Gasquet, p. 199, quoting a letter by Gasquet to Fleming, November 29, 1903.

[20]Copy of a letter by Barry, November 23, 1903, Ward Papers.

[21]Bedoyere, Baron von Hügel, pp. 154-55.

[22]Ibid., pp. 156-57. Besides L'Évangile et l'Église and Autour d'un petit livre, three other works by Loisy were censured: La Religion d'Israël, Etudes évangéliques, and Quatrième Évangile.

[23]Loisy, My Duel with the Vatican, Appendix 10, "Decree of the Holy Office and letter from Cardinal Merry del Val to Cardinal Richard," pp. 341-42. For a detailed account of the exchanges between Loisy and the ecclesiastical authorities that followed the decree and letter, see ibid., pp. 250-70.

[24]Catholicus, letter to the editor, The Times, January 25, 1904, p. 4; Romanus, letter to the editor, The Times, March 2, 1904, p. 15. Bedoyere, Baron von Hügel, pp. 155-56, identifies "Catholicus" as Fleming and refers to a letter by Hügel to Ward in which Hügel spoke of Fleming's letter to The Times as treacherous. Jean Steinmann, Friedrich von Hügel (Paris, 1962), p. 175, identifies Hügel as the author of the "Romanus" letter and quotes from Loisy, Mémoires, II, 328, evidencing the fact. Bedoyere, Baron von Hügel, pp. 155-56, indicates the same in writing that Hügel "joined in a correspondence in The Times where Fr. Fleming, over the pseudonym 'Catholicus,' was now showing himself hostile to Loisy."

[25]Catholicus, letter to the editor, The Times, January 25, 1904, p. 4.

[26]Romanus, letter to the editor, The Times, March 2, 1904, p. 15.

[27]The Times, January 25, 1904, p. 4.

[28]The Times, March 2, 1904, p. 15.

[29]Bedoyere, Baron von Hügel, p. 157.

[30]The Times, March 2, 1904, p. 15.

[31]Bedoyere, Baron von Hügel, p. 166.

[32]See "Official Authority and Living Religion" in Friedrich von Hügel, Essays and Addresses on the Philosophy of Religion, 2nd ser. (London and Toronto, 1930), pp. 1-23.

[33]Cf. Maurice Nédoncelle, La Pensée religieuse de Friedrich von Hügel (1852-1925) (Paris, 1935), p. 201.

[34]Bedoyere, Baron von Hügel, pp. 166-67, quoting from a letter by Blondel to Hügel, June 24, 1904, and from a letter by Ward to Hügel, July 6, 1904.

NOTES TO CHAPTER IV

[35]In its strict sense, the term "mystic" denotes a
temperament characterized by a "passion for union with the
object of religious devotion. . . ." But Hügel tended to
use the term in a broader sense to refer to all interior or
personal experiential religion; he did not perhaps adequately
distinguish this sense of the term from its strict sense.
Moreover, he considered it unwholesome in cultivating
interior religion to isolate the mystical element from the
institutional and intellectual elements, from discipline
and learning. Clement C. J. Webb, A Study of Religious
Thought in England from 1850 (Oxford, 1933), pp. 139-40.

[36]Bedoyere, Baron von Hügel, pp. 158-59.

[37]Loisy, Mémoires, II, 397; quoted in Maisie Ward,
Insurrection versus Resurrection, pp. 504-505. Loisy's
journal entry is dated June 7, 1904.

[38]In his book, Baron Friedrich von Hügel and the
Modernist Crisis in England (Cambridge, Eng., 1972),
Lawrence F. Barmann showed that Hügel was very much involved
in the modernist movement. In Dr. Barmann's book, however,
the anti-immanentism and antisubjectivism that developed in
Hügel's thought and that distinguished him from some of the
other modernists receive only passing mention, although
Hügel ultimately attached great importance to these issues,
which were, indeed, central ones in the modernist crisis.
This is a substantial weakness in Barmann's book, as I noted
in my review of the book in the American Historical Review,
LXXVIII (April, 1973), 447-48. See also Thomas Michael
Loome, "The Enigma of Baron Friedrich von Hügel--as
Modernist," Downside Review, XCI (January, 1973), 13-34;
(April, 1973), 123-40; (July, 1973), 204-30. Over and above
providing a balanced view of Hügel, I believe my study of
the intellectual crisis in English Catholicism demonstrates,
so far as England is concerned, a very important point suggested by Loome in his recently published book, Liberal
Catholicism, Reform Catholicism, Modernism: A Contribution
to a New Orientation in Modernist Research (Mainz, Germany,
1979): "It is only when one stresses one crisis manifest in
many highly diverse controversies that one can do justice to
the complexity of the crisis and make room for the widely
differing controversies through which the crisis unfolded"
(p. 195). However, my use of the term "modernist" differs
from his. Whereas he employs "modernist" as a synonym for
"liberal Catholic," I use "modernist" to indicate a subgroup

that emerged among the larger "liberal Catholic" group as the intellectual crisis unfolded.

[39]Whelan, The Spirituality of Friedrich von Hügel (London, 1971), p. 112.

[40]Hügel to Tyrrell, May 30, 1903, Add. Ms. 44928. Cited in Whelan, Spirituality of von Hügel, p. 112.

[41]See Hügel to Petre, April 20, 1902, Add. Ms. 45361.

[42]Hügel to Tyrrell, June 4, 1902, Add. Ms. 44928.

[43]See Vidler, A Variety of Catholic Modernists, pp. 121-22, 145.

[44]Hügel to Petre, April 20, 1902, Add. Ms. 45361.

[45]Bedoyere, Baron von Hügel, p. 164.

[46]Ibid., p. 156.

[47]Maisie Ward, Insurrection versus Resurrection, pp. 497-98.

[48]Hügel to Petre, October 5, 1903, Add. Ms. 45361.

[49]Tyrrell to Hügel, November 20, 1904, Add. Ms. 44928.

[50]Hügel to Tyrrell, January 28 and February 5, 1904, Add. Ms. 44928; cited in Bedoyere, Baron von Hügel, p. 161. An attack of typhoid fever in 1870 had left Hügel delicate in health, nervous, and deaf.

[51]Bedoyere, Baron von Hügel, p. 195; Loisy, My Duel with the Vatican, p. 303.

[52]John Corbett, "The Biblical Commission," Catholic Encyclopedia (New York, 1913), II, 558.

[53]See Vidler, The Modernist Movement, pp. 185-88, 193-96, for brief commentaries on Laberthonnière and Fogazzaro.

[54]Ibid., p. 187.

[55]Bedoyere, Baron von Hügel, p. 182, quoting a letter by Hügel to Petre, April 17, 1906.

[56]Loisy, Mémoires, II, 449; quoted in Bedoyere, Baron von Hügel, p. 172. Hügel's letter to Loisy and Loisy's response are dated August, 1905.

[57]Webb, Religious Thought in England, p. 12.

[58]The above paragraph is partially based on ibid., Ch. i, "Introductory."

[59]Linguistic analysis and existentialism became the popular philosophies. In England and the United States, linguistic analysis predominated within the philosophical schools.

[60]Knox and Vidler, Development of Modern Catholicism, p. 181.

[61]Macquarrie, Twentieth-Century Religious Thought, pp. 178-79, 191.

[62]Of the Catholic intellectuals mentioned in this paragraph, Blondel, whose thought is very complex and who publicly disagreed with Loisy, is usually not considered to be a modernist.

[63]M[aude] D. Petre, My Way of Faith (London, 1937), pp. 290-93; Maisie Ward, Insurrection versus Resurrection, pp. 186-87.

[64]Tyrrell to Hügel, January 3, [1902], Add. Ms. 44928.

[65]Hügel to Tyrrell, December 4, 1902, and Tyrrell to Hügel, December 5, 1902, Add. Ms. 44928. David G. Schultenover, George Tyrrell: In Search of Catholicism (Shepherdstown, W. Va., 1981), a book which appeared almost too late (August, 1981) to note here, describes Tyrrell's intellectual development in detail up to and including the year 1903. It, however, does not treat in detail his works from 1904 down to his death in 1909. For further comments, see my forthcoming review in the American Historical Review.

[66]See Petre, <u>Life of George Tyrrell</u>, II, 193-94;
J. Lewis May, <u>Father Tyrrell and the Modernist Movement</u>
(London, 1932), pp. 215-16; Vidler, <u>The Modernist Movement</u>,
p. 168.

[67]Maude D. Petre's Diary, Add. Mss. 52372 and 52373.

[68]George Tyrrell, <u>A Much-Abused Letter</u>, new impression (London, 1907), pp. 40-41, 48-52. This little book is
a publication of Tyrrell's "A Letter to a Professor of
Anthropology."

[69]<u>Ibid.</u>, pp. 53-56.

[70]<u>Ibid.</u>, pp. 65-66.

[71]Vidler, <u>The Modernist Movement</u>, p. 164. For
Tyrrell's admission of drawing on James' pragmatism, see
Petre, ed., <u>George Tyrrell's Letters</u>, p. 22, Tyrrell to
Rev. J. H. R. Abbott, August 11, 1904.

[72]Tyrrell, <u>A Much-Abused Letter</u>, pp. 78-79.

[73]<u>Ibid.</u>, pp. 63, 87, 89,

[74]See George Tyrrell, "Semper Eadem (I)," in his
<u>Through Scylla and Charybdis: Or the Old Theology and the
New</u> (London, 1907), pp. 107-32. It is a reprint of the
"Semper Eadem" article in the <u>Month</u>, January, 1904.

[75]See Maisie Ward, <u>Insurrection versus Resurrection</u>,
p. 165; Tyrrell, <u>Through Scylla and Charybdis</u>, pp. 106-107,
note by Tyrrell on "Semper Eadem."

[76]Tyrrell, "Semper Eadem (I)," in his <u>Through Scylla
and Charybdis</u>, pp. 107-11.

[77]<u>Ibid.</u>, pp. 111-14.

[78]<u>Ibid.</u>, pp. 115-21, 129.

[79]<u>Ibid.</u>, pp. 130-32.

[80]See Tyrrell, Through Scylla and Charybdis, p. 107, note by Tyrrell on "Semper Eadem."

[81]See ibid., p. 133, and Tyrrell to Ward, January 4, 14, 19, and 25, 1904, Ward Papers.

[82]Maisie Ward, Insurrection versus Resurrection, pp. 167-68.

[83]John Gerard, S.J., to Ward, January 20 and 21, 1904, Ward Papers. Gerard subsequently sent Ward the letter (Tyrrell to Gerard, December 5, 1903) in which Tyrrell had proposed the article.

[84]Gerard to Ward, January 26, 1904, Ward Papers. Cited in Maisie Ward, Insurrection versus Resurrection, p. 168.

[85]Tyrrell to Ward, December 1, 1904, Ward Papers, quoted in Maisie Ward, Insurrection versus Resurrection, pp. 169-70.

[86]Bedoyere, Baron von Hügel, pp. 172-74; Bernard Holland, ed., Baron Friedrich von Hügel: Selected Letters, 1896-1924 (London and Toronto, 1927), pp. 129-32. Bedoyere cites a letter by Hügel to Tyrrell, June 12, 1905, which is printed in Holland's selection of Hügel's letters.

[87]George Tyrrell, Lex Credendi, new impression (London, 1907), pp. 15-16, 31-32, 38-41.

[88]Macquarrie, Twentieth-Century Religious Thought, p. 190.

[89]In 1903, he had published a book entitled Lex Orandi. Lex Credendi was a sequel to it.

[90]Tyrrell, Lex Credendi, pp. xi-xii, 240, 253-55.

[91]For an enumeration of these works and brief commentaries on them, see Petre, Life of George Tyrrell, Vol. II, Ch. viii, "Last Works of the Jesuit Period."

[92]May, Father Tyrrell, p. 218. May quotes the letter on pp. 218-21. The letter is printed at fuller length in Petre, ed., George Tyrrell's Letters, pp. 56-61, Tyrrell to Hügel, February 10, 1907.

[93]Petre, ed., George Tyrrell's Letters, pp. 56-58, Tyrrell to Hügel, February 10, 1907.

[94]Ibid., pp. 58-61, Tyrrell to Hügel, February 10, 1907.

[95]Vidler, The Modernist Movement, p. 174.

[96]Bedoyere, Baron von Hügel, pp. 173-76.

[97]For a detailed account of Tyrrell's relationship with the Jesuit order after 1900, see Petre, Life of George Tyrrell, Vol. II, Ch. x, "Rupture with the Society (1901-1906)."

[98]See ibid., pp. 249-55, 297-307. On p. 249 of Petre's work, it is incorrectly stated that the extracts from Tyrrell's "Letter to a Professor of Anthropology" were published in the Corriere della Sera on December 31, 1905. Thomas Michael Loome, "A Bibliography of the Published Writings of George Tyrrell (1861-1909)," Heythrop Journal, X (July, 1969), p. 290, gives January 1, 1906, as the correct date and notes the error.

[99]Hedley, however, was not actively engaged in the attempts to reconcile Catholicism with contemporary culture. "The circumstances of his career kept the Bishop apart from the chief centres of Catholic activity, so that he was not called upon to guide or direct the wider movements of thought and action around him." In addition, he had little faith in public controversy. Wilson, Life of Bishop Hedley, pp. vii-viii, 210-11.

[100]Leslie, Cardinal Gasquet, pp. 81-82.

[101]Abercrombie, Life of Edmund Bishop, p. 333.

[102]See Leslie, Cardinal Gasquet, pp. 84-85, "Memorandum of Abbot Gasquet on the Election of the Archbishop of Westminster, 1903.

[103]Maisie Ward, Insurrection versus Resurrection, p. 151.

[104]Bedoyere, Baron von Hügel, p. 152.

[105]Leslie, Cardinal Gasquet, p. 83, quoting a letter by Gasquet to Bishop, September 7, 1903. For another account of the appointment of Bourne to Westminster, see Ernest Oldmeadow, Francis Cardinal Bourne (London, 1940), I, 207-11.

[106]Leslie, Cardinal Gasquet, pp. 82-83, 86-87, quoting a letter by Fleming to Gasquet, October 22, 1903.

[107]Maisie Ward, Insurrection versus Resurrection, pp. 150-51.

[108]Bedoyere, Baron von Hügel, p. 152.

[109]Leslie, Cardinal Gasquet, p. 83, quoting a letter by Gasquet to Bishop, September 7, 1903.

[110]Maisie Ward, Insurrection versus Resurrection, pp. 212-13.

[111]Hedley to Ward, January 22, 1906, Ward Papers.

[112]Maisie Ward, Insurrection versus Resurrection, pp. 205, 213-15.

NOTES TO CHAPTER V

[1]Loisy, My Duel with the Vatican, p. 309.

[2]Petre, ed., George Tyrrell's Letters, p. 133,
letter by Tyrrell to William Scott-Palmer (Mrs. Dowson),
August 29, 1907.

[3]Petre, Life of George Tyrrell, II, 356, quoting a
letter by Tyrrell to Emil Wolff, February 5, 1908.

[4]Petre, Von Hügel and Tyrrell, p. 160, quoting a
letter by Hügel to Tyrrell written shortly after the
promulgation of the encyclical condemning modernism.

[5]"Decree of the Holy Roman and Universal Inquisition
(Lamentabili Sane Exitu)" [English translation reprinted
from the Tablet], in Paul Sabatier, Modernism, trans. C. A.
Miles (London, 1908), Appendix 3, p. 217.

[6]Maisie Ward, Insurrection versus Resurrection,
p. 255, quoting a letter by Wilfrid Ward to Paul Sabatier,
August, 1906.

[7]Barry to Ward, May 8, 1906, Ward Papers.

[8]Maisie Ward, Insurrection versus Resurrection,
pp. 220-21, 235; Bedoyere, Baron von Hügel, pp. 182-83.
Ward's Dublin articles, "The Functions of Prejudice" (April,
1906) and "For Truth or for Life" (October, 1906 and April,
1907), displeased Bagshawe, who had been made an archbishop
in partibus.

[9]See Maisie Ward, Insurrection versus Resurrection,
pp. 222-30.

[10]Maturin to Ward, June 18, 1907, Ward Papers.
Basil William Maturin (1847-1915), Catholic preacher and
writer, took his degree at Trinity College, Dublin, and was
ordained deacon in the Anglican Church in 1870. From 1873
to 1897, he was a member of the Society of St. John the
Evangelist, Cowley. He converted to Roman Catholicism in
1897, and was ordained a priest in 1898 after studying
theology in Rome. The Dictionary of National Biography,
1912-1921, ed. H. W. C. Davis and J. R. H. Weaver (London,
1927; rpt. 1953), pp. 371-72. When George Tyrrell died in
1909, Robert Dell wrote of Maturin: "It was very nice of
Maturin to come to the funeral; he was the only priest there
except [Henri] Bremond, and of course he did not agree with
Tyrrell. But he was very fond of him and he happens to be
a Christian." Dell to Edmund Bishop, August 6, 1909,
Bishop Papers. Maturin died during World War I--torpedoed
on the Lusitania returning from a visit to America.

[11]Maisie Ward, Insurrection versus Resurrection,
pp. 227-30, quoting a letter by Croke-Robinson to Ward,
August 15, 1907, and a letter by Ward replying to Croke-
Robinson.

[12]Ibid., p. 234, quoting from a letter by Bourne to
Ward, date unspecified.

[13]Ibid., pp. 217-19, quoting a letter by Ward to
Bourne, June, 1907, and p. 226, quoting from a letter by
Ward to Bourne, date unspecified.

[14]Ibid., pp. 230-31, quoting a statement by Bishop
Hedley, dated September 19, 1907, and p. 270, quoting a
letter by Ward to Fr. John Norris, November 4, 1907, in
which Ward said that Bagshawe told Bourne that he was
delating Ward to Rome, Bourne advised Ward to appeal to
Hedley, and Hedley wrote strongly to Rome on Ward's behalf.

[15]Ibid., p. 231, quoting from a letter by Merry del
Val to Hedley, date unspecified.

[16]Bedoyere, Baron von Hügel, pp. 182-84; Abercrombie,
Life of Edmund Bishop, pp. 355-56. For a detailed study of
Hügel's involvement in the modernist movement, see Lawrence
F. Barmann's Baron Friedrich von Hügel and the Modernist
Crisis in England. The book emphasizes Hügel's involvement

in the modernist movement in his English environment but also treats his international activities in its behalf. For criticisms of Barmann's interpretation of Hügel, see Thomas Michael Loome, "The Enigma of Baron Friedrich von Hügel--as Modernist" [Installments I and III], <u>Downside Review</u>, XCI (January, 1973), 13-34; (July, 1973), 204-30. In the present chapter and, especially, in Ch. vi, I have sought to present a balanced view of Hügel in relation to modernism.

[17]Bedoyere, <u>Baron von Hügel</u>, pp. 186-87, quoting from a letter by Mignot to Hügel, November 23, 1906.

[18]Holland, ed., <u>Hügel: Selected Letters</u>, pp. 136-37, letter by Hügel to Tyrrell, December 18, 1906. The letter is cited in Bedoyere, <u>Baron von Hügel</u>, pp. 188-89.

[19]Bedoyere, <u>Baron von Hügel</u>, p. 189, citing Loisy, <u>Mémoires</u>, II, 498-500.

[20]Hügel to Petre, July 3, 1906, Add. Ms. 45361.

[21]Norfolk to Wilfrid Ward, July 15, 1906, Ward Papers.

[22]Petre, <u>Life of George Tyrrell</u>, II, 257-58, 283-84, 307-15. Among the friends with whom Tyrrell stayed were the English liberal Catholics W. J. Williams and William Gibson with whom he felt a mutual sympathy. His cousin William Tyrrell (later Lord Tyrrell) of the British Foreign Office also offered his hospitality.

[23]See Friedrich von Hügel, "Father Tyrrell: Some Memorials of the Last Twelve Years of His Life," <u>Hibbert Journal</u>, VIII (January, 1910), 235.

[24]See Petre, <u>Life of George Tyrrell</u>, II, 315-22, for information on the preparation of <u>Through Scylla and Charybdis</u> and for comments on the work.

[25]George Tyrrell, "From Heaven, or of Men?" in his <u>Through Scylla and Charybdis</u>, pp. 361-65, 369-72, 381-82, 384.

NOTES TO CHAPTER V

²⁶_Through Scylla and Charybdis_, pp. 355-57, note by Tyrrell on "From Heaven, or of Men?"

²⁷Holland, ed., _Hügel: Selected Letters_, pp. 138-39, letter by Hügel to Tyrrell, May 14, 1907.

²⁸Loisy, _My Duel with the Vatican_, pp. 280-86.

²⁹_Ibid._, pp. 286, 296-97.

³⁰Bedoyere, _Baron von Hügel_, pp. 191-92.

³¹Loisy, _My Duel with the Vatican_, pp. 297-98, 302-303.

³²Fr. David [Fleming] to Wilfrid Ward, May 3, 1907, Ward Papers.

³³_Ibid._

³⁴Cf. Ratté, _Three Modernists_, p. 18.

³⁵"Decree of the Holy Roman and Universal Inquisition (_Lamentabili Sane Exitu_)" [English translation reprinted from the _Tablet_], in Sabatier, _Modernism_, Appendix 3, pp. 217-30.

³⁶Loisy, _My Duel with the Vatican_, pp. 303-304.

³⁷Petre, ed., _George Tyrrell's Letters_, pp. 106-107, letter by Tyrrell to Robert Dell, August 2, 1907.

³⁸Bedoyere, _Baron von Hügel_, p. 195, quoting from a letter by Hügel to Tyrrell, July 27, 1907.

³⁹Barry to Ward, July 23, 1907, Ward Papers.

⁴⁰Petre, _Life of George Tyrrell_, II, 322-31.

[41]See "Encyclical Letter ('Pascendi Gregis')" [reprint of official English translation], in Sabatier, Modernism, Appendix 4, pp. 231-346.

[42]Pascendi Gregis, in Sabatier, Modernism, pp. 234, 236-37.

[43]Ibid., pp. 237-40, 245-46.

[44]Ibid., pp. 252-53, 257-60.

[45]Ibid., pp. 263-67.

[46]Ibid., pp. 268-69, 271-72.

[47]Ibid., pp. 273-74, 278-79.

[48]Ibid., pp. 280, 283-84, 286-87.

[49]Ibid., pp. 288-89, 291, 299, 304.

[50]Ibid., pp. 309, 312-14.

[51]Ibid., pp. 314-18, 322-23.

[52]Ibid., pp. 324-30.

[53]Ibid., pp. 330-35, 337-41, 344.

[54]Ibid., pp. 344-45.

[55]Maisie Ward, Insurrection versus Resurrection, pp. 254-55.

[56]Ch. xiv, in Maisie Ward, Insurrection versus Resurrection. Notwithstanding my criticism of this chapter, her work remains, in my opinion, a really good biography of Wilfrid Ward; by and large, she understood Wilfrid Ward's thought very well, and much better than some recent minor commenters.

NOTES TO CHAPTER V

[57]Copy of a letter by Ward to Father John [Norris], n.d., Ward Papers.

[58]Norfolk to Ward, October 2, 1907, Ward Papers.

[59]Copy of a letter by Ward to Norfolk, October 10, 1907, Ward Papers.

[60]Norfolk to Ward, October 11, 1907, Ward Papers.

[61]Letter by Williams to The Times, November 2, 1907, p. 10.

[62]Copy of a letter by Ward to Norfolk, November 2, 1907, Ward Papers. Ward thought that Pascendi had hit such staples of Newman's thought as his non-scholastic approach to religious belief and assent, and his idea of doctrinal development--even though Newman opposed the view that dogmas could be cast aside as obsolete.

[63]Letter by Norris to The Times, November 4, 1907, p. 10; Maisie Ward, Insurrection versus Resurrection, pp. 268-69, quoting a letter by Ward to Norris, November 4, 1907.

[64]Copy of a draft of an unpublished letter by Ward to The Times, Ward Papers. For contrast and comparison of Newman and modernism, see B[ernard] M. G. Reardon, "Newman and the Catholic Modernist Movement," Church Quarterly, IV (July, 1971), 50-60; J. Derek Holmes, "Newman and Modernism," Baptist Quarterly, XXIV (July, 1972), 335-41; Edward E. Kelly, "Newman, Wilfrid Ward, and the Modernist Crisis," Thought, XLVIII (Winter, 1973), 508-19.

[65]Letter by Gasquet to The Times, November 5, 1907, p. 8.

[66]Copy of a letter by Ward to W. S. Lilly, November 5, 1907, Ward Papers.

[67]Letter by Williams to The Times, November 6, 1907, p. 13.

[68]Letter by Norris to The Times, November 7, 1907, p. 4.

[69]"The Pope and Modernism," [from The Times correspondent in Rome], The Times, November 6, 1907, p. 7.

[70]Letter by Gasquet to The Times, November 7, 1907, p. 4.

[71]Letter by Dell to The Times, November 13, 1907, p. 19.

[72]Leslie, Cardinal Gasquet, p. 200, quoting from a letter by Gasquet to Fleming, November 28, 1907.

[73]Vaughan to Ward, December 12, 1907, Ward Papers.

[74]Vaughan to Ward, November 28, 1907, Ward Papers.

[75]Copy of a draft of an unpublished letter by Ward to The Times, Ward Papers.

[76]Copy of a letter by Ward to Williams, December 14, 1907, Ward Papers.

[77]Copy of a letter by Ward to Williams, December 24, 1907, Ward Papers. Maisie Ward, Insurrection versus Resurrection, Appendix B, "Difficulties in the Encyclical Pascendi," pp. 559-62, proffers a solution of difficulties that Wilfrid Ward saw in Pascendi.

[78]Williams to Ward, n.d., Ward Papers.

[79]Williams to Ward, n.d., Ward Papers.

[80]Williams to Ward, n.d., Ward Papers.

[81]Williams to Ward, n.d., Ward Papers.

[82] [Wilfrid Ward], "The Encyclical 'Pascendi,'" Dublin Review, CXLII (January, 1908), 1-10. Maisie Ward identifies this article as Wilfrid Ward's article on Pascendi and gives incidents connected with its publication. Maisie Ward, Insurrection versus Resurrection, pp. 288-92.

[83] [Wilfrid Ward], "The Encyclical 'Pascendi,'" pp. 1-3, 5-6.

[84] Ibid., pp. 9-10.

[85] Barry to Ward, January 3, 1908, Ward Papers.

[86] Hügel to Ward, February 10, 1908, Ward-Hügel correspondence, St. Andrews University Library. Quoted, with no date given, in Maisie Ward, Insurrection versus Resurrection, p. 290.

[87] Maisie Ward, Insurrection versus Resurrection, pp. 290-91.

[88] Abercrombie, Life of Edmund Bishop, pp. 374-75, 405, n. 1.

[89] Ward Papers. James Hope was Ward's brother-in-law.

[90] Bishop to Green, August 1, 1908, Bishop Papers.

[91] Edmund Bishop to W. C. Bishop, August 9, 1908, Bishop Papers.

[92] Bedoyere, Baron von Hügel, pp. 200-201, 203, quoting from a letter by Hügel to Tyrrell, October 1, 1907.

[93] Ibid., pp. 200-201, 204-207.

[94] Bedoyere, Baron von Hügel, pp. 213, 221. The book, published in 1908, was his magnum opus. It revealed two basic characteristics of his thought: (1) it was not a treatise on mysticism but an attempt to find the mystical element's right place in man's entire knowledge and experience of his relationship with God, and (2) it treated the

subject not by systematic philosophical reasoning but by the
historical record of the mystic Catherine of Genoa's experience. Although "written throughout the Modernist crisis, it
bore little or no trace of the Modernist views. . . ."
Ibid., pp. 225, 227.

[95]Petre, Von Hügel and Tyrrell, pp. 147 (quoting
from a letter by Tyrrell to Dell, May 3, 1908), 197-98.
See also Dell to Edmund Bishop, August 6, 1909: "he [Hügel]
has intervals of courage, but they are intervals" (Bishop
Papers).

[96]Petre, Von Hügel and Tyrrell, pp. 147-48.

[97]Loisy, My Duel with the Vatican, pp. 307-11
(quoting from a letter by Loisy to Merry del Val, September
29, 1907), 314-15. On p. 314, Loisy explicitly says that
he did not conceal from himself that his actual opinions
were censured, in and together with those he might be able
to disavow.

[98]Bedoyere, Baron von Hügel, p. 204.

[99]Loisy, My Duel with the Vatican, pp. 311-18. See
Appendix 11, pp. 343-44, for the ordinance by the Archbishop of Paris condemning Les Évangiles Synoptiques and
Simples réflexions, and Appendix 12, pp. 344-45, for the
decree of the Holy Office excommunicating Loisy.

[100]Hügel to Petre, February 20, 1908, Add. Ms. 45361.
Quoted in Bedoyere, Baron von Hügel, p. 208.

[101]Bedoyere, Baron von Hügel, pp. 208-209, 215.
Bedoyere quotes from a letter by Mignot to Hügel, March 9,
1908, and Loisy's Mémoires, III, 20.

[102]Hügel, "Father Tyrrell: Some Memorials of the
Last Twelve Years of His Life," pp. 245-46.

[103]See ibid., p. 246; Bedoyere, Baron von Hügel,
p. 201.

[104]Petre, Life of George Tyrrell, II, 335, 338-39, quoting a letter by Tyrrell to Hügel, October 3, 1907.

[105]Petre, Von Hügel and Tyrrell, p. 160, quoting a letter by Hügel to Tyrrell.

[106]George Tyrrell, "The Pope and Modernism," The Times, September 30, 1907, p. 4. Noting the modernist complaint that the Roman Church had made faith a matter of yielding intellectual assent to propositions, John Macquarrie has commented: "it is of course true that the Roman Catholic Church more than any other precisely defines its dogmas in propositional form. . . . No doubt many Catholics have identified and do identify faith with mere intellectual assent, yet here is what a leading Catholic theologian, Karl Adam, says of those who hold their faith in an intellectualist way only: 'Their faith often is reduced to a purely intellectual and therefore shallow awareness of the teaching of the Church, and to a mere assent of the mind. And yet every Credo, if said in the spirit of the Church, ought to be an act of completest dedication of the entire man to God, an assent springing from the great and ineffable distress of our finite nature and our sin.' Such a statement makes it clear that the Catholic conception of faith is a richer one than some of its critics will allow it to be, and that it is indeed inseparable from the wider life of the Church." Thus Macquarrie suggests that the Roman Church does not equate faith with mere intellectual assent. Macquarrie, Twentieth-Century Religious Thought, p. 291.

[107]George Tyrrell, "The Pope and Modernism (II)," The Times, October 1, 1907, p. 5.

[108]Petre, Von Hügel and Tyrrell, pp. 161-63, quoting letters by Hügel to Tyrrell, September 30 and October 1, 1907, and Tyrrell to Hügel, October 3, 1907. Hügel's letter of October 1 is printed at greater length in Holland, ed., Hügel: Selected Letters, pp. 141-42.

[109]Petre, Life of George Tyrrell, II, 341.

[110]Vidler, The Modernist Movement, p. 211.

[111]Copy of a letter by Ward to Norfolk, October 10, 1907, Ward Papers.

[112]Williams to Ward, n.d., Ward Papers.

[113]Petre, Life of George Tyrrell, II, 349, quoting from a letter by Tyrrell to V. [this unidentified V. was Maude Petre], March 22, 1908, and p. 355, quoting a letter by Tyrrell to Emil Wolff, November 20, 1907.

[114]Ibid., pp. 414-15, quoting a letter by Tyrrell to an unnamed French friend, January 11, 1908.

[115]Hügel to Petre, February 20, 1908, Add. Ms. 45361. Cited in Bedoyere, Baron von Hügel, p. 208.

[116]Holland, ed., Hügel: Selected Letters, p. 147, letter by Hügel to Tyrrell, March 25, 1908.

[117]Bedoyere, Baron von Hügel, pp. 217-18, quoting from a letter by Hügel to Tyrrell, June 27, 1908. The letter is printed at full length in Holland, ed., Hügel: Selected Letters, pp. 152-53.

[118]Petre, Life of George Tyrrell, II, 362.

[119]May, Father Tyrrell, p. 242, quoting from Tyrrell's Medievalism.

[120]See Petre, Life of George Tyrrell, Vol. II, Ch. xviii, "The Church of His Baptism."

[121]Petre, Von Hügel and Tyrrell, p. 173, quoting a letter by Tyrrell to Hügel, June 22, 1908.

[122]Ibid., pp. 183-84, quoting a letter by Hügel to Tyrrell, December 7, 1908.

[123]May, Father Tyrrell, pp. 271-72, quoting a letter by Tyrrell to Hügel. Bedoyere, Baron von Hügel, p. 216, quotes from the same letter and gives its date, April 9, 1909.

[124]Petre, _Life of George Tyrrell_, II, 399-400,
quoting a letter by Tyrrell to Fawkes, June 3, 1909. Alfred
Fawkes (1850-1930) was educated at Eton and Balliol. In
1875, he converted to Roman Catholicism after a brief period
as a High Anglican curate; he was ordained a priest by
Cardinal Manning in 1881. To Loisy in 1903, Hügel intro-
duced him as a secular priest at Brighton and a writer. He
apparently had no parochial duties at the time and was free
to write and travel. Vidler, _A Variety of Catholic Modern-
ists_, pp. 155-56. Fawkes was more of the type of liberal
Protestant that Tyrrell criticized before his death than a
supporter of modernist principles. Thus Fawkes cannot be
considered an actual adherent of Catholic modernism but only
a figure who was in touch with it and reported on it.
Vidler, _The Modernist Movement_, pp. 204, 209-11. Hügel,
especially, was critical of Fawkes. He told Maude Petre in
1902 that he had seen much of Fawkes in Rome, "and was again
struck with his extraordinary gift for writing--a born
writer he is, not as great but as genuine as ever are
Duchesne or Father Tyrrell. But how impatient and impoverishing is his mind! There is a constant lapsing and
relapsing into the 'No Metaphysics' error, the getting the
whole case far too simple, clear and easy." Hügel to Petre,
April 20, 1902, Add. Ms. 45361. In 1908 Hügel told Edmund
Bishop that he had long had doubts whether Fawkes should
ever have joined the Roman Catholic Church: "his views,
for the last 10 years at least, have been more purely and
pointedly individualist, than those of any of the non-
Catholic German and English scholars and philosophers with
whom I am intimate." Hügel to Bishop, June 16, 1908, in
Nigel Abercrombie, "Friedrich von Hügel's Letters to Edmund
Bishop (concluded)," _Dublin Review_, CCXXVII (Fourth Quarter,
1953), 425. Fawkes left the Roman Church to return to
Anglicanism in 1909. In 1913, he published a book, _Studies
in Modernism_, which was a collection of articles that he
had written earlier on the modernist movement.

[125]See Vidler, _The Modernist Movement_, pp. 175-77;
Petre, _Life of George Tyrrell_, II, 400-403; May, _Father
Tyrrell_, pp. 255-56.

[126]Hügel, "Father Tyrrell: Some Memorials of the
Last Twelve Years of His Life," p. 252.

[127]See Petre, _Life of George Tyrrell_, Vol. II, Ch.
xxii, "The End of the Journey," Ch. xxiii, "The Resting-
Place"; Bedoyere, _Baron von Hügel_, pp. 231-35.

[128]*Christianity at the Cross-roads*, 3rd impression (London, 1910), Pref., pp. xx-xxi.

[129]*Ibid.*, pp. 36, 50, 65-66, 87-90, 93-94. Some writers use the term "modernism" instead of "liberal Protestantism." As Loisy's criticism of Harnack (in *L'Évangile et l'Église*) and Tyrrell's criticism of liberal Protestantism (in *Christianity at the Cross-roads*) show, Catholic modernism was very different from liberal Protestantism. The differences between moderate liberal Catholicism and liberal Protestantism were even greater.

[130]*Ibid.*, pp. 95, 98, 102, 261, 278.

[131]*Ibid.*, pp. 118-19, 127.

[132]*Ibid.*, pp. 120, 156, 167.

[133]*Ibid.*, pp. 220, 232-38, 246-47, 254-55.

[134]*Ibid.*, p. 280 and Pref., p. xix.

[135]See Macquarrie, *Twentieth-Century Religious Thought*, pp. 291-99.

[136]Cf. J[ohn] J. Heaney, "Modernism," *New Catholic Encyclopedia* (New York, 1967), IX, 995. Heaney observes that, before modernism arose, many of these insights were already present in the writings of Möhler, Newman, Blondel, and other orthodox thinkers, who had begun to examine these questions. He suggests that such insights were hampered, not helped, in their development in the Church by modernism's appearance and by the strong measures taken against it.

[137]Vidler, *The Modernist Movement*, p. 177.

[138]*Ibid.*, pp. 219-22.

NOTES TO CHAPTER VI

[1]Vidler, The Modernist Movement, pp. 223-25; Maisie Ward, Insurrection versus Resurrection, pp. 308-10.

[2]Maisie Ward, Insurrection versus Resurrection, pp. 303-306.

[3]Gasquet to the Duke of Norfolk, January 11, 1911, Ward Papers.'

[4]Maisie Ward, Insurrection versus Resurrection, p. 331.

[5]Bourne to Mrs. [Wilfrid] Ward, February 10, 1918, Ward Papers.

[6]Maisie Ward, Insurrection versus Resurrection, pp. 310-11, quoting from Mignot's "Memoir to Cardinal Ferrata" cited in N. Fontaine, Saint Siège, Action francaise et Catholiques integraux (1928), p. 133.

[7]Jean Levie, The Bible, Word of God in Words of Men, trans. S. H. Treman (New York, [1962]), pp. 122-24; Vidler, The Modernist Movement, p. 228.

[8]Levie, The Bible, Word of God, pp. 125 (quoting from his article in the Nouvelle Revue Théologique, June, 1929), 131.

[9]Alec R. Vidler, Twentieth Century Defenders of the Faith (New York, 1965), pp. 36-37, quoting from Hügel's papers.

[10]Adrian Hastings, "Some Reflexions on the English Catholicism of the Late 1930's," in Hastings, ed., Bishops and Writers: Aspects of the Evolution of Modern English Catholicism (Wheathampstead, Eng., 1977), p. 108.

[11]Vidler, The Modernist Movement, pp. 204, 209-11.

[12]See ibid., pp. 211-12.

[13]Maisie Ward, Insurrection versus Resurrection, p. 135.

[14]See Robert Dell, My Second Country (France) (London and New York, 1920), the concluding chapter, Ch. viii, "Back to Voltaire." Vidler, A Variety of Catholic Modernists, Ch. vii, "Lesser Lights and Fellow Travellers," names H. C. Corrance, E. J. Dillon, and Joseph P. Thorp as other lesser lights or minor characters among the modernists; he also refers to William Gibson as a modernist. Henry Clemence Corrance (1858-1939) was the son of a Suffolk rector. He took a second class degree in theology at Christ Church, Oxford. After serving as rector of West Bergholt, near Colchester, in the 1890's, he converted to Roman Catholicism in 1898. During the modernist controversy, he subscribed to Loisy's distinction between science and faith. In 1911, Hügel wrote to a friend as though he considered that Corrance was falling into pure immanentism. During World War I, Corrance became a captain in the army. In 1939, he died in Australia. His body was cremated; the officiating minister was an Anglican clergyman. According to Corrance's daughter-in-law, he was an Anglican in his latter years, though he did not often attend a church. Emile Joseph Dillon (1854-1933), an Irishman, studied oriental languages at seven European universities and theology in the seminary of Saint Sulpice. He became a professor of comparative philology at the University of Kharkov, before embarking on a career in journalism. He was correspondent of the Daily Telegraph in Russia from 1887 to 1914. He was very interested in the works of Loisy, who for forty years continued to regard him as a devoted friend. Joseph P. Thorp had been a Jesuit novice and a friend of Tyrrell with whom he kept in contact until Tyrrell's death. For many years he was the dramatic critic of Punch using the nom de plume "T." He returned to the Catholic Church after a lapse of thirty years. Vidler, A Variety of Catholic Modernists, pp. 160-70.

[15]Knox and Vidler, Development of Modern Catholicism, pp. 173, 175. For a rather similar statement regarding Hügel, see Edward Hutton, "Catholic English Literature, 1850-1950," The English Catholics, 1850-1950, ed. George Andrew Beck (London, 1950), p. 556. For all practical

purposes, only among theologians in the Catholic section of the Anglican Church was there any definite and conscious effort to continue the work of the Roman Catholic modernists. Modernism, however, was not an influence on the High Church party as a whole. Vidler, The Modernist Movement, p. 247.

[16]Knox and Vidler, Development of Modern Catholicism, p. 176.

[17]Barry to Ward, April 13, 1909, Ward Papers.

[18]See Vidler, Twentieth Century Defenders, p. 64.

[19]Maritain, Challenges and Renewals, selected readings edited by Joseph W. Evans and Leo R. Ward (Cleveland, 1968), p. 139. The excerpt is taken from Maritain's On the Use of Philosophy (1961).

[20]Maisie Ward, Insurrection versus Resurrection, pp. 292, 312-13 (quoting Bourne's letter to Ward, January 26, 1908, and from Ward's reply), 314.

[21]The two articles were "Reduced Christianity: Its Advocates and Its Critics" (October, 1912) and "Some Oxford Essays" (July, 1913).

[22]Barry to Ward, April 22, 1915, Ward Papers.

[23]Maturin to Ward, January 12, 1910, Ward Papers.

[24]Maisie Ward, Insurrection versus Resurrection, pp. 314-20.

[25]Ibid., p. 323, quoting from Ward's memorandum to Cardinal Rampolla.

[26]Wilfrid Ward, "Preface," in his Men and Matters (London, 1914), pp. vi-vii; quoted in Maisie Ward, Insurrection versus Resurrection, p. 326.

[27]Wilfrid Ward, Men and Matters, pp. vii-ix.

[28]Hügel to Ward, January 28, 1914, Ward-Hügel correspondence, St. Andrews University Library.

[29]Leslie, Cardinal Gasquet, p. 188.

[30]Maisie Ward, Insurrection versus Resurrection, Ch. xvi, "The Newman Biography," especially pp. 344, 347-51.

[31]Ibid., pp. 567-70, quoting letters by Ward to Lord Hugh Cecil, September 16, and September 21, 1911.

[32]Ibid., p. 566, quoting a letter by Ward to Cecil, September 2, 1911.

[33]Abercrombie, Life of Edmund Bishop, pp. 403-404, quoting a letter by Bishop to Everard Green, 1909.

[34]Ibid., p. 383.

[35]Ibid., pp. 382 (quoting from a letter by Bishop to Dr. H. B. Swete, 1908), 396-97.

[36]Bishop to Green, October 24, 1909, Bishop Papers.

[37]Petre, My Way of Faith, p. 213, quoting from a letter by Bishop to Petre, March 12, 1913.

[38]Holland, ed., Hügel: Selected Letters, p. 362, Hügel to Mrs. Lillie, November 29, 1922.

[39]Bishop's annotations of M[aude] D. Petre's Life of George Tyrrell from 1884 to 1909, Vol. II of Autobiography and Life of George Tyrrell (London, 1912; 2nd impression), p. 407, in the Edmund Bishop Library at Downside Abbey.

[40]Bishop's annotations of Petre's Life of George Tyrrell, Vol. II of Autobiography and Life of George Tyrrell, pp. 295-96, in the Edmund Bishop Library at Downside Abbey.

[41]Abercrombie, Life of Edmund Bishop, pp. 383, 442.

[42]M. D[avid] Knowles, Cardinal Gasquet as an Historian (London, 1957), pp. 9, 16. See also Alban Baer, "The Careers of Cardinal Gasquet," American Benedictine Review, V (Summer, 1954), 118.

[43]Knowles, Cardinal Gasquet as an Historian, pp. 23-24. Knowles gives the factors which he considers responsible for the decline of Gasquet's scholarship.

[44]See Leslie, Cardinal Gasquet, Ch. xi, "The Great War."

[45]Hügel to Maude Petre, December 7, 1909, Add. Ms. 45361.

[46]See Webb, Religious Thought in England, pp. 135-36; Bedoyere, Baron von Hügel, p. 247.

[47]Hügel to Petre, February 18, 1910, Add. Ms. 45361.

[48]Holland, ed., Hügel: Selected Letters, p. 182, Hügel to Webb, October 3, 1910.

[49]Bedoyere, Baron von Hügel, p. 242, quoting from Loisy, Mémoires, III, 156.

[50]Bedoyere, Baron von Hügel, p. 239, quoting from Holland, ed., Hügel: Selected Letters, p. 334, Hügel to Professor René Guisan, July 11, 1921. The letter is printed in full in French in the aforementioned work, pp. 333-37. Thomas Michael Loome, "The Enigma of Baron Friedrich von Hügel--as Modernist--I," Downside Review, XCI (January, 1973), p. 13, n. 1, notes that Guisan's name is incorrectly given as "Guiran" there and in subsequent literature on Hügel.

[51]See Loome, "Enigma of Baron von Hügel," p. 24.

[52]Hügel to Petre, February 16, 1911, Add. Ms. 45362; quoted in Bedoyere, Baron von Hügel, p. 255.

[53]Hügel, "On Certain Central Needs of Religion, and the Difficulties of Liberal Movements in Face of the Needs: As Experienced within the Roman Catholic Church during the Last Forty Years," in his Essays and Addresses on the Philosophy of Religion, 2nd ser. (London and Toronto, 1930), pp. 104-105.

[54]Hügel, "Religion and Reality," in his Essays and Addresses on the Philosophy of Religion, 1st ser. (London and Toronto, 1921), p. 48. The passage is cited in Knox and Vidler, Development of Modern Catholicism, p. 2, n. 1.

[55]Hügel to Petre, June 15, 1918, Add. Ms. 45362. Quoted in Holland, ed., Hügel: Selected Letters, p. 251.

[56]Bedoyere, Baron von Hügel, pp. 264-65. For a detailed study of Hügel's views on the problem of authority in the Church, see John J. Heaney, The Modernist Crisis: Von Hügel (Washington, 1968). The book studies that particular element in Hügel's thought.

[57]Hügel to Petre, November 3, 1910, Add. Ms. 45362.

[58]See Bedoyere, Baron von Hügel, pp. 273, 317, 343-44.

[59]See Webb, Religious Thought in England, pp. 140-41.

[60]Hügel, letter [on Louis Duchesne] to The Times Literary Supplement, May 25, 1922, p. 342.

[61]Hügel, Eternal Life (Edinburgh, 1912), pp. 150-51.

[62]Bedoyere, Baron von Hügel, p. 338, quoting from a letter by Hügel to A. Thorold, August 15, 1921.

[63]Ibid., pp. 317, 328-29, quoting from Holland, ed., Hügel: Selected Letters, p. 334, Hügel to Guisan, July 11, 1921. Cf. Hügel to Petre, June 8, 1922, Add. Ms. 45362: "It is very clear now (precisely, I think, to the more vigorous and independent of the thinkers coming on) that Kant was simply obsessed by a mistaken presumption when he argued that the mere fact of my having, or attaining to, a conception of anything renders absurd the notion that this conception bears any likeness to the thing conceived" [my underlining].

NOTES TO CHAPTER VI

[64]Bedoyere, Baron von Hügel, pp. 290-91.

[65]Hügel, "The Idea of God," Essays and Addresses, 2nd ser., pp. 137, 143. For another specific warning by Hügel against pantheism and subjectivism, see "Central Needs of Religion" in the same book, pp. 119-21.

[66]Bedoyere, Baron von Hügel, pp. 290-91, quoting Hügel's notes prepared for a discussion of a paper at the London Society for the Study of Religion meeting in December 1916.

[67]Hügel, Eternal Life, p. 339.

[68]Ibid., pp. 342, 346-47.

[69]Hügel, "The Essentials of Catholicism," Essays and Addresses, 1st ser., p. 240.

[70]Hügel, "Central Needs of Religion," Essays and Addresses, 2nd ser., pp. 109-10.

[71]John J. Heaney, "The Enigma of the Later Von Hügel," Heythrop Journal, VI (April, 1965), 146-47. See also Heaney, The Modernist Crisis: Von Hügel, pp. 134-40. Heaney gives February 13, 1907, as the date of Tyrrell's letter to Hügel.

[72]Nédoncelle, La Pensée religieuse de Friedrich von Hügel, pp. 204-205.

[73]Hügel, "The Case of the Abbe Loisy," Pilot, January 9, 1904, p. 31.

[74]Hügel, "Institutional Christianity or the Church, Its Nature and Necessity," Essays and Addresses, 1st ser., p. 273.

[75]Hügel, "Central Needs of Religion," Essays and Addresses, 2nd ser., p. 121.

[76]See his letter to the mother of a son at Downside, quoted above.

[77]Hügel, Eternal Life, pp. 360, 363-64.

[78]See Michael Hanbury, "Von Hügel Today: A Fore-runner of Vatican II," Tablet, November 20, 1965, pp. 1291-93.

[79]Ibid., pp. 1291-92. The quotation from Hügel is from the Preface to his Mystical Element of Religion, p. x.

[80]Hügel to Ward, June 4, 1907, Ward-Hügel corre-spondence, St. Andrews University Library.

[81]See Chapter iii above and my article, "George Tyrrell and the English Liberal Catholic Crisis, 1900-01," Downside Review, XCII (July, 1974), 180-83.

[82]Hügel, "The Essentials of Catholicism," Essays and Addresses, 1st ser., pp. 238-39.

[83]Holland, ed., Hügel: Selected Letters, p. 220, Hügel to Bishop Edward Talbot, March 20, 1915.

[84]Hügel to Petre, March 13, 1918, Add. Ms. 45362. Quoted in Holland, ed., Hügel: Selected Letters, pp. 248-49.

[85]See Loome, "Enigma of Baron von Hügel," p. 23, n. 27.

[86]Wilfrid Ward, "Pope Pius X," Dublin Review, CLV (October, 1914), 224; Maisie Ward, Insurrection versus Resurrection, pp. 294-95.

[87]Wilfrid Ward, Men and Matters, p. 193; quoted in Maisie Ward, Insurrection versus Resurrection, p. 164.

[88]Wilfrid Ward, Last Lectures, ed. Josephine Ward and Maisie Ward (London, 1918), pp. 281-82, 290.

A SELECTED BIBLIOGRAPHY

MANUSCRIPT SOURCES

British Museum: Friedrich von Hügel, George Tyrrell, and Maude Petre Mss.

Cambridge University Library: Papers of Lord Acton.

Downside Abbey: Edmund Bishop Papers and Francis Cardinal Gasquet Papers.

Hickleton Papers, Archives of the Wood Family of Hickleton and Garrowby: Copies (made by Wilfrid Ward in 1910 and sent to Lord Halifax) of some letters of George Tyrrell to Ward.

St. Andrews University Library: Letters of Edmund Bishop to Friedrich von Hügel; Wilfrid Ward-Friedrich von Hügel correspondence; George Tyrrell's correspondence with Wilfrid Ward.

Westminster (Archives of the Archdiocese of): Papers of Herbert Cardinal Vaughan, especially George Tyrrell's correspondence with Vaughan.

Wilfrid Ward Family Papers, formerly in the care of Rosemary Sheed Middleton; now in the St. Andrews University Library.

BOOKS

Abercrombie, Nigel. The Life and Work of Edmund Bishop. London: Longmans, Green, 1959.

Altholz, Josef L. The Liberal Catholic Movement in England: The "Rambler" and Its Contributors, 1848-1864. London: Burns and Oates, 1962.

Barmann, Lawrence F. Baron Friedrich von Hügel and the Modernist Crisis in England. Cambridge, England: Cambridge University Press, 1972.

_____. The Letters of Friedrich von Hügel and Norman
    Kemp Smith. New York: Fordham University Press,
    1981.* [*This book appeared too late to note in
    the present study other than in the Bibliography.]

Barry, William. Memories and Opinions. London and New
    York: G. P. Putnam's Sons, 1926.

Beck, George Andrew, ed. The English Catholics, 1850-1950.
    Essays to Commemorate the Centenary of the
    Restoration of the Hierarchy of England and Wales.
    London: Burns Oates, 1950.

Bedoyere, Michael de la. The Life of Baron von Hügel.
    London: J. M. Dent and Sons, 1951.

Benson, Arthur C. The Life of Edward White Benson: Some-
    time Archbishop of Canterbury. 2 vols. London:
    Macmillan, 1899.

Blehl, Vincent Ferrer, ed. The Essential Newman. New York:
    New American Library Mentor-Omega Books, 1963.

Blondel, Maurice. The Letter on Apologetics and History
    and Dogma. Texts presented and translated by
    Alexander Dru and Illtyd Trethowan. New York:
    Holt, Rinehart and Winston, 1964.

Burtchaell, James Tunstead. Catholic Theories of Biblical
    Inspiration since 1810: A Review and Critique.
    Cambridge, England: Cambridge University Press,
    1969.

Carpenter, James. Gore: A Study in Liberal Catholic
    Thought. London: Faith Press, 1960.

Cockshut, A. O. J. Anglican Attitudes: A Study of
    Victorian Religious Controversies. London:
    Collins, 1959.

Daly, Gabriel. Transcendence and Immanence: A Study
    in Catholic Modernism and Integralism. Oxford:
    Clarendon Press, 1980.

Dell, Robert. My Second Country (France). London and
    New York: John Lane, 1920.

Dodd, C. H. The Founder of Christianity. New York:
    Macmillan; London: Collier-Macmillan, 2nd
    printing, 1970.

_____. History and the Gospel. New York: Charles Scribner's Sons, 1938.

Fawkes, Alfred. Studies in Modernism. London: John Murray, 1913.

Gasquet, Francis Aidan. Henry VIII and the English Monasteries: An Attempt to Illustrate the History of Their Suppression. 2 vols. Vol. I, 2nd ed.; Vol. II, 3rd ed. London: John Hodges, 1888-89.

_____, and Edmund Bishop. Edward VI and the Book of Common Prayer: An Examination into Its Origin and Early History with an Appendix of Unpublished Documents. London: John Hodges, 1890.

Gore, Charles, ed. Lux Mundi: A Series of Studies in the Religion of the Incarnation. From the 5th English ed. New York: John W. Lovell Co., n.d.

Gruber, Jacob W. A Conscience in Conflict: The Life of St. George Jackson Mivart. New York: Published for Temple University Publications by Columbia University Press, 1960.

Hales, E. E. Y. Pio Nono: A Study in European Politics and Religion in the Nineteenth Century. Garden City, New York: Doubleday Image Books, 1962.

Halifax, [Charles Lindley Wood, 2nd] Viscount. Leo XIII and Anglican Orders. London and New York: Longmans, Green, 1912.

Hastings, Adrian, ed. Bishops and Writers: Aspects of the Evolution of Modern English Catholicism. Wheathampstead, England: Anthony Clarke, 1977.

Heaney, John J. The Modernist Crisis: Von Hügel. Washington: Corpus Books, 1968.

Holland, Bernard, ed. Baron Friedrich von Hügel: Selected Letters, 1896-1924. With a memoir by Bernard Holland. London and Toronto: J. M. Dent and Sons, 1927.

Holmes, J. Derek. More Roman than Rome: English Catholicism in the Nineteenth Century. London: Burns and Oates; Shepherdstown, West Virginia: Patmos Press, 1978.

Hügel, Friedrich von. Essays and Addresses on the
    Philosophy of Religion. 2 series. London and
    Toronto: J. M. Dent and Sons, 1921-30.

_____. Eternal Life: A Study of Its Implications and
    Applications. Edinburgh: T. and T. Clark, 1912.

Hughes, John Jay. Absolutely Null and Utterly Void: The
    Papal Condemnation of Anglican Orders, 1896.
    Washington: Corpus Books, 1968.

Knowles, M. D[avid]. Cardinal Gasquet as an Historian.
    London: University of London, Athlone Press, 1957.

Knox, Wilfred L., and Alec R. Vidler. The Development of
    Modern Catholicism. Milwaukee: Morehouse Pub-
    lishing Co., 1933.

Leslie, Shane. Cardinal Gasquet: A Memoir. London:
    Burns Oates, 1953.

Levie, Jean. The Bible, Word of God in Words of Men.
    Trans. S. H. Treman. New York: P. J. Kenedy and
    Sons, [1962].

Loisy, Alfred. The Gospel and the Church. Tr. Christopher
    Home. New edition. London: Sir Isaac Pitman and
    Sons, 1908.

_____. Mémoires pour servir à l'histoire religieuse de
    notre temps. 3 vols. Paris: E. Nourry, 1930-31.

_____. My Duel with the Vatican: The Autobiography of
    a Catholic Modernist. Authorized translation by
    Richard Wilson Boynton. New York: E. P. Dutton,
    1924.

Loome, Thomas Michael. Liberal Catholicism, Reform
    Catholicism, Modernism: A Contribution to a New
    Orientation in Modernist Research. Mainz, Germany:
    Matthias-Grünewald-Verlag, 1979.

Louis-David, A[nne], ed. Lettres de George Tyrrell a Henri
    Bremond. Paris: Aubier Montaigne, 1971.

McAvoy, Thomas T. The Americanist Heresy in Roman
    Catholicism, 1895-1900. Notre Dame, Indiana:
    University of Notre Dame Press, 1963.

McClelland, Vincent Alan. Cardinal Manning: His Public
    Life and Influence, 1865-1892. London: Oxford
    University Press, 1962.

McCormack, Arthur. Cardinal Vaughan: The Life of the
    Third Archbishop of Westminster, Founder of St.
    Joseph's Missionary Society, Mill Hill. London:
    Burns and Oates, 1966.

MacDougall, Hugh A. The Acton-Newman Relations: The
    Dilemma of Christian Liberalism. New York:
    Fordham University Press, 1962.

McElrath, Damian. Richard Simpson, 1820-1876: A Study in
    XIXth Century English Liberal Catholicism. Louvain:
    Publications Universitaires de Louvain, 1972.

Macquarrie, John. Twentieth-Century Religious Thought:
    The Frontiers of Philosophy and Theology, 1900-
    1960. New York: Harper and Row, 1963.

Manning, H[enry] E., ed. Essays on Religion and Literature.
    2 series. London: Longman, 1865-67.

Maritain, Jacques. Challenges and Renewals. Selected
    readings edited by Joseph W. Evans and Leo R. Ward.
    Cleveland: World Publishing Co. Meridian Books,
    1968.

May, J. Lewis. Father Tyrrell and the Modernist Movement.
    London: Eyre and Spottiswoode, 1932.

Mivart, St. George. Under the Ban. A correspondence
    between Dr. St. George Mivart and Herbert Cardinal
    Vaughan, Archbishop of Westminster. Accompanied by
    two articles by Dr. Mivart on "Some Recent Catholic
    Apologists" and "The Continuity of Catholicism."
    New York: Tucker Publishing Co., 1900.

Mott, Lewis Freeman. Ernest Renan. New York and London:
    D. Appleton, 1921.

Mozley, John Kenneth. Some Tendencies in British Theology:
    From the Publication of Lux Mundi to the Present
    Day. London: S.P.C.K., 1951.

Nédoncelle, Maurice. La Pensée religieuse de Friedrich von
    Hügel (1852-1925). Paris: Librairie Philosophique
    J. Vrin, 1935.

Newman, John Henry. An Essay on the Development of
     Christian Doctrine. New edition, edited with a
     preface and introduction by Charles Frederick
     Harrold with an appendix on Newman's textual
     changes by Ottis Ivan Schreiber. New York, London,
     and Toronto: Longmans, Green, 1949.

_____. The Idea of a University. New edition, edited
     with a preface and introduction by Charles Frederick
     Harrold. New York, London, and Toronto: Longmans,
     Green, 1947.

Oldmeadow, Ernest. Francis Cardinal Bourne. Vol. I.
     London: Burns Oates and Washbourne, 1940.

Petre, M[aude] D. Autobiography and Life of George Tyrrell.
     Vol. II: Life of George Tyrrell from 1884 to 1909.
     2nd impression. London: Edward Arnold, 1912.

_____, ed. George Tyrrell's Letters. London: T. Fisher
     Unwin, 1920.

_____. Modernism: Its Failure and Its Fruits. London:
     T. C. and E. C. Jack, 1918.

_____. My Way of Faith. London: J. M. Dent and Sons,
     1937.

_____. Von Hügel and Tyrrell: The Story of a Friend-
     ship. London: J. M. Dent and Sons, 1937.

Prestige, G. L. The Life of Charles Gore: A Great English-
     man. London and Toronto: William Heinemann,
     September, 1935; rpt. December, 1935.

Purcell, Edmund Sheridan. Life of Cardinal Manning:
     Archbishop of Westminster. 2 vols. 2nd ed.
     London: Macmillan, 1896.

Ramsey, Arthur Michael. An Era in Anglican Theology: From
     Gore to Temple. New York: Charles Scribner's Sons,
     1960.

Ratté, John. Three Modernists: Alfred Loisy, George
     Tyrrell, William L. Sullivan. New York: Sheed and
     Ward, 1967.

Reardon, Bernard M. G., ed. Roman Catholic Modernism.
     Stanford: Stanford University Press, 1970.

Schultenover, David G. George Tyrrell: In Search of
     Catholicism. Shepherdstown, West Virginia: Patmos
     Press, 1981.

Snead-Cox, J. G. The Life of Cardinal Vaughan. 2 vols.
     London: Herbert and Daniel, 1910.

Stam, Johannes Jacobus. George Tyrrell (1861-1909).
     Utrecht: H. Honig, 1938.

Steinmann, Jean. Friedrich von Hügel: Sa vie, son œuvre
     et ses amitiés. Paris: Aubier, Éditions Montaigne,
     1962.

Turvasi, Francesco. The Condemnation of Alfred Loisy and
     the Historical Method. Rome: Edizioni di Storia e
     Letteratura, 1979.

Tyrrell, George. Christianity at the Cross-roads. 3rd
     impression. London: Longmans, Green, 1910.

_____. Lex Credendi: A Sequel to Lex Orandi. New
     impression. London: Longmans, Green, 1907.

_____. Medievalism: A Reply to Cardinal Mercier.
     London: Longmans, Green, 1908.

_____. A Much-Abused Letter. New impression. London:
     Longmans, Green, 1907.

Vidler, Alec R. The Modernist Movement in the Roman Church:
     Its Origins and Outcome. Cambridge, England:
     Cambridge University Press, 1934.

_____. Twentieth Century Defenders of the Faith. New
     York: Seabury Press, 1965.

_____. A Variety of Catholic Modernists. Cambridge,
     England: Cambridge University Press, 1970.

Ward, Maisie. Father Maturin: A Memoir. London:
     Longmans, 1920.

_____. Insurrection versus Resurrection. The Wilfrid
     Wards and the Transition: Vol. II. New York:
     Sheed and Ward, 1937.

_____. The Wilfrid Wards and the Transition. Vol. I:
     The Nineteenth Century. London: Sheed and Ward,
     1934.

Ward, Wilfrid. Last Lectures. Being the Lowell Lectures,
    1914, and three lectures delivered at the Royal
    Institution, 1915. Edited by Josephine Ward and
    Maisie Ward. With an introductory study by Mrs.
    Wilfrid [Josephine] Ward. London: Longmans, Green,
    1918.

_____. The Life and Times of Cardinal Wiseman. 2 vols.
    London: Longmans, Green, 1897.

_____. The Life of John Henry Cardinal Newman. Based
    on his private journals and correspondence. 2 vols.
    London: Longmans, Green, 1912; new impression 1921.

_____. Men and Matters. London: Longmans, Green, 1914.

_____. William George Ward and the Catholic Revival.
    Re-issue with a new preface. London: Longmans,
    Green, 1912.

_____. William George Ward and the Oxford Movement.
    London: Macmillan, 1889.

Wardman, H. W. Ernest Renan: A Critical Biography.
    London: University of London, Athlone Press, 1964.

Weaver, Mary Jo, ed. Letters from a "Modernist": The
    Letters of George Tyrrell to Wilfrid Ward, 1893-
    1908. Shepherdstown, West Virginia: Patmos Press,
    1981.

Webb, Clement C. J. A Study of Religious Thought in England
    from 1850. Oxford: Clarendon Press, 1933.

Whelan, Joseph P. The Spirituality of Friedrich von Hügel.
    London: Collins, 1971.

Wilson, J[oseph] Anselm. The Life of Bishop Hedley. New
    York: P. J. Kenedy and Sons, 1930.

Wood, H. G. Belief and Unbelief since 1850. Cambridge,
    England: Cambridge University Press, 1955.

Wynne, John J., ed. The Great Encyclical Letters of Pope
    Leo XIII. New York: Benziger Brothers, 1903.

ARTICLES

Abercrombie, N[igel] J. "Edmund Bishop and St. George Mivart." The Month, CXCIII (March, 1952), 176-80.

_____. "Friedrich von Hügel's Letters to Edmund Bishop." Dublin Review, CCXXVII (First Quarter, 1953), 68-78; (Second Quarter, 1953), 179-89; (Third Quarter, 1953), 285-98; (Fourth Quarter, 1953), 419-38.

Baer, Alban. "The Careers of Cardinal Gasquet." The American Benedictine Review, V (Summer, 1954), 113-22.

Barry, William. "An American Religious Crusade." The National Review, XXXIII (March, 1899), 115-28.

_____. "'Americanism,' True and False." The North American Review, CLXIX (July, 1899), 33-49.

_____. "The Troubles of a Catholic Democracy." The Contemporary Review, LXXVI (July, 1899), 70-86.

Burke, Ronald. "An Orthodox Modernist [Friedrich von Hügel] with a Modern View of Truth." The Journal of Religion, LVII (April, 1977), 124-43.

Burtchaell, James Tunstead. "The Biblical Question and the English Liberal Catholics." The Review of Politics, XXXI (January, 1969), 108-20.

Cameron, J. M. "Newman and Liberalism." Cross Currents, XXX (Summer, 1980), 153-66.

Cuthbert, O.S.F.C., Father. "Wilfrid Ward." Dublin Review, CLIX (July, 1916), 1-22.

Dell, Robert Edward. "A Liberal Catholic View of the Case of Dr. Mivart." The Nineteenth Century, XLVII (April, 1900), 669-84.

_____. "Mr. Wilfrid Ward's Apologetics." The Nineteenth Century, XLVIII (July, 1900), 127-36.

Dillon, E. J. "Intellectual Liberty and Contemporary Catholicism." The Contemporary Review, LXVI (August, 1894), 280-304.

_____. "The Papal Encyclical on the Bible." The Contemporary Review, LXV (April, 1894), 576-608.

_____. "Theological Book-Keeping by Double Entry." The Contemporary Review, LXVI (September, 1894), 351-73.

"Evolution and Its Upholders." The Tablet, June 24, 1899, pp. 969-70.

Fidelis, pseud. "A Convert's Experiences of the Catholic Church." The Contemporary Review, LXXVII (June, 1900), 817-34.

_____. "The Movement for Reform within the Catholic Church." The Contemporary Review, LXXVIII (November, 1900), 693-709.

Gibson, William. "An Outburst of Activity in the Roman Congregations." The Nineteenth Century, XLV (May, 1899), 785-94.

Gilley, Sheridan. "Wilfrid Ward and His Life of Newman." The Journal of Ecclesiastical History, XXIX (April, 1978), 177-93.

Gore, Charles. "The Encyclical Letter Recently Issued by Pope Leo XIII on the Study of Holy Scripture." The Guardian, XLIX (April 11, 1894), 530-31.

Halifax, [Charles Lindley Wood, 2nd] Viscount. "The Recent Anglo-Roman Pastoral." The Nineteenth Century and After, XLIX (May, 1901), 736-54.

Hanbury, Michael. "Von Hügel Today: A Forerunner of Vatican II." The Tablet, November 20, 1965, pp. 1291-93.

Healey, Charles J. "Maude Petre: Her Life and Signifi-cance." Recusant History, XV (May, 1979), 23-42.

Heaney, John J. "The Enigma of the Later Von Hügel." The Heythrop Journal, VI (April, 1965), 145-59.

_____. "Modernism." New Catholic Encyclopedia (New York, 1967), IX, 991-95.

Hedley, John Cuthbert. "Dr. Mivart on Faith and Science." The Dublin Review, CI (October, 1887), 401-19.

_____. "Physical Science and Faith." The Dublin Review, CXXIII (October, 1898), 241-61.

Holmes, J. Derek. "Newman and Modernism." The Baptist Quarterly, XXIV (July, 1972), 335-41.

Hügel, Friedrich von. "The Case of the Abbe Loisy." The Pilot, January 9, 1904, pp. 30-31.

_____. "The Church and the Bible: The Two Stages of Their Interrelation." The Dublin Review, CXV (October, 1894), 313-41; CXVI (April, 1895), 306-37; CXVII (October, 1895), 275-304.

_____. "Father Tyrrell: Some Memorials of the Last Twelve Years of His Life." The Hibbert Journal, VIII (January, 1910), 233-52.

"The Joint Pastoral." The Tablet, January 5, 1901, pp. 5-6.

Kelly, Edward E. "Newman, Wilfrid Ward, and the Modernist Crisis." Thought, XLVIII (Winter, 1973), 508-19.

Kelly, James J. "The Modernist Controversy in England: The Correspondence between Friedrich von Hügel and Percy Gardner." The Downside Review, XCIX (January, 1981), 40-58.

Kerlin, Michael J. "Blondel and Von Hügel: The Debate about History and Dogma." The American Benedictine Review, XXVIII (June, 1977), 210-25.

Loome, Thomas Michael. "A Bibliography of the Printed Works of George Tyrrell: Supplement." The Heythrop Journal, XI (April, 1970), 161-69.

_____. "A Bibliography of the Published Writings of George Tyrrell (1861-1909)." The Heythrop Journal, X (July, 1969), 280-314.

_____. "The Enigma of Baron Friedrich von Hügel--as Modernist." The Downside Review, XCI (January, 1973), 13-34; (April, 1973), 123-40; (July, 1973), 204-30.

McClelland, Vincent Alan. "Manning and the Universities: A Reappraisal of the Background to the Kensington Venture." The Tablet, March 30, 1963, pp. 335-37.

Manning, H[enry] E. "The Work and the Wants of the Catholic Church in England." The Dublin Review, n.s., I (July, 1863), 139-66.

"Mr. Gore on the Pope's Encyclical." The Spectator, LXXII (April 28, 1894), 578-79.

Mivart, St. George. "The Catholic Church and Biblical Criticism." The Nineteenth Century, XXII (July, 1887), 31-51.

_____. "The Continuity of Catholicism." The Nineteenth Century, XLVII (January, 1900), 51-72.

_____. "Happiness in Hell." The Nineteenth Century, XXXII (December, 1892), 899-919.

_____. "The Happiness in Hell: A Rejoinder." The Nineteenth Century, XXXIII (February, 1893), 320-38.

_____. "Last Words on the Happiness in Hell: A Rejoinder." The Nineteenth Century, XXXIII (April, 1893), 637-51.

_____. "Some Recent Catholic Apologists." The Fortnightly Review, N.S., LXVII (January, 1900), 24-44.

"The Pope and Modernism." [From The Times correspondent in Rome.] The Times (London), November 6, 1907, p. 7.

Reardon, B[ernard] M. G. "Newman and the Catholic Modernist Movement." The Church Quarterly, IV (July, 1971), 50-60.

Rickaby, Joseph. "The Church and Liberal Catholicism." The Month, XCVII (April, 1901), 337-46.

"The Roman Catholic Church and the Dreyfus Case." The Times (London), September 18, 1899, p. 7; October 17, 1899, p. 9.

Root, John D. "English Catholic Modernism and Science: The Case of George Tyrrell." The Heythrop Journal, XVIII (July, 1977), 271-88.

Schoenl, William J. "George Tyrrell and the English Liberal Catholic Crisis, 1900-01." The Downside Review, XCII (July, 1974), 171-84.

_____. "The Reappearance of English Liberal Catholicism in the Early 1890's." The Clergy Review, LXII (March, 1977), 92-105.

_____. "Von Hügel after the Modernist Controversy." The Clergy Review, LXIII (June, 1978), 211-19.

330

Stephen, J[ames] F[itzjames]. "Mr. Mivart's Modern Catholicism." The Nineteenth Century, XXII (October, 1887), 581-600.

Trevor, Meriol. "Manning's University and Newman's Aloofness." The Tablet, January 5, 1963, pp. 7-8.

"A Triangular Duel." The Saturday Review of Politics, Literature, Science, and Art, LXIV (December 3, 1887), 760-61.

Tyrrell, George. "A Perverted Devotion," in his Essays on Faith and Immortality. Arranged by M[aude] D. Petre. London: Edward Arnold, 1914.

_____. "The Pope and Modernism." The Times (London), September 30, 1907, p. 4; October 1, 1907, p. 5.

_____. "Semper Eadem (I)" and "From Heaven, or of Men?" in his Through Scylla and Charybdis: Or the Old Theology and the New. London: Longmans, Green, 1907.

Vidler, A[lec] R. "Last Conversations with Alfred Loisy." The Journal of Theological Studies, N.S., XXVIII (April, 1977), 84-89.

Ward, Wilfrid. "Catholic Apologetics: A Reply." The Nineteenth Century, XLV (June, 1899), 955-61.

_____. "Doctores Ecclesiæ." The Pilot, June 22, 1901, pp. 774-76.

_____. "The Encyclical 'Pascendi.'" The Dublin Review, CXLII (January, 1908), 1-10.

_____. "The Ethics of Religious Conformity." The Quarterly Review, CLXXXIX (January, 1899), 103-36.

_____. "For Truth or for Life." The Dublin Review, CXXXIX (October, 1906), 233-51; CXL (April, 1907), 271-79.

_____. "The Functions of Prejudice." The Dublin Review, CXXXVIII (April, 1906), 99-118.

_____. "Liberalism and Intransigeance." The Nineteenth Century, XLVII (June, 1900), 960-73.

_____. "New Wine in Old Bottles." The Nineteenth Century, XXVII (June, 1890), 942-56.

_____. "Pope Pius X." The Dublin Review, CLV (October, 1914), 217-25.

_____. "Reduced Christianity: Its Advocates and Its Critics." The Dublin Review, CLI (October, 1912), 217-40.

_____. "The Rigidity of Rome." The Nineteenth Century, XXXVIII (November, 1895), 786-804.

_____. "Some Oxford Essays." The Dublin Review, CLIII (July, 1913), 53-64.

Weaver, Mary Jo. "A Bibliography of the Published Works of Wilfrid Ward." The Heythrop Journal, XX (October, 1979), 399-420.

_____. "George Tyrrell and the Joint Pastoral Letter." The Downside Review, XCIX (January, 1981), 18-39.

_____. "Wilfrid Ward, George Tyrrell and the Meanings of Modernism." The Downside Review, XCVI (January, 1978), 21-34.

_____. "A Working Catalogue of the Ward Family Papers." Recusant History, XV (May, 1979), 43-71.

LETTERS TO THE EDITOR

Catholicus [David Fleming]. The Times (London), January 25, 1904, p. 4. On Loisy and the Holy Office.

A Conservative Catholic [George Tyrrell]. The Pilot, March 2, 1901, p. 282. On the joint pastoral censuring English liberal Catholicism.

Dell, Robert [E.] The Times (London), November 13, 1907, p. 19. On the Vatican and Newman.

_____. The Tablet, March 3, 1900, p. 336. On Mivart and The New Era.

E. F. G. [George Tyrrell]. The Pilot, July 6, 1901, pp. 23-24. On the joint pastoral.

Gasquet, Francis A. The Times (London), November 5, 1907, p. 8. On the Vatican and Newman.

_____. The Times (London), November 7, 1907, p. 4. On Roman Catholics and modernism.

Hedley, J[ohn] C. The Tablet, January 14, 1899, p. 59. On physical science and faith.

Hügel, Friedrich von. The Spectator, LXXII (May 19, 1894), 684-85. On the papal encyclical Providentissimus Deus and Charles Gore.

_____. The Times Literary Supplement (London), May 25, 1922, p. 342. On Louis Duchesne.

Mivart, St. George. The Times (London), October 17, 1899, pp. 13-14. On the Roman Catholic Church and the Dreyfus Affair.

Norris, John. The Times (London), November 4, 1907, p. 10. On the Vatican and Newman.

_____. The Times (London), November 7, 1907, p. 4. On Roman Catholics and modernism.

Romanus [Friedrich von Hügel]. The Times (London), March 2, 1904, p. 15. On Loisy and the Holy Office.

Vaughan, Herbert Cardinal. The Times (London), September 18, 1899, p. 9. On the Roman Catholic Church and the Dreyfus Affair.

Ward, Wilfrid. The Times (London), September 21, 1899, p. 10. On the Roman Catholic Church and the Dreyfus Affair.

Williams, W. J. The Times (London), November 2, 1907, p. 10. On the Vatican, Tyrrell, and Newman.

_____. The Times (London), November 6, 1907, p. 13. On the Vatican and Newman.

MISCELLANEOUS

"The Church and Liberal Catholicism: Joint Pastoral Letter by the Cardinal Archbishop and the Bishops of the Province of Westminster." The Tablet, January 5, 1901, pp. 8-12; January 12, 1901, pp. 50-52 [concluded].

"Decree of the Holy Roman and Universal Inquisition
(Lamentabili Sane Exitu)" [English translation
reprinted from The Tablet], Appendix 3, pp. 217-30,
in Paul Sabatier, Modernism. Trans. C. A. Miles.
London: T. Fisher Unwin, 1908.

"Encyclical Letter ('Pascendi Gregis')" [reprint of
official English translation], Appendix 4, pp. 231-
346, in Paul Sabatier, Modernism. Trans. C. A.
Miles. London: T. Fisher Unwin, 1908.

"The Pope and Liberal Catholicism: Letter to the English
Bishops." [From Leo XIII, Pope]. The Tablet,
March 23, 1901, p. 441.

INDEX

339